THE SOVIET UNION
IN THE MIDDLE EAST

The Royal Institute of International Affairs is an unofficial body which promotes the scientific study of international questions and does not express opinions of its own. The opinions expressed in this publication are the responsibility of the authors.

The Institute and its Research Committee are grateful for the comments and suggestions made by Malcolm Mackintosh and David Pool, who were asked to review the manuscript of this book.

THE SOVIET UNION IN THE MIDDLE EAST

Policies and Perspectives

Edited by
Adeed Dawisha and Karen Dawisha

HM

Published by
Holmes & Meier Publishers
for the Royal Institute of International Affairs

First published in the United States of America 1982 by
Holmes & Meier Publishers, Inc.
30 Irving Place, New York, N.Y. 10003

Library of Congress Cataloging in Publication Data
Main entry under title:

The Soviet Union in the Middle East.

  Includes index.
  1. Near East – Foreign relations – Soviet Union –
Addresses, essays, lectures.   2. Soviet Union – Foreign
relations – Near East – Addresses, essays, lectures.
I. Dawisha, A. I.   II. Dawisha, Karen.   III. Royal
Institute of International Affairs.
DS63.2.S55S67 1982   327.47056   82-953
ISBN 0-8419-0796-X   AACR2
ISBN 0-8419-0797-8 (pbk.)

Printed in Great Britain

Contents

Editors' Acknowledgements   vii

Contributors   x

1   Perspectives on Soviet Policy in the Middle East by
    Adeed Dawisha and Karen Dawisha   1

2   The Soviet Union in the Arab World: The Limits to
    Superpower Influence by *Adeed Dawisha*   8

3   Soviet Relations with the Countries of the Northern
    Tier by *Malcolm Yapp*   24

4   Ideology, Soviet Policy and Realignment in the Horn
    by *Robert Patman*   45

5   The East Europeans and the Cubans in the Middle
    East: Surrogates or Allies? by *Edwina Moreton*   62

6   Energy as a Factor in Soviet Relations with the Middle
    East by *Anthony Stacpoole*   85

7   The Influence of Trade on Soviet Relations with the
    Middle East by *Alan H. Smith*   103

8   Soviet–American Rivalry in the Middle East: The
    Political Dimension by *Shahram Chubin*   124

9   Soviet–American Rivalry in the Middle East: The
    Military Dimension by *Jonathan Alford*   134

10 The Correlation of Forces and Soviet Policy in the
    Middle East by *Karen Dawisha*   147

Index   167

Tables

5.1 Communist military technicians in the Middle East, 1979   64

5.2 Communist training of Middle East military personnel in communist countries, 1955–79   66

6.1 Soviet production of energy   86

6.2 Soviet energy trade   90

6.3 Soviet consumption of energy   94

6.4 Estimated CMEA energy consumption, 1980   96

7.1 Unspecified residuals in Soviet exports   107

7.2 Soviet exports to Middle Eastern countries   110

7.3 Soviet imports from Middle Eastern countries   111

7.4 Quarterly data for Soviet trade with Iran, Iraq and Afghanistan   112

7.5 Differences between Soviet data and partners' data   116

7.6 Commodity structure of major Soviet imports from Middle Eastern countries   118

7.7 Commodity structure of Soviet exports to the Middle East   119

Editors' Acknowledgements

We are indebted to a number of people and organizations for help in the preparation of this volume. The essays in this book grew from papers delivered initially at meetings of an ongoing study group on Soviet foreign policy which was organized by the Royal Institute of International Affairs and which, in 1980–1, discussed Soviet–Middle Eastern relations. These meetings were funded by a small subvention from a larger Ford Foundation grant which had been given to the Institute to prepare a study on the relations of the Muslim world with other parts of the contemporary international system. We are therefore thankful to the Ford Foundation for providing the funds, and to the Royal Institute of International Affairs for making available its excellent facilities and support services for the study group meetings. In this, we are especially grateful to Dr William Wallace, Dr Lawrence Freedman and Mr Robin Edmonds for chairing various meetings of the study group. Along with other contributors to the symposium, we owe a great deal to all the members of the study group, who provided many pertinent comments on earlier drafts of the esssays that follow. At the Institute, we are thankful to Miss Elizabeth Watson and Mrs Heather Weeks for typing the manuscripts so efficiently, to Miss Ann De'Ath for her organizational work during the pre-publication period, and to Miss Pauline Wickham, whose meticulous copy-editing made an invaluable contribution to the book.

September 1981   A.D.
K.D.

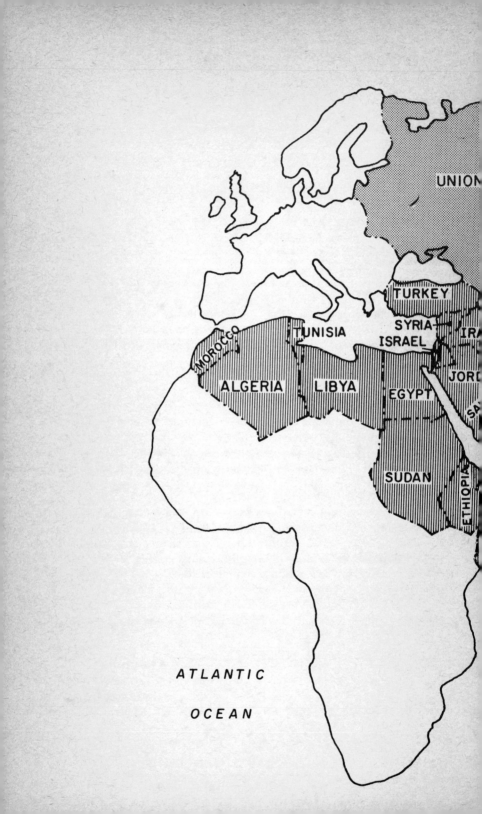

OF SOVIET SOCIALIST REPUBLICS

Mongolia

China

AFGHANISTAN

RAN

PAKISTAN   Tibet

GULF
STATES

India

OMAN

YEMEN

PDRY

ARABIAN
SEA

MALIA

INDIAN OCEAN

ADAGASCAR

Contributors

Jonathan Alford, International Institute for Strategic Studies

Shahram Chubin, Graduate Institute of International Studies, Geneva

Adeed Dawisha, Royal Institute of International Affairs

Karen Dawisha, Centre for International Studies, London School of Economics, University of London

Edwina Moreton, *The Economist*

Robert Patman, Department of Politics, University of Southampton

Alan H. Smith, School of Slavonic and East European Studies, University of London

Anthony Stacpoole, British Petroleum Company Ltd

Malcolm Yapp, School of Oriental and African Studies, University of London

1 Perspectives on Soviet Policy in the Middle East
Adeed Dawisha and Karen Dawisha

Soviet interest in the area south of its border has been long-standing. Of all the nineteenth-century European powers with interests in the area called the Middle East, Czarist Russia was the one that, with much justification, could consider itself a local power. From the 1917 Russian Revolution until the Second World War, Soviet concerns in the area centred on Iran, Afghanistan and Turkey, but in the mid-1950s Soviet involvement spread rapidly to cover many countries of the Middle East, spanning the two continents of Asia and Africa. Indeed by the late 1950s and early 1960s, some Western observers and political leaders were identifying the Soviet Union as the dominant power in the region.

But what constitutes the Middle East? There has been very little consensus among either academics or political commentators on the exact geographical delineation of the area. Like its forerunner, 'the Near East', a term employed by nineteenth-century Europeans and usually taken to include the Balkans, 'the Middle East' is used to designate the area between Europe and the Far East. Even disregarding the blatant Eurocentrism of the phrase, there still is no general agreement on the definition of its geographical boundary. For the purpose of this book, the Middle East is defined in its broadest sense: the Arab countries of south-west Asia and north Africa, Afghanistan, Iran, Turkey, Israel and, in the Horn of Africa, Ethiopia and Somalia. Not only does this area appear to possess geographic continuity, but, more important, in terms of the policies of the powers, it seems to be perceived by decision-makers in the Soviet Union as well as in the United States as a single and integral strategic concern.

This area has witnessed increasing Soviet activity in the 1970s. In addition to the recent invasion of Afghanistan, the Soviet Union has treaties with Iraq, Syria, Ethiopia and the People's Democratic Republic of Yemen (PDRY); Soviet, East European and Cuban military personnel or combat troops are operational in Ethiopia, the PDRY, Syria, Libya and of course Afghanistan; and Syria, a central actor in inter-Arab, as well as Arab–Israeli, relations, is now almost totally dependent on Soviet arms and equipment. Moreover, Soviet naval activity in the Mediterranean and in the Indian Ocean has increased considerably since the October 1973 war. It thus seems that the Soviet leaders now consider the Middle East to be as critically important to them as it has always been to the West. This is hardly surprising since, apart from its strategic centrality, the region contains over half of the world's oil reserves and currently supplies most of Western Europe's and Japan's energy needs. Given its chronic instability, epitomized by the perennial Arab–Israeli conflict, the Iranian Islamic revolution, the Ethiopian–Somali and Iraqi–Iranian confrontations, the opportunities that the Soviet Union has to exploit the political situation in the area appear limitless.

This book analyses the scope and direction of Soviet involvement in this strategically and economically crucial region, and explores the Kremlin's intentions and methods of achieving policy objectives. Additionally, it examines the response of indigenous states to Soviet overtures and activities, thus assessing the chances of success of the Soviet effort.

The three chapters by Adeed Dawisha, Malcolm Yapp and Robert Patman, which describe and explain Soviet involvement in the Arab world, the Northern Tier and the Horn of Africa respectively, illustrate both the common factors underlying Soviet strategy towards the region as a whole and the divergent and sometimes contradictory policies pursued by the Kremlin towards individual states or groups of states within the Middle East. They also show clearly that Soviet policy suffered from constraints, relating to local factors, which were outside the control of Soviet policy-makers.

The extent to which Soviet activity and endeavours in the Middle East were a hostage to indigenous political attitudes and local rivalries is illustrated by Adeed Dawisha, who traces the development of Soviet fortunes in the Arab world since Egypt's signing of the Czech arms deal in September 1955. He maintains that Soviet penetration of the Arab world was aided by the West's colonial legacy and by the Western governments' misperception of the nationalist tide sweeping through the area at the time. The Soviet Union, therefore, maximized its gains by backing and encouraging 'anti-Western' nationalist leanings in the Arab world, even at the expense of local communist groupings. However, according to Dawisha, it was these very factors that later on militated against continued Soviet success in the area. While the Soviets, during their quarter of a century's flirtation with the Arab world, did sometimes pursue erroneous, ideologically based policies that ran contrary to Arab sensitivities, it nevertheless seems that, on the whole, it has been indigenous factors which limited the spread of Soviet influence in the Arab world.

Malcolm Yapp, in his chapter, argues that a clear distinction must be drawn between Soviet policy towards the Northern Tier states of Turkey, Iran and Afghanistan, and Soviet policy towards the Arab world and the rest of the Middle East. First of all, Russia, even in pre-revolutionary times, had close relations with the Northern Tier states, while similarly close ties with the Arab world did not develop until well after the Second World War. Moreoever, the impulse to maintain secure borders has had an abiding and overriding influence on Soviet policy towards Turkey, Iran and Afghanistan which has been absent from Soviet policy towards the rest of the region. Yet ideology and consideration of prestige are also present as factors motivating Soviet policy, and Yapp argues that whereas in the past Soviet strategy possessed a certain coherence, the invasion of Afghanistan showed not just the importance of ideology but also the distorting influence it exerted on the Soviet decision to invade – a decision which has done little to strengthen the security of the Soviet border.

Many of the contradictions inherent in Soviet policy are illustrated by the Soviet involvement in the Horn of Africa. Robert Patman concentrates on the circumstances surrounding the switch-over from Somalia to Ethiopia in 1977, and analyses the extent to which this shift was motivated in Moscow by a clear conception of Soviet aims and interests. Patman concludes that although the USSR initially had gained influence in Somalia through the provision of weaponry and military assistance, Moscow never supported Somalia's irredentist claims in the Ogaden, not least because to have done so would have flaunted the OAU principle concerning the inviolability of territorial borders at independence. The switch from Somalia to Ethiopia also took cognizance of Ethiopia's greater status within the African community and the better prospects which that country offered for long-term economic and political gains along socialist lines. Yet Soviet policy on the Horn has not been without its failings. In particular, Patman cites Moscow's efforts to form a Marxist-Leninist federation of the PDRY, Ethiopia, Somalia and Djibouti as indicative of the more general failure to appreciate the depth of indigenous rivalries and conflicts within and amongst the states of the Horn – a major weakness also, as Dawisha points out, of Soviet policy elsewhere in the region.

Soviet activity in the Middle East over the last three decades has been conducted through political, ideological, economic and military means. One of the most interesting, and still largely unexplored, aspects of Soviet involvement in the area is the Kremlin's use of Cubans and East Europeans seemingly as instruments of Soviet foreign policy. Edwina Moreton, however, paints a much more complex picture than the conventional 'proxy' thesis. She argues that there is ample evidence to suggest that the Cuban and East German regimes, for example, have more than sufficient reasons of their own for cultivating Third World contacts. In most cases, though, the interests that these two countries have pursued have run parallel to those of the Soviet Union. But there have been signs that the Soviet leaders, perhaps because of the importance of the Middle East, would not allow the Cubans the same freedom of manoeuvre in Ethiopia that they had enjoyed in Angola. Moreton concludes that 'to point to overall Soviet command is not to confirm the "proxy" thesis, if those commanded are there because they want to be. On the other hand, voluntary self-assignment to the Soviet cause does not amount to partnership if, when push comes to shove, the junior allies are unable to make their influence felt in Moscow.' The relationship is obviously complex and multifaceted.

In addition to historical, geostrategic and political factors, Soviet policy towards the Middle East has been influenced by economic considerations. This dimension is addressed by Anthony Stacpoole, who writes on Soviet energy concerns in relation to the Middle East, and by Alan Smith, who analyses Soviet trade with the various countries of the Middle East.

Stacpoole maintains that, with the exception of coal, Soviet energy production – of gas, nuclear power and hydroelectric power – is satisfactory. Most important, Soviet targets for oil production for 1985 could be met, but significant growth to 1990 is improbable. This seems to suggest that at present, or even by the mid-1980s, the Soviet Union possesses enough oil and gas (of which it has the largest reserves in the world) to cater for its own domestic needs. However, in all this, one inescapable conclusion emerges: since the Soviets do not seem to be in a position to use much of Middle Eastern oil themselves, it is reasonable to assume that they have in mind supply to the East Europeans. To understand fully, therefore, Soviet motivations for an 'energy relationship' with the countries of the Middle East, the analysis cannot be confined to the Soviet Union alone, but must take into consideration the needs and demands of 'the Six'.

Alan Smith, in his chapter on trade between the USSR and the Middle East, seeks to determine the comparative costs and benefits derived by the USSR from trade with the countries of the region. In this, he distinguishes between those states with observer status within the Council for Mutual Economic Assistance (CMEA) – Afghanistan, Ethiopia and the PDRY – and other Middle Eastern trading partners. The first group happens to be amongst the poorest and least developed of all the states in the area, and it is not entirely surprising that relations with these states constitute a net economic cost to the Soviet economy, a cost increased by the garrisoning of Soviet troops in Afghanistan. In its trade with other states, Moscow has been able to derive considerable economic benefit. In a detailed discussion of the commodity composition of trade, Smith examines the various explanations for the growth of 'unspecified residuals' in Soviet trade statistics, including the possibility that the growing salience of trade in this category is accounted for by arms transfers.

Arms transfer is one stark example of the rivalry that exists between the two superpowers for influence in the Middle East. The political dimension of this rivalry is analysed by Shahram Chubin, who takes as his starting-points the shift to the Gulf of the epicentre of Middle East politics and the preponderance of Soviet military power there. While conceding that in the region as a whole the USSR has air and naval facilities only in Ethiopia, the PDRY and Afghanistan, Chubin maintains that it is primarily through its contiguity to the region that Moscow possesses such potential for directly and indirectly influencing events. He also suggests that the continued failure to solve the Palestinian problem provides the USSR with influence not only amongst the Arab confrontation states but in Gulf countries sensitive to pressure on the Palestinian issue. He suggests, therefore, that in order to meet the challenge of Soviet power the West must evolve a unified political and military strategy which, first of all, increases the West's direct military presence in the area and, secondly, takes greater cognizance of the priorities and concerns of the states indigenous to the area. In particular, he argues that while the West must take measures to protect its oil supplies and meet the Soviet threat, at the same time to judge the Middle Eastern states merely as oil suppliers or as pro- or anti-Soviet is self-defeating for the long-term success of Western policy.

Jonathan Alford begins his chapter on Soviet–American military rivalry in the Middle East by noting that the military dimension should be seen as only one component of the overall and larger political and strategic competition between the two superpowers in the area. On the role of military power, Alford discusses the importance of the West enhancing the aura of its military presence in the region, both as a direct deterrent to the USSR and as a statement to indigenous countries that there is an overall East–West balance. As for Soviet military capabilities, he asserts that the uncomfortable military reality is that the USSR could, with relative ease, bring preponderant power to bear on the countries of the Northern Tier. However, in the other areas of the Middle East, the Soviet threat lacks some credibility because it is unable to match US amphibious and carrier-based capability. As a result, it is his view that 'without airfields in the Gulf, air operations would present considerable problems for the Soviet Union'. The building of American forces in the area, however, is also constrained by a number of factors, not least of which is the reluctance of indigenous leaders to grant Washington basing facilities for the Rapid Deployment Force. Nevertheless, it is Alford's conclusion that while the Middle East constitutes an enduring vulnerability for the West, Moscow is likely to be deterred from any move southward, both by continued problems in power projection beyond non-contiguous areas and by American willingness to risk escalation in the event of a Soviet move.

Karen Dawisha concludes the volume with an overview of Soviet strategy in the Middle East. She seeks to analyse Soviet policy as it is seen in Moscow, and for this she utilizes the various components in the Soviet calculus of the correlation of forces. After examining the notion that the correlation constitutes the dynamic balance between all class forces in the Middle East and not just static evaluations of the balance of power between states, she turns to the relationship between short-term policies and long-term goals. While the former are supposed to serve the latter, Moscow finds itself constantly having to take actions which gain an initial foothold, but which undermine the likelihood of achieving long-term objectives. Also, in the case of the relationship between Moscow's regional policy and its global strategy, although in theory the former is supposed to serve the latter, in fact the invasion of Afghanistan, combined with the US policy of linkage and Washington's new determination to enhance its own presence in the area, has led to the 'globalization' of Moscow's Middle East policy, with its activism in this sector – very much against its own wishes and interests – determining the parameters of conflict and cooperation at the global, East–West level.

The chapters that follow, therefore, chronicle both the successes and the failures of Soviet policy in the Middle East over the last thirty years. The book does not take 'the Soviet threat' as its starting-point. Rather, it examines the nature and scope of Soviet power, intentions and capabilities in the political, economic and military domains, and scrutinizes assumptions currently prevalent in the West about Soviet policy. The growth of Soviet military power is accepted and documented, but the long-term prospects of the Soviet Union translating that power into political and economic control is questioned. In this respect, the following chapters seek to present a fresh perspective on the policies of the Soviet Union in the Middle East.

2   The Soviet Union in the Arab World: The Limits to Superpower Influence
Adeed Dawisha

For all intents and purposes, the first important point of Soviet entry into the politics of the Arab world in the post-war period occurred in September 1955 with the signature of the Czech arms deal.[1] Until then, the Soviet Union was almost completely excluded from the Arabic-speaking regions of Asia and North Africa. Soviet policy was ill-conceived and lacking in consistency and understanding of the area, being formulated almost exclusively by the Communist International. Nor did the Soviet Union possess any economic interest worth pursuing or defending in an area still dominated by the old Western colonial powers. And as one of the first countries to recognize the new state of Israel in 1948, it naturally had attracted much hostility from the Arab countries. In the early 1950s, therefore, the opportunities for Soviet entry into the Arab world were extremely limited: the Kremlin did not seem particularly interested; and indigenous attitudes and political conditions were hardly welcoming or sympathetic.

The decision by President Gamal Abd al-Nasser of Egypt to buy arms from the Soviet-led Eastern bloc in September 1955 signalled a dramatic shift in the international relations of the Arab world, which hitherto had been completely dominated by the Western powers. This transformation occurred partly because of changes in Soviet policy and partly as a result of changes in the local environment itself. It was after Khrushchev's rise to prominence in 1954–5 that Soviet policy began to take account of the area's strategic and, to a lesser extent, economic importance. This coincided with the rise of nationalist, 'anti-imperialist' (and in consequence anti-Western) movements in the Arab world, at the helm of which stood Nasser's Egypt. It was in their intense hostility to the Baghdad Pact, signed in 1955 and designed as a crucial link in the West's effort to contain the alleged spread of 'international Communism', that the interests of the Soviet Union and the Arab nationalist forces converged. The Kremlin perceived the Pact as a major threat to Soviet security, and the Arab nationalists saw it as a further proof of the old colonial powers' determination to keep the local states under their tutelage. In April 1955, the Soviet Union publicly condemned the Pact and promised 'to support and develop cooperation with the countries of the Middle East and to work toward strengthening the national independence of these countries and consolidating peace and friendly cooperation among the people'.[2] Five months later, after the West's refusal to meet President Nasser's demand for arms to modernize his army, the Egyptian leader signed the Czech arms deal to the almost unanimous delight of the Arab nationalist forces. Within less than three years, Soviet influence had grown to such an extent that many Western politicians and analysts would predict the imminent absorption of Egypt and other key Arab states into the Soviet orbit.

The rapid spread of Soviet influence in the area in the mid and late 1950s could be attributed to a combination of factors. Most of these were in the form of indigenous nationalist and independence-orientated attitudes and sentiments which, by virtue of the West's colonialist tradition, were basically anti-Western, and were sweeping through the Arab countries and indeed through much of the contemporary underdeveloped world. And through this good fortune, plus conscious political manipulation, the Soviet Union was able to entrench itself in the area in a relatively short period of time.

The 1950s were politically volatile years in the Middle East. Anti-colonialist and 'anti-imperialist' sentiments were increasingly manifesting themselves in violent demonstrations of national assertiveness. In most cases, these were directed against the two dominant colonial powers, Britain and France; but the United States too, owing to the total obsession of the Eisenhower Administration, particularly Secretary of State John Foster Dulles, with 'anti-communist' alliances, was being increasingly perceived as another imperialist power. There was, thus, bitter nationalist hostility to the Eisenhower Doctrine, announced in January 1957, which pledged American assistance, including the dispatch of armed forces, to nations requesting Washington's help against 'armed aggression from any nation controlled by international communism'.[3] In fact, through the Eisenhower Doctrine, which in reality was aimed at protecting the traditionalist, monarchical regimes of Jordan, Saudi Arabia and Iraq and the pro-Western, Christian government of Lebanon against the rising tide of revolutionary nationalism, the Western powers played into Soviet hands. For there could be no doubt that in the inevitable division of the area between the 'conservative', *status-quo* and pro-Western regimes, and the emergent, radical and nationalist anti-Western forces, the latter were in the ascendancy.

The Soviet Union, therefore, began its penetration of the Arab world at a most opportune time. Helped by the West's colonialist legacy and by the Western governments' misperceptions of rapidly changing indigenous attitudes and loyalties, it entered the area on the winning side. Though having interests in the area which were no less 'imperialistic' than those of the United States, Britain or France, the Soviet Union was perceived at the popular level as a friendly and supportive power, simply because it was backing the indigenous 'nationalist' forces. Thus, immediately after the 1958 Iraqi revolution, which overthrew a virulently pro-West monarchy, Baghdad established diplomatic relations with Moscow, and when the new Soviet ambassador arrived in the Iraqi capital, he was met by a jubilant crowd, 100,000-strong while his American, British and French colleagues were all being protected by the army from an angry and abusive populace.

The Soviet aim remained stable: namely, to exclude American and Western interests from the area, and thereby to eradicate Western threats to the Soviet Union, while simultaneously increasing Moscow's influence and power *vis-à-vis* the West in a strategically important region. In the pursuit of this objective, the Soviet leaders endeavoured to emphasize and strengthen the Middle Eastern perception of Moscow as the champion of nationalist forces, even when these were 'bourgeois nationalists' who were often at odds with the local communists. There were of course a few aberrations. When in 1959 President Nasser attacked the seeming ascendancy of the Communist Party in Iraq's new revolutionary government, Khrushchev reminded him that such behaviour could 'give rise to complications for discharging Soviet obligations under the agreement for the construction of the Aswan Dam'.[4] However, such manifestations of Soviet support for indigenous communists were few and far between. As always in the past, local communists had to subordinate their interests to the higher 'good' of Soviet well-being. And Moscow could well see that, in the Arab world, it was the nationalist bourgeoisie and not the communist parties who had sufficient popular support to stand against and push back Western influence, thereby serving Soviet strategic, and ultimately political and ideological, interests. During this period, therefore, very rarely did Moscow deliberately try to impose on indigenous nationalist leaderships its communist beliefs. This attitude was epitomized by a statement made in 1957 by Khrushchev in an interview: 'Many Arabs . . . are very remote from Communist

ideas. In Egypt, for instance, many Communists are held in prison
. . . Is Nasser a Communist? Certainly not. But nevertheless, we
support Nasser. We do not want to turn him into a Communist and
he does not want to turn us into nationalists.'[5] The exclusion of
Western influence from the area through bolstering existing
nationalist populist leaderships, and not the erection of Soviet-style
political and social systems, was Moscow's highest priority during
this period.

Active Soviet support for the indigenous nationalist forces was
undertaken in a variety of ways. Moscow vigorously backed
nationalist 'progressive' causes in the United Nations and other
international forums. It supplied its allies in the areas with the most
modern weaponry, thereby increasing not only the military power
but, even more important, the prestige and stature of its clients
vis-à-vis other competitive regimes in the region. Furthermore,
every time Soviet armour was paraded in a friendly Middle Eastern
capital, it served as a subtle, yet potent, reminder to other peoples
in the area of the value of Soviet patronage. Economically, Moscow's trade and aid patterns during the period showed a clear
orientation towards achieving political and strategic goals rather
than, and often at the expense of, economic objectives. In an
economically asymmetrical relationship, it is invariably the client
state that gains economic advantage. Not only were the Soviets
aware of this but they pursued their line regardless of the economic
cost. It is interesting to note, for example, that by 1977 Egypt's debt
to the Soviet Union, which President Sadat decided not to repay,
was estimated to be in the region of $11 billion.* Finally, although
one of the first states to recognize Israel, the Soviet Union quickly
espoused the Palestinian cause, thus placing itself firmly at the side
of the Arab and Islamic worlds. The indigenous populations could
then contrast Soviet unequivocal support for what they considered
to be Arab and Muslim legitimate rights with the West's seemingly
unbending commitment to the maintenance and defence of Israel.
And this seems to be an enduring Arab image. Thus, according to
the Syrian semi-official newspaper *al-Thawra*, the Treaty of Friendship and Cooperation signed between Syria and the Soviet Union
in October 1980 was 'the natural crowning of our friendship with a
nation that has always supported the Arab struggle against Zionism'.[6]

While calculating that an imposition of Marxist-Leninist beliefs
on leaderships and populations imbued with the spirit of nationalism would, for the time being, prove counter-productive to Soviet

*Billion is used to denote one thousand million.

strategic interests, the Soviet leaders no doubt hoped that, by means of gentle and subtle Soviet help and persuasion, the local states themselves would ultimately develop political and economic systems more attuned to Soviet ideological imperatives. For instance, most of the Soviet Union's aid to its Arab clients was in the form of project aid – that is, aid granted to cover the costs of specific projects. This kind of aid was designed to benefit the development of the state sector at the expense of the private sector, and to encourage the introduction of long-term central planning.

In a similar, even more important, vein, the Soviet Union tried to aid the development in these countries of a one-party system. Indeed, in many cases, it encouraged the local communists to join forces with, or enter, the relevant country's party organization. In 1965, the Egyptian Communist Party was voluntarily disbanded, and its members subsequently joined the Arab Socialist Union (ASU), Egypt's sole party organization. The Soviets seemed optimistic that the ASU gradually would be transformed 'into a vanguard party which could carry out the revolution from above'.[7] Similarly, active Soviet encouragement compelled the Syrian and Iraqi Communist parties in the early 1970s to join forces with the ruling Baath parties in both of these pro-Soviet Arab countries. In 1972, the Syrians formed the Progressive National Front, whose central leadership consisted of seventeen members, two of whom were communists. A year later, in the first parliamentary elections in Syria for ten years, the communists ran with their Baathists allies in a unified 'national progressive' ticket which won over 67 per cent of the vote.[8] In Iraq, under the instigation of Brezhnev, the Communist Party stopped its underground activities (a decision it regretted later) and allied itself to the Baath Party in 1972. The Baathist government incorporated two communist leaders into the Cabinet, and a year later permitted the Communist Party to publish and distribute unhindered its newspapers.[9] It was obvious from these manoeuvres that the Soviet Union placed much hope on the future potential of the Arab one-party system. Organizational help and advice were also accorded to the Algerian FLN and the NLF of the People's Democratic Republic of Yemen (PDRY).

It was not that the Arab leaderships and populations needed much encouragement to develop one-party systems, which during the late 1950s and 1960s seemed more attractive to most of the newly emerging political elites than Western-type multi-party systems. In the 1940s and 1950s, some Arab countries, such as Iraq, Lebanon, Jordan and Syria (and the non-Arab Middle Eastern Islamic countries of Turkey and Iran), at one time or another boasted parliamentary systems with a number of parties supposedly competing for electoral votes. In reality, democratic practices were very rarely applied: corruption was rampant; elections were invariably rigged; more often than not, it was patronage rather than representation which dictated the parliamentary codes of conduct; and popular participation was in most cases limited to a very narrow, semi-feudal social structure.

The emerging elites (particularly the military elites) of the Arab world during this period had become distrustful of the 'sham democracy' of the traditional political systems, and, except for Lebanon, they had come to believe that, in the economically and socially underdeveloped societies, a multi-party system simply served to perpetuate and reinforce the political and economic interests of the feudal and business classes and their external backers. For example, when President Nasser once was asked why he did not allow the emergence of a multi-party system, he replied: 'If I did that, there would be one party acting as an agent for the American CIA, another upholding British interests, and a third working for the Soviets.'[10] Furthermore, the new elite perceived their major preoccupation to be the struggle against 'imperialist' influence and interests in the region, and to them this 'sacred duty' had to be pursued through a unified national endeavour. They therefore considered a multi-party system to be decidedly counter-productive to the effective direction and execution of this struggle. Accordingly, in that particular historical period of Arab and Middle Eastern political development, the Soviet model of an ideologically based, centrally controlled, one-party system seemed to be more attuned to the needs and interests of the emergent ruling elites.

By the mid-1960s, after no more than ten years of Soviet involvement in the Arab world, Moscow's influence had extended to the three core Arab states of Egypt, Iraq and Syria, and to Yemen and Algeria. The two primary pro-West Arab states, Jordan and Saudi Arabia, were reeling under the pressure of the rising tide of indigenous nationalist anti-Western sentiment. During that stage of Soviet activity, Moscow was clearly on the ascendancy, and the Western powers were being pushed back on to the defensive.

The period immediately after the 1967 Arab–Israeli war, witnessed, if anything, an increase in Soviet influence. It was the Soviet leaders themselves who decided to upgrade and intensify their presence in the region. The Kremlin sensed correctly the ensuing vulnerability of the Arab radical and 'progressive' regime *vis-à-vis* the conservative states in the wake of their humiliating defeat in June 1967. Consequently, it looked likely that the defeated Arab regimes would become more willing to accept greater Soviet participation in the economic and military reconstruction of their countries. Moroeover, at that time, Soviet strategic thinking was shifting towards establishing a greater conventional military presence to challenge Western domination in conventional arms in areas such as the Middle East. The securing of military facilities in Egypt, and to a lesser extent Syria, Iraq and Algeria, therefore became high priority. Indeed, by the early 1970s, thousands of Soviet military advisers had been dispatched to Egypt and Syria to rebuild the armies from the ashes of 1967. At the same time, the annual number of Soviet ships in the Mediterranean was dramatically increased,[11] and the Soviet navy obtained repair and resupply facilities at the Egyptian ports of Alexandria, Port Said, Mersa Matruh and Sollum; at the Iraqi port of Um Kasr; at Berbera in Somalia; and at Aden in the PDRY. To crown and cement this increasing Soviet visibility, Moscow signed treaties of friendship and cooperation with Egypt in 1971 and Iraq in 1972. At that time, there seemed little that could stop the triumphant Soviet march.

It is clear, however, that in the post-October-war period, the Soviet march began to be halted, and in some cases reversed. Thus, in 1980, Soviet influence in the Arab world was confined to Syria, Libya and the PDRY. In the 1970s, while gaining the PDRY and Libya, Moscow lost Egypt, Sudan, Somalia and North Yemen, and seemed to be in the process of losing Iraq. Jordan and Saudi Arabia, the most loyal Arab allies of the West, who in the late 1950s and early 1960s had been extremely vulnerable to the nationalist, pro-Soviet tide, emerged in the mid- and late 1970s as central actors in inter-Arab relations and regional politics. And the growing Saudi–Iraqi–Jordanian entente, if it continues, could prove to be a most potent pro-West alliance in the area, much more powerful than anything the Soviets could muster locally.

This picture is not one which seems to be confined to the Arab world. The revolution in Iran could be considered a loss to the West, but, given present indications, it is difficult to conceive of the clergy-dominated Iranian order as a gain for 'atheistic' Moscow. And Moscow's inability after all these years to effect fundamental attitudinal reorientations in the indigenous populations of the area is nowhere more evident than in Afghanistan, where political and ideological influence failed so miserably that, in order not to suffer yet another setback in the region, Moscow embarked on an invasion in which, after two years, the most powerful army in the world is still nowhere near 'pacifying' a weak and tribally divided country.

Although not immediately apparent, the decline actually began in 1971 when, for a short time, a coup engineered by the Sudanese Communist Party looked like succeeding before it was crushed by

President Jaafar Numeiry. For the Soviet Union, the writing was on the wall, since the man who played the main role in reinstituting Numeiry was no other than Egypt's President Anwar Sadat. This show of independence, coming from such a supposedly dependent client, should have worried the Soviet leaders. Other similar indications came later on. When Moscow refused to supply Egypt with weapons, in either the quality or the quantity that the Egyptian government demanded, Sadat decided to expel over 15,000 Soviet experts stationed in Egypt,[12] and more or less severed Soviet–Egyptian relations until Moscow relented, and in 1973 began supplying him with the weapons he needed. Worse was to come. In spite of Soviet protestations, in September 1975 Sadat signed with Israel, under American auspices, a disengagement agreement providing for the withdrawal of Israeli forces from the Sinai passes, which had been under Israeli occupation since the June 1967 Arab–Israeli war. He also began to accuse the Soviets, yet again, of reneging on their promise to supply Egypt with arms. Moscow's response was immediate and full of bitterness: 'Only after having lost all sense of shame can some people now say that [following the October 1973 war] Egypt received "only a few cases of spare parts" from the Soviet Union . . . The Soviet Union has been consistently continuing the policy of furthering friendly cooperation with Egypt in the military field in accordance with the existing agreements. But cooperation, of course, is a two-sided matter. It cannot develop if one of the sides is pursuing a policy of undermining it.'[13] Of course, it was the beginning of the end. Sadat had finally made up his mind to dispense with his Soviet mentors. He had decided that in the Middle East, and particularly as regards the perennial Arab–Israeli conflict, the Americans held all the trump cards, and that the Russians had become not just a nuisance, but a positive obstacle to his future Middle Eastern and international policies. And, in any case, moving over to the West not only suited Sadat's conservative temperament but also afforded him yet another opportunity to break with the policies of his predecessor, in the face of whose memory and towering presence he had consistently been trying to establish a separate identity and credibility. Egypt, the glittering prize of the area, the country which had commanded something like 43 per cent of all Soviet aid to the Third World between 1954 and 1971, was finally, and seemingly irrevocably, slipping away from Moscow's grasp. It was hardly a surprise, therefore, when on 14 March 1976 in a speech to the Egyptian Parliament, President Sadat unilaterally abrogated the Soviet-Egyptian treaty. To add injury to insult, eighteen months later, the Egyptian leader announced that he had suspended for ten years Egypt's repayment of its $11 billion debt to the Soviet Union. The Soviets were naturally irate, but could do nothing.

Relations with other Arab countries in which the Soviets had invested much time and effort were likewise attended by trouble and disappointments. After the withdrawal from Yemen in December 1967 of the Egyptian forces, which had been shoring up the Republican regime against the Saudi-backed Royalist forces, it was only the massive and rapid Soviet military aid that ensured the survival of the Sana' government. And for a while Yemen was referred to as a staging post for the Soviet Union, from which Moscow would launch its subversive attacks against Western interests and clients in the Peninsula. Yet here, too, Soviet influence was short-lived, and Western fears of Moscow's potential for further expansion through control of weak states was misplaced. Inevitably, the conservative instincts and social customs of the Yemenis, as well as their religious affiliations, meant that sooner rather than later Sana' would replace Moscow's protection by that of Riadh. By the mid- and late 1970s, it had become obvious that the survival of the Sana' government depended not so much on the Russian tank as on the Saudi riyal.[14]

Iraq is another case in point. The accession to power of the present Baathist regime in July 1968 signalled a gradual strengthening of relations between Moscow and Baghdad. Sophisticated military equipment was supplied to Iraq, and a training programme was agreed upon. Economic and technical agreements followed. These were designed to help the Iraqis in the development of the oil industry, nuclear power, agriculture, and a broader industrial base. By mid-1971, over sixteen agreements between Iraq and the Soviet Union, spanning the military, economic, technological and cultural fields, had been concluded.[15] Additionally, and more crucially, increasing contacts, and a firm bilateral relationship, had been established between the Soviet Communist Party and the Iraqi Baath Party. All this led to the signing of the Treaty of Friendship and Cooperation between the two countries in April 1972, which, to the Iraqi Baathist leadership, represented 'a strategic and ideological alliance between two regimes bound by a common revolutionary bond against Zionism and Western imperialism'.[16] For the next five or six years, Iraq's internal and foreign policies vindicated the perception that the Baghdad government had become one of the Soviet Union's main surrogates in the area. And no doubt the Kremlin had great hopes in Iraq's 'revolutionary' government.

The Kremlin, however, was soon to be served with yet another dose of Arab unpredictability. In mid-1978, and later in April 1979, a total of forty-eight members of the Iraqi Communist Party (ICP) were executed by the pro-Soviet regime for allegedly trying to establish a communist underground organization in the Iraqi armed forces. This was followed by wholesale arrests and persecution of communists that resulted in driving the ICP underground. Whatever their private feelings, the Soviet leaders could do, and indeed said, very little in the face of the Iraqi assertion, voiced publicly, that preceding the signature of the Treaty of Friendship and Cooperation in 1972 the Soviets had given assurances that relations between the Iraqi Baath and Communist parties were not subject to Soviet interference, and that under no circumstances would the USSR conduct its relations with Iraq through the Communist party.[17] By 1980, the 'ideological alliance' and 'revolutionary bond', which the Iraqis said bound the two regimes in 1972, seemed to be loosening rapidly. In fact, the Iraqis were now beginning to maintain that there were various political differences between the two countries, especially as Iraq's policy 'derived from national and pan-Arab interests'.[18] Indeed, President Saddam Hussein went as far as calling the communists 'a rotten, atheistic, yellow storm which has plagued Iraq'.[19] This verbal onslaught was accompanied by a gradual decrease, initiated primarily by Iraq, in the intensity of actual bilateral relations, so that by 1981, Iraq's trade with the Soviet Union, including the purchase of military equipment, had declined considerably. And to emphasize Iraq's alienation from the Soviet Union, the Baghdad government publicly and unequivocally condemned the Soviet invasion of Afghanistan.

The Iraqi experience should serve as a sombre reminder to those Kremlin leaders who might be thinking that through the Treaty of Friendship and Cooperation signed with Syria in October 1980, they can now concentrate on Damascus as the linchpin for their influence in the area. Although it is true that the Soviets have had consistently good relations with the Baathist regime of President Asad, and that, as the only supplier of military equipment to Syria, their influence is considerable, they have nevertheless experienced the limits of that influence.

On 1 June 1976, the Syrian armed forces invaded Lebanon to fight alongside pro-West, Christian Lebanese militias against Lebanese leftist and Palestinian forces. The Soviets were put in an untenable position as they watched their 'client' state in the area launching an offensive against a 'liberation movement' which had always been a close Soviet ally. A week after the Syrian entry into Lebanon, the official Soviet agency Tass issued a statement calling for an end to foreign intervention and demanding an immediate cease-fire. It reminded the Syrians that they had repeatedly claimed that their intervention was aimed at stopping the bloodshed. However, 'notice should be called to the fact that bloodshed continued in Lebanon today and blood flows in even greater streams'.[20] Soviet displeasure at the Syrian action was such that Brezhnev was moved to dispatch two letters to President Asad, in one of which he insisted 'that the Syrian leadership should take all possible measures to end its military operations against the [Palestinian] Resistance and the Lebanese National Movement'. He urged Asad to contribute to the establishment of peace in Lebanon by withdrawing his troops, adding that such an action 'corresponded with Syria's own interests.'[21] Indeed, the CIA suggested that in the wake of the Syrian invasion, Soviet military aid to the Damascus regime had 'dwindled to a trickle'[22] as an expression of Moscow's displeasure.

Yet, against Soviet wishes and in the face of Soviet severance of military supplies, the Syrians not only soldiered on with their invasion, but actually launched a subsequent massive offensive against the Palestinians which left Yasser Arafat, the leader of the Palestinian Liberation Organization, feverishly demanding help to 'save the Palestinians from this new massacre'.[23] The Soviets, however, were unable to impose their view of the situation on the Syrian leadership. President Asad stated simply: 'We have a different point of view which is not subject to compromise because it is based on our firm national principles and interest.'[24]

The Soviet leaders would do well to remember this encounter, as well as their loss of paramountcy in Egypt, Iraq, Yemen and Somalia, when they come to assess their influence in the Arab world. Of the three client states of the PDRY, Libya and Syria, the last two are ruled by vehemently Islamic and nationalist governments, whose ideological orientations are antithetical to those of the Soviet Union. Soviet-style Marxism-Leninism has no place in Asad's deeply ingrained Baathist nationalism or in Gaddafi's Islamic 'Third International Theory'. In fact, the Soviet leaders seem to have tacitly recognized this inevitable constraint on their ambitions in the area. In his speech to the 26th Party Congress in February 1981, Brezhnev singled out, of all his present Arab allies, the PDRY as a country of 'Socialist orientation'. After more than a quarter of a century of active political, economic and military involvement in the Arab world, the Soviet Union could name only one Arab state, which happens to be the poorest of them all, that could be considered anything more than a transient and unreliable ally – hardly the success story that need worry Western analysts or political leaders.

One of the reasons why the USSR was unable to maintain and reinforce its early advantage was inherent in the very policies it pursued so successfully in the late 1950s and early 1960s. Its efforts to encourage nationalist and Islamic tendencies were aimed at strengthening the forces in the area which at the time were fighting British and French colonial presence and perceived American imperialism. As long as the struggle for political and economic independence from the West continued, nationalism and Islam constituted weapons aimed at Western influence and as such needed to be vigorously encouraged by the Soviet Union. However, once independence was more or less achieved, and once local states, mainly through economic advances, no longer suffered from a consistently unequal relationship with Western powers, the forces of nationalism and Islam became as potent weapons against Soviet interests in the 1970s as they had been against the West ten to twenty years earlier.

The Soviet leaders, moreover, committed several mistakes in their dealings with local states, which were due primarily to a lack of understanding of indigenous attitudes, customs and rivalries. These misunderstandings probably occurred as a result of their tendency to view and analyse social and political activity from an ideological perspective. Thus, for example, they seemed unable to appreciate that local antagonisms, brought about by many years of ethnic, religious, cultural or geostrategic differences, could supersede seemingly ideological proximity. In the wake of the Ethiopian coup in early 1977, and the emergence of a 'progressive', neo-Marxist regime in Addis Ababa, Moscow tried to create a pro-Soviet alliance between Ethiopia and neighbouring 'progressive' Somalia (which was to include the PDRY), ignoring in the process the long-standing suspicion and mistrust which existed between the two countries as a result of their territorial dispute over the Ogaden. The net result was the almost immediate Somali defection to the West. Similar Soviet efforts abounded in the Arab world. In the early 1970s Moscow encouraged other neighbouring 'pro-Soviet' states, such as Egypt and Libya, the two Yemens, and Iraq and Syria, into various forms of closer relationships entailing stricter coordination of their 'anti-Western' policies. These Soviet endeavours inevitably came to nothing and, in many instances, eventually led to the alienation from Moscow of one or the other of the local states in question.

Furthermore, the influence of ideology on Soviet assessments and activities led Moscow to attribute too much importance to the structure and performance of the ruling party and the centrally-directed economic system. To the Soviets, it was the strengthening and cementing of these institutions which would guarantee the eventual and hopefully permanent transformation of the local states to a Soviet-style socialist system. This basically 'ideological' view admittedly was given credence by the seeming preference of the indigenous nationalist elites for the single party over the Western-type multi-party system. Yet the Soviet leaders seem to have taken this simple preference by the indigenous elites as a total acceptance of the paramountcy of the single-party system over all the institutions. In the process, Moscow completely underestimated the susceptibility of Middle Eastern and Islamic populations to the phenomenon of personalized leadership. The social and cultural backgrounds of these populations incline them to be particularly amenable to the idea of a single, clearly identifiable source of authority. Socially, the extended family, the tribe and the village for centuries had formed the main units of Middle Eastern societies, and in all these cases the pattern of authority always had been hierarchical, being bestowed upon one person. Culturally, Islam prescribes the concentration of religious and political power in the hands of one man, al-Khalifa, the successor to the Prophet Muhammed, the final arbiter of political power and the ultimate dispenser of justice. While al-Khalifa, as an institution, has been politically extinct since the collapse of the Ottoman Empire, the idea of an identifiable and personalized authority still forms an important part of the cultural norms and values of Middle Eastern Muslim societies. Consequently, social and cultural factors have tended to give the Chief Executive greater power than competitive political institutions, a fact which sometimes the Soviets did not seem to grasp.

The starkest example of this failure to understand basic indigenous attitudes was the Soviets' over-emphasis, after Nasser's death in 1970, on courting key members of Egypt's Arab Socialist Union (ASU) at the expense of the new and allegedly inconsequential President Sadat. They seem to have calculated that in any future power struggle it would be Ali Sabri, the ASU's General Secretary, backed by an extremely effective party organization (modelled on Soviet lines), who would emerge victorious against President Sadat. In the event, it was not Sabri and his party organization who won the political battle, but the 'ineffectual' Sadat who, even though he had been Chief Executive for barely seven months, nevertheless commanded enough loyalty generally to overcome Ali Sabri who, for years, had worked at establishing a secure power base in what was supposedly a grass-roots organization.

Perhaps the most important reason for the Soviets' failure to realize fully their early promise in the Arab world could be attributed to a significant change in the mood and attitudes of the Arab populations themselves – a factor which lay outside the control of the Soviet Union. The revolutionary nationalism of the 1950s and 1960s gave way to the political pragmatism of the 1970s: revolutionary leaders were replaced by more pragmatic ones, or simply by men who had moderated their views as time went on. Thus, while it was Egypt's Nasser with his fiery brand of revolutionary anti-Western oratory who dominated the Arab political theatre in the earlier period, the principal actors in the 1970s were pro-Western, *status-quo* leaders such as King Faisal and Prince Fahd of Saudi Arabia and President Sadat of Egypt. Not only was Nasser succeeded by the infinitely more conservative Sadat, but in Syria the neo-Marxist Salah Jadid gave way to the more pragmatic Hafiz al-Asad. Other 'revolutionary' leaders, such as Numeiry of Sudan, Boumédienne of Algeria, Siad Barre of Somalia, and lately Hussein of Iraq, gradually moderated their views, and only the Libyans and South Yemenis (PDRY) have so far remained faithful to the revolutionary creed. The decrease in revolutionary activism is attested to by the fact that the majority of Arab leaders who were in office at the beginning of the 1970s were still holding on to the reins of power as the decade ended – an amazing feat, given the previous domestic volatility of the region.

As the move away from nationalist, revolutionary politics gathered momentum, and as the conservative, pro-West leaders, hitherto on the defensive, emerged to play central roles in the international relations of the region, the influence of the Soviet Union began to wane. Indeed, the conservative states, at whose helm stood Saudi Arabia, went on the offensive to try to exclude the Soviet Union from the area. This was clearly spelled out in a statement made by Saudi Arabia's Crown Prince Fahd in 1974: 'I intend to get the Russian Communists out of Somalia. My policy will be to help the moderate forces in South Yemen. I will help the Sudan resist Communist subversion.'[25] And the Prince was true to his word. By 1980, Saudi aid to the Sultanate of Oman, a country which had been fighting communist insurgents for long periods, amounted to over $3,000 million. Saudi aid was also instrumental in persuading North Yemen to expel considerable numbers of Soviet advisers and reduce her reliance on the USSR. Similar tactics were used successfully with Somalia, and the Saudis publicly handed a cheque of $25 million to the Afghan rebels at the Islamabad Islamic Conference in May 1980. The Riadh government has also extended financial support to the Eritrean insurrection against the Marxist Ethiopian regime. Indeed, Saudi aid has gone to distant countries such as South Korea, Taiwan and Zaire simply because of their governments' anti-communism.

While the Soviet Union did sometimes pursue erroneous, ideologically based policies in the Arab world, which did not take account of local attitudes and sensitivities, it nevertheless seems that, on the whole, it has been mainly indigenous factors that militated against the spread of Soviet influence in the Arab world. And at present Moscow's influence seems to be almost entirely contingent on regional factors, relating primarily to inter-state rivalries, which, as has been proved in the past, can be too volatile for comfort. And, in all this, one inescapable conclusion remains: after a quarter of a century of active, indeed vigorous, involvement, nowhere in the Arab world, except in the PDRY, has the Soviet Union been able to establish a more than transient foothold. Moscow's footprints, implanted on many and various parts of the region in the 1950s and 1960s, had disappeared by the 1980s in the treacherous quicksand of Arab politics.

Notes

[1]   For an analysis of the pre-war Soviet policy in the area, see Hélène Carrère d'Encausse and Stuart R. Schram. *Marxism in Asia* (London, Allen Lane, 1969).

[2]   Karen Dawisha, *Soviet Foreign Policy Towards Egypt* (London, Macmillan, 1979), p. 11.

[3]   P. E. Zinner (ed.), *Documents on American Foreign Relations, 1957* (New York, Harper and Brothers, 1958), p. 201.

[4]   Adeed Dawisha, *Egypt in the Arab World: The Elements of Foreign Policy* (London, Macmillan, 1976), p. 86.

[5]   *New York Times*, 10 October 1957; quoted in Karen Dawisha, 'Soviet Policy in the Arab World: Permanent Interests and Changing Influence', *Arab Studies Quarterly*, vol. 2, no. 1 (1980), p. 21.

[6]   *Al-Thawra* (Damascus), 18 October 1980.

[7]   Quoted in Karen Dawisha, *Soviet Foreign Policy Towards Egypt*, p. 157.

[8]   Adeed Dawisha, *Syria and the Lebanese Crisis* (London, Macmillan, 1980), p. 47.

[9]   See Adeed Dawisha, 'The Transnational Party in Regional Politics: The Arab Baath Party', *Asian Affairs*, February 1974, pp. 23–31.

[10] *Egyptian Gazette* (Cairo), 9 May 1966.

[11] Robert G. Weinland, 'Land Support for Naval Forces: Egypt and the Soviet Escadra, 1967–1976', *Survival*, vol. 20 no. 2 (1978), pp. 73–80.

[12] *The Observer*, 19 March 1972; see also Mohamed Heikal, *The Road to Ramadan* (London, Fontana, 1976), pp. 171–5.

[13] Karen Dawisha, *Soviet Foreign Policy Towards Egypt*, p. 76.

[14] See Adeed Dawisha, *Saudi Arabia's Search for Security*, Adelphi Paper No. 158 (London, International Institute for Strategic Studies, 1979), pp. 20–1.

[15] Majid Khadduri, *Socialist Iraq: A Study in Iraqi Politics Since 1968* (Washington, D.C., The Middle East Institute, 1978), pp. 144–5.

[16] *Al-Thawra* (Baghdad), 12 April 1972.

[17] *Al-Destour* (London), 2–8 April 1979, pp. 6–7.

[18] *Al-Jumhuriya* (Baghdad), 13 July 1980.

[19] Adeed Dawisha, 'Iraq: The West's Opportunity', *Foreign Policy*, no. 41, Winter 1980/81, p. 138.

[20] *Soviet News* (London), 15 June 1976.

[21] *Events* (London), 1 October 1976, p. 23.

[22] *International Herald Tribune*, 3 October 1977; *Events* (London), 21 October 1977, p. 5.

[23] *The Times,* 29 September 1976.

[24] *Events* (London), 1 October 1976, p. 20.

[25] The quotation later appeared in *The New York Times* 23 December 1977.

3 Soviet Relations with Countries of the Northern Tier
Malcolm Yapp

A clear distinction may be made between Soviet policy towards the Northern Tier – Turkey, Iran and Afghanistan – and Soviet policy towards the Arab countries of the southern part of the Middle East.[1] Russian and Soviet relations with the northern countries are old and close: the first clash with Turkey (the Ottoman Empire) took place in the seventeenth century; that with Iran in the eighteenth century; and that with Afghanistan in the nineteenth century. Relations with the Arab countries are of very recent origin and very much less important to the Soviet Union: if one leaves out of account Russian campaigns against the Ottomans in the eastern Mediterranean in the eighteenth century, there is only the nineteenth-century Orthodox interest in Syria and Palestine to represent an enduring source of involvement until the Soviet move into the Arab world in the mid-1950s.[2] The relative importance of the two areas in Soviet eyes may be shown by comparing the Soviet reaction to developments in Egypt with its response to events in Afghanistan: in 1972, the Soviet Union was ousted from its expensive, carefully constructed position in Egypt and went without demur; in 1979, faced with the prospect of losing its influence in Afghanistan, the Soviet Union sent in combat troops to save its position.[3]

How may this difference in the Soviet approach to the two areas be explained? In this paper the various factors which appear to influence Soviet policies to the Northern Tier will be discussed. But first let us briefly consider the history of Soviet policies towards the countries of the Northern Tier.[4]

History
For convenience the history of Soviet relations with the countries of the Northern Tier may be divided into four phases: revolution (1917–21), symbiosis (1921–41), aggression (1941–53), and court-

ship (1953–78). The Afghan and Iranian revolutions of 1978–9 opened a new phase, the nature of which will be discussed at the end of this paper.

The revolutionary character of the first phase was determined partly by the heady, ideological enthusiasm of the early days of the revolution, but more by the precarious situation of the young Soviet state, menaced by civil war and by foreign intervention. In this situation it was important to use whatever means lay to hand to frustrate the purposes of the enemies of the state. The chief enemy appeared to be Britain and the support of revolutionary and anti-British movements in Turkey, Iran and Afghanistan. These movements not only posed a threat to British India, but also offered the hope of inducing Britain to abandon its policy of intervention, recognize the Soviet state, and negotiate a fervently desired trade treaty with it. This policy succeeded better in its ends than in its means: communist revolution was a damp squib, and the nationalist revolutions which brought new regimes to power in Turkey, Iran and Afghanistan owed little to Soviet support; on the other hand Britain did what was wanted of it.

The objectives of Soviet policy having been achieved, support for revolution was abandoned, and treaties were signed in 1921 with each of the three Middle Eastern states, ushering in the second phase, a period when, despite deep mistrust, the Soviet Union and the Northern Tier states managed to live together. The states of the Northern Tier continued to seek some countervailing force, some disinterested and powerful state which could reduce their commercial dependence on the Soviet Union and provide them with some political support. During the 1930s they began to think that Nazi Germany might be such a saviour, only to discover in 1941 that they had confused disinterest with uninterest.

The German invasion of Russia in 1941 caused Britain and the Soviet Union to bury their differences, combine their forces and eventually impose their will upon the states of the Northern Tier – the beginning of the third phase. Afghanistan was obliged to cast off its German connections, Iran was invaded and occupied, and although Turkey's geographical position and diplomatic skill enabled it to maintain its neutrality for most of the war, it, too, ultimately threw in its lot with the victorious alliance. As a consequence of these events and of the progress of the war, the power of the Soviet Union *vis-à-vis* the Northern Tier was greatly increased, and in 1945 it elected to try to convert its advantage into permanent gain by demanding from Iran and Turkey concessions which would have given her a commanding position in those countries. The Soviet demands proved to be a turning-point in the development of the Cold War, for the United States came to the support of Iran and Turkey, the Soviet Union backed down, and relations between the Soviet Union and the Northern Tier degenerated into snarls directed at one another across their borders.

The fourth phase of Soviet policy in the Middle East began after the death of Stalin. The new policy had two features. One, which is not the concern of this chapter, was a movement into the Arab world with the apparent intention of disrupting Western interests there as a means of inducing the Western alliance to relax its support for the states of the Northern Tier. The other is a movement into the Northern Tier itself. Afghanistan became a major recipient of Soviet economic and military aid, the largest *per capita* ever of such aid outside the Soviet bloc. Iran and Turkey, now members of CENTO, were less responsive but, despite repeated rebuffs, the Soviet Union persisted in presenting its most amiable countenance towards these states, and in the 1960s began to enjoy some signs of requited affection. The military aspects of CENTO faded from view, and Turkey and Iran exhibited an increasingly conciliatory demeanour towards the Soviet Union. Cultural exchanges, economic agreements and political discussions followed one another. By the late 1970s the Soviet Union could take real satisfaction from the results of its policies in the Northern Tier. Its influence in Afghanistan was predominant; its economic transactions with Iran had greatly increased; and in the summer of 1978 its developing ties with Turkey were crowned by a political document on the principles of good neighbourliness and friendly cooperation, a modest enough agreement but one proudly displayed by the Soviet Union as representing a new, higher stage in Soviet–Turkish relations.[5]

It is the success of a Soviet policy pursued consistently for a quarter of a century that makes it difficult to suppose that the Soviet Union deliberately abandoned this policy in favour of an aggressive orientation, similar to that which was tried under the very different circumstances of 1917–21 and 1941–6. On the contrary, if past patterns are any guide to the future, one would declare that the USSR will continue to seek good relations with stable states on its southern frontier. No doubt, if there were no other factors to be considered, the USSR would like something more and would wish to bring the Northern Tier into a state of greater dependence; but, given the existing balance of power or correlation of forces, it is evident that the USSR had settled happily for good relations. The policy of disruption by encouragement of revolutionary or separatist elements was pursued only in extreme circumstances and as a last resort. The Soviet Union deplored the instability, anarchy and terror which prevailed in Turkey until recently.

I have discussed elsewhere the question of Soviet involvement in the Afghan revolution of April 1978 and the Iranian revolution of 1978–9, and have concluded that there was none.[6] The USSR was obliged to deal with a new situation which had come into being as a result of developments which it did not control and had not sought. Before discussing the shape of the new Soviet policy, I shall examine some of the factors which have been held to influence Soviet policies towards the Northern Tier.

The economic argument

The contention that the USSR seeks economic advantage is discussed in Chapter 7. Although the level of Soviet commercial dealings with the countries of the Northern Tier increased considerably after the mid-1960s, it remained a very small part of Soviet foreign trade.[7] Nor are the commodities exchanged of particular value. Afghanistan has many minerals, but they are very expensive to extract. So absurd an economic proposition is an Afghan steel industry that when the late President Da'ud sought finance for this purpose the Soviet Union turned him down, and even the sympathetic Shah was reluctant to assist. Soviet import of natural gas from Iran and Afghanistan is a convenience not a necessity, one which enables the USSR to make a profit on the difference between what it pays for Northern Tier natural gas and what it receives for its own gas exported across the western frontier, taking into consideration the costs of transport. Nor can one have much confidence in the theory that the Soviet Union is running out of oil and hoped to gain access to Middle Eastern oil through the Northern Tier.[8] The Soviet Union is not running out of oil, and if it wanted Middle Eastern oil, it would be much cheaper to buy it on the open market than to incur the costs of dominating the Northern Tier to obtain it. It is true that Afghanistan, now a CMEA observer, may be herded into full membership of that institution, but that would be a political not an economic decision.

The 'stepping-stone' theory

A second explanatory theory which is employed is the stepping-stone theory. This theory alleges that, for a variety of reasons, the USSR seeks to dominate the Northern Tier in order to gain access to the Indian Ocean. The theory derives from two sources: history and the exigencies of present-day superpower conflict. The argument from history is worthless. It is alleged that from the time of Peter the Great, Russia and the Soviet Union have always sought access to a warm-water port in the Gulf area. In support of this argument, various documents and episodes are cited, invariably out of context, beginning with the forged will of Peter the Great. There is little evidence to suggest that it had been Tsarist or Soviet policy to seek a naval base on the Gulf, or anywhere in the Indian Ocean area, or to desire the possession of India.

Because of its speculative nature, the argument from present-day superpower conflict cannot be so easily dismissed. The argument offers four reasons why the Soviet Union should seek to dominate the Northern Tier: to enable it to neutralize Western naval strength in the Indian Ocean, especially with reference to the possibility that missiles might be launched from submarines in the area against the southern parts of the Soviet Union; to enable it to support by military means a political policy of the containment of China; to enable it to interdict supplies of oil from the Gulf area to Western countries and Japan, either by military or political action in the Gulf area or by threatening shipping lanes; and to enable it to support and extend its political influence in countries of the southern Middle East and Africa.[9] Each of these possibilities is worth a separate paper, but here only a few comments can be offered about each of them.

The missile defence argument, which appeared strong in the late 1960s, has been disposed of by technological advances. On the question of neutralizing Western naval strength it may be noted that the USSR has said only that it aspires to equality and, in fact, is nowhere near that position. Without bases, the desire for which it denies, it is difficult to see how the USSR could equal Western naval strength in the Indian Ocean. Of course, if the USSR dominated Iran she could obtain a naval base on the Gulf or the Arabian Sea, but contemplation of this possibility at once exposes one of the principal reasons for Soviet unwillingness to seek a base. Such a base would be vulnerable to attack from the sea and it would require Soviet control of a long line of land communications through what would be hostile country. The base would be nothing more than a hostage to fortune. In short, the purely naval argument seems to lead nowhere.

The Chinese question has been a prominent feature of Soviet policy in the region for more than ten years. The circumstance that states in South-East and South Asia felt threatened by China has enabled the Soviet Union to find some local support for what amounts to a policy of containment. Soviet policy has had three elements: a collective security scheme; bilateral agreements with individual states; and support for the non-aligned movement's policy of declaring the Indian Ocean a zone of peace, by which the

USSR means that outside powers should not have bases but should be free to sail their navies on the high seas. The first project (of the collective security scheme), with which Brezhnev has been closely associated, has made no progress and much less has been heard of it lately.[10] As for the third policy, of the zone of peace, it is manifestly impossible to harmonize that policy with one of domination of the Northern Tier and with the creation of bases in the area.

By far the most important is the policy of bilateral agreements represented by Soviet agreements with the states of Indo-China and by the Soviet–Indian entente. Plainly, these agreements involve the ability both to supply the states concerned and, in certain circumstances, to lend them aid against the threat of China. It can reasonably be argued that to give such support would be easier if the Soviet Union could dominate the Northern Tier. Command of Afghanistan provides the means to put the pressure on China's ally Pakistan; command of the Gulf gives access to the Indian Ocean and a better chance of forestalling the spread of Chinese influence in the area; and command of Turkey would give greater freedom of movement for the Black Sea fleet. As far as the states of Indo-China are concerned, there is no evidence that their benevolent feelings towards the Soviet Union are diminished by Soviet activities in the Northern Tier. In the case of India, however, it would seem that there is much less enthusiasm for Soviet intervention in Afghanistan, which suggests that a more naked policy of domination in the Northern Tier might be counter-productive in relation to India. If Indian attitudes towards the Soviet Union changed, it would be considerably more difficult for the USSR to aid the states of Indo-China. India's commitment is firmly to the zone of peace policy and to the exclusion of outside powers from the Indian Ocean. A friendly but distant Soviet Union is one thing; a Soviet Union on one's back doorstep would be another. Consequently, a more aggressive policy of Soviet expansion in the Northern Tier might bring on a Sino-Indian rapprochement, which for the Soviets would adversely change the disposition of affairs in the Indian Ocean. The recent agreement by India and China to discuss matters in dispute between them may be the first sign of that change.[11]

The interdiction of Western oil supplies by obstructing the sea lanes would be the equivalent of a declaration of war and need not be considered further. The question whether a Soviet presence in the Gulf area would enable the USSR to disrupt the political systems of Gulf states is a difficult one to answer. One is tempted to remark that the powers of self-destruction among the Gulf states are so great that any Soviet assistance would be superfluous;

indeed, a Soviet presence on the Gulf might be a stabilizing factor among the Gulf states. But the Gulf states themselves obviously do not believe that the Soviet Union presents any threat to them, and they sympathize with the Soviet argument that the West is using the alleged Soviet threat as a pretext for intervention in their internal affairs.[12] There are also arguments which question whether the Soviet Union would see any benefit to itself in disrupting Western economies. These, however, cannot be conclusive, since the possibility must remain that even if the USSR saw no present benefit in such a policy, it might nevertheless wish to secure a position from which it could mount such action if the international situation required it: for example, if it became desirable to try to deter the West from pursuing a policy contrary to Soviet interests in Eastern Europe.

The last argument in the stepping-stone theory is the most difficult of all to discuss, for it involves a consideration of what value the USSR sets upon its stake in the Middle East and Africa, notably the People's Democratic Republic of Yemen (PDRY) and Ethiopia, but also including interest in several other countries in the region. Contemplating the poverty and instability of the states involved and their doubtful strategic value, one is inclined to think that the USSR would not set too high a value on the investment it has built up in them, and to suppose that the effort of dominating the Northern Tier would be wholly disproportionate to the objective desired. But this line of reasoning excludes the linked questions of ideology and prestige, which will be discussed later and may be deferred for the moment.

Finally, the opportunity argument should be noted. Proponents of this argument assert that whatever the motives for any Soviet advance (and they concede that such a movement may be dictated by purely defensive impulses), the positions obtained create opportunities for future action and may even inspire ambition. Students of British imperial history will indeed remember on how many occasions advances were made for one reason and subsequently defended by quite different arguments. Strategy sometimes becomes a rationalization of accident. It is not inconceivable that the USSR may come to adopt goals previously disdained merely because it has achieved positions which bring them nearer realization and which require the adoption of those goals in order to make the retention of the positions seem a rational choice. An imperial logic so compounded from a mixture of Alice and Lady Macbeth carries a fearsome plausibility. But before we agree to enter into the spirit of the game, we must look at the question of opportunity costs.

Reviewing the arguments in favour of the theory that the USSR seeks the domination of the Northern Tier because of its superpower conflicts, one can note that some have little or no value, while others may have some substance and may influence Soviet policy in so far as they can be seen to offer the Soviet Union some possible advantage in the future, if not now. But the question which must always be asked is: what price is one prepared to pay, now or in the future, in direct or in opportunity costs, in order to guard against some prospective danger or to secure some possible advantage which may not materialize and which may be capable of containment or access by other, cheaper means? To the question put in this fashion the answer is likely to be 'not much', as, historically, the answer has almost always been. While recognizing the force of the arguments of imperial inertia and springboard – that it is often easier to rationalize the decision to stay in a position rather than to abandon it, and that, as a consequence, the new position becomes the starting-point for new ventures – one may yet note that, historically, empires have usually been willing to call it a day when the bill became too costly. Market forces may prevail even in international relations and even in command economies. And the Soviet Union is not short of urgent demands upon its resources.

From these speculative questions of Soviet ambition we may turn to almost equally speculative questions of Soviet defence. Here we may consider three aspects: the Straits,[13] the border and the Soviet Muslims.[14]

The Straits question
The Straits of the Bosphorus and the Dardanelles form the only sea passage linking the Black Sea with the Mediterranean. Through them Russia was attacked in 1854 and 1914; and they formed a major gap in Soviet defences in 1919–20 and 1940–2. One half of Soviet sea-borne trade passes through the Straits. Use of the passage is governed by the Montreux Convention of 1936, which recognizes Turkish sovereignty over the Straits and affirms the principle of free navigation, to be regulated by a convention. The convention provides for free commercial navigation in peacetime and for the passage of small warships subject to certain limitations. Different regulations govern the use of the Straits in time of war. The Montreux Convention ensures that no enemy fleet more powerful than the Soviet Black Sea fleet can threaten the coasts and shipping of the USSR in that region. It also permits some Soviet warships to pass into the Mediterranean. But from the Soviet viewpoint, it has some deficiencies: it limits the size and character of the warships which the USSR can pass through the Straits into

the Mediterranean; and, because the USSR has no base in the Straits, it gives no guarantee that a hostile Turkey will not prevent the USSR from exercising its rights under the convention, or, at least, oblige the Soviet Union to observe the limitations of the convention much more precisely than that power does at present. The Straits are vital to the defence and commerce of the Soviet Union, and Soviet strategists must smile ruefully when they read of Western fears of a possible Soviet stranglehold upon the oil lifeline in the Indian Ocean, for a member of NATO is already in actual physical control of a passage essential to the well-being of the USSR. The Soviet Union has not raised the question of the revision of the Montreux Convention since the failure of its disastrous attempt to do so in 1945, which pushed Turkey into the arms of the USA. It cannot, however, be supposed that the USSR is content with the present situation, and the question of the Straits must always inform Soviet policy towards Turkey. The Soviet Union could secure no greater prize in the region than to bring Turkey into the CMEA and the Warsaw Pact.

Border defence
The importance to the Soviet Union of the defence of its borders is too obvious to require much discussion and is regularly trumpeted by the Soviet Union itself. The Soviet Union has the longest land frontiers of the world, and to protect them by the control of strategic positions, by the disposition of its troops, and by the maintenance of a number of buffer states has been a feature of the policies of both Tsarist Russia and the USSR. Plainly, the Middle Eastern frontier is not as sensitive as those of Central Europe and China, if for no other reason than that no major international enemy faces the USSR across the Middle Eastern frontier. Nevertheless the same preoccupations have been visible throughout history. The western Iranian frontier is that which was selected by Russia in the early nineteenth century and achieved in 1828. The eastern Iranian frontier has remained undisturbed since the late nineteenth century. The eastern Turkish frontier is a less satisfactory solution, which was questioned by the Soviet Union (or at least the Republics of Georgia and Armenia) as late as 1946. The frontier with Afghanistan is a frontier achieved by compromise with British India at the end of the nineteenth century, and represents a renunciation by Russia of its long-held view that the proper frontier was the Hindu Kush range and not the Amu Darya. In the event of the disintegration of the Afghan state, it might well be that the USSR would reopen the question of the alignment of that frontier and could find some support for such a move through the

ethnic claims of the Soviet Republics. A similar move could be made in relation to Iran by the incorporation of Azerbaijan.

Such frontier changes are unlikely except in the event of a major upheaval in the area and the collapse of states. The shape of Soviet policy since 1921 indicates a preference for the continuation of the Tsarist policy of seeking to maintain weak, dependent states along the Middle Eastern frontier as the best protection for its borders. Iran may have denounced that provision in the Soviet-Iranian treaty of 1921 which gave the USSR the right of armed intervention in Iran under certain circumstances, but the USSR has not consented to this alteration. And, although the 1978 Afghan-Soviet treaty gives the Soviet Union no right of intervention, the December 1979 invasion was justified partly by reference to that treaty. It would be no surprise to discover that the unpublished March 1980 Moscow agreement contained a more definite provision for the independent action of Soviet troops in Afghanistan. Only in Turkey does the USSR not have some legal basis for intervention, although, to some extent, the Montreux Convention could provide a substitute in the case of a Turkish regime which pursued a policy of outright hostility towards the USSR. The Afghan invasion also suggests the emergence of a new type of control over the states of the Northern Tier, namely the maintenance in power of regimes ideologically sympathetic to the USSR, a circumstance which could make the Northern Tier situation similar to that of Eastern Europe and provide a valuable insulation for the Soviet frontiers in the area. Finally, another weapon is to tie these states to the USSR by means of economic links and the supply of weapons and military advice, although in this respect comparatively little progress has been made in relation to Iran or Turkey. It must be questioned, however, whether a policy which was appropriate some years ago can still be suitable today. Sovereign countries of the size and vigour of Iran and Turkey cannot be kept in a state of weak dependence as their predecessors might have been.

The Soviet Muslim factor
A special circumstance, not shared by the European or Chinese frontiers, distinguishes the Middle Eastern frontier of the USSR. This is the fact that the population of the USSR adjacent to much of the border speaks Turkish and Persian languages and by religion is Muslim. There has been much speculation about the extent to which the need to insulate these peoples from contact with an Islamic resurgence in the areas to the south may have influenced Soviet policy towards Afghanistan and Iran. There is little or no direct evidence to support the assertion that the insulation of

Soviet Muslims has played much part in Soviet thinking (nor in the nature of things could there be), and the argument rests on the interpretation of indirect evidence which must now be examined.

The first element in the argument is that of population growth. The birth rate among Soviet Muslims is much higher than that among European Russians, leading to the presumption that, by the year 2000, up to one in four of Soviet citizens may be Muslim. This population growth could have three effects: first, Muslims can demand and receive a greater voice in Soviet policy-making; second, the Soviet army may be increasingly composed of Soviet Muslims; and, third, in order to give employment to the new Muslims, there may have to be either a massive shift of industrial investment into Central Asia or a major movement of the Central Asian population into other regions of the USSR. If certain assumptions are correct, each of these effects holds out the prospect of increased dissension within the USSR. The most important of these assumptions is that Soviet Muslims should feel themselves to be distinct from other members of the Soviet Union. Orthodox Soviet theory supposes that, under socialism, religion withers away, remaining only as an unimportant private activity of a minority of citizens and having no effect upon public policy, and that political nationalism does not appear, it being essentially a product of bourgeois capitalism. If Soviet theory is correct, then the Soviet Union has nothing to fear from the rise of the Soviet Muslims. But there is good reason to suppose that Soviet theory offers an inadequate description of the nature of the formation of political identities.[15]

With regard to religion, it may be observed that in certain respects Soviet Muslims remain Muslims: that is, that they observe Muslim festivals, practise circumcision and go through religious marriages and funerals. This, however, is only to say that they are what may be called 'cultural' Muslims and does not contradict Soviet theory. The question we must ask is whether this cultural identity has the possibility of transformation into a political identity in the fashion with which events in other parts of the Muslim world have made us familiar.

There is good evidence of the persistence or revival on a large scale of Muslim mystical (Sufi) brotherhoods among the Muslims of the North Caucasus, and of their political character inasmuch as they play a primary role in regulating the lives of the people of the area. The phenomenon is interesting and certainly militates against Soviet theory, but in itself it is not especially menacing to the Soviet Union. First, the Muslims of the North Caucasus are not numerous. They are virtually surrounded by non-Muslims, are insulated from the border, and speak languages distinct from those spoken on the other side of the border. Second, the movement appears to be largely a rural movement, although it is alleged that some urban intellectuals also belong to the Sufi orders. Third, the North Caucasus Muslims constitute a peculiar case. Their nineteenth-century resistance to Russian conquest was by far the most determined and prolonged of all the conquered peoples; their hostility to Russian and Soviet rule has always been evident (in the Second World War they collaborated with the Germans and many were deported for several years); and the Sufi Naqshbandi order in the North Caucasus has a militarist character which is by no means common to other branches of the Naqshbandiyya, still less to other Sufi orders. It is also claimed that Sufi orders are on the increase among Muslims of Central Asia. If this were so, it would be a much more serious matter, but the evidence is very slight and relates mainly to the minor Republic of Kirgizia. The vitality of the Sufi orders, therefore, is a difficulty for Soviet ideologists but not necessarily a permanent one, and it is not a menace to the security of the Soviet state. There can be little doubt, however, that organizations like the Sufi brotherhoods would be likely to derive encouragement from the Islamic resurgence outside the USSR, even though the Islamic revival elsewhere has not usually been associated with Sufi organizations.

The Islamic revival in general has been especially associated with urban groups and particularly with new immigrants to towns.[16] It is therefore a phenomenon of the process of modernization, and if there were to be a corresponding movement in the Soviet Union, one would expect to find evidence of it in towns like Baku, Alma Ata, Tashkent and Dushanbe. In fact there are no reported signs of a revival of orthodox Islam in these towns. And it is difficult to see how any such revival could take place because of the position of the Sharia. So far the Sharia has been the essential reference point of Islamic revivalism; revivalists have attacked the secularist rulers of Muslim states on the grounds that they had not ruled according to the Sharia. The Sharia is a code around which the revivalists rally and through which they legitimize their critique of the existing order. In the Soviet Union, the Sharia does not exist except with regard to certain matters of worship. Its role in law and education disappeared after the revolution and there is no evidence of any demand for its return. In this respect Soviet Muslims resemble most closely the Muslims of Turkey, another state which ordained a secular system of government and society, and banished religion to the sphere of private life. Whilst the hold of religion has remained strong in private life, it has reasserted itself in public life only in a minor way in Turkey. The urban masses of Turkey support secular political parties.

Whether Soviet Central Asia will follow the Turkish or Iranian pattern is uncertain. For a variety of reasons, the emigration of Central Asians to towns has been slower than similar movements in other areas of the region. If, as seems possible, the rate of urbanization should quicken, the situation may change. Islam might then seem a suitable political identity with which to oppose the claims of those who owed their positions to Soviet power. In such a case the official Soviet Muslim hierarchy, an organization created primarily to impress non-Soviet Muslims, might become much more important, revealing itself as a ready-made leadership, capable of articulating Muslim grievances. But, on the evidence which has so far appeared, one would conclude that urban Central Asian Muslims tend to regard religion as a private activity and to adopt a secular attitude to public life. The situation of Islam in the Soviet Union, therefore, seems to be one which calls for some circumspection on the part of the Soviet authorities, particularly in relation to any plans for rapid modernization, but not for urgent and violent solutions. In short, one would suppose that some more modest means of insulation would be more appropriate than the invasion of Afghanistan.

If one supposes it more likely that Soviet Muslims will choose a secular rather than a religious political identity, the question arises whether that identity is likely to be a Soviet one or, say, an Uzbek, a Turkman, or a Kazakh one. (For various reasons one would be inclined to rule out a Central Asian or Pan-Turkish identity.) The evidence suggests little assimilation by Soviet Muslims to the Soviet model. Soviet Muslims lead separate social lives; they rarely intermarry with non-Muslims; they learn Russian increasingly as a second language, but apparently often very badly, and almost never adopt it as a first language; and they tend to stay in their own republics and, increasingly, to monopolize the public organizations within them. It is also clear that they are not regarded as equal Soviet citizens by Russians: they are under-represented in Union institutions; they are virtually excluded from any positions of power in the army; and there is some evidence of racial feeling against them. There have been a few (although remarkably few) examples of prominent officials being dismissed for what are recognizable as nationalist deviations. There have been, and continue to be, arguments about the allocation of resources, notably about transport, the location of industry and the question of the southwards diversion of the northward flowing rivers of Siberia to supply water essential for agriculture and industrial expansion in Central Asia.

What significance should be read into these phenomena? One might think very little; most of what has been said could be said of Scots and Welsh in relation to England, and it is evident that political nationalism and the desire for separation from Britain are the programmes of only a minority of Scots and Welsh. A further safety factor within the Soviet system lies in the probability that Central Asians are not necessarily united against Russians but have their own conflicts: in particular, the dynamism and prosperity of the largest ethnic group, the Uzbeks, can appear as a threat to Turkomans and Tajiks, by whom the Soviet system thus may be perceived as a guarantee of their own separate national life. Within the republics, the position of certain groups, operating through regional, family, clan or tribal links, is, in effect, guaranteed by the Soviet system. And, of course, the Soviet grip, through the presence of large numbers of Russians and Ukrainians, of the Communist Party and other organizations, and of the army, is unshakable under present circumstances.

Should one therefore conclude that Soviet Muslims present no significant threat to the Soviet system? Not necessarily. Two factors may alter the situation. The question of manpower has already been mentioned, which means that it might become imperative for either industry to move into Central Asia or labour to move out if the Soviet system is to run smoothly. If the Soviet planners will not (often for good economic reasons) move industry into Central Asia, and if Central Asians decline to move out (and they are not wanted in Russian and Ukrainian towns), the one obvious possibility is the movement back to European Russia or Siberia of the large numbers of Russians and Ukrainians who emigrated to Central Asia during the last hundred years. Such a movement could be accelerated by the competition for jobs in Central Asia, in which Central Asians have a natural advantage.

The second factor is the circumstance that Central Asian Muslims are now reasonably prosperous, literate and more assertive than in years past, and have come to dominate state organizations within the republics. Fifty or thirty years ago the presence of Russians at all levels of the system acted as a mechanism of detailed control. It is now more difficult to operate controls at lower levels, and recourse must be had to higher levels. One may compare the situation to fire-fighting. Fires may be dealt with either by local defence (sprinklers, extinguishers, and even the humble bucket of sand or water) or by central defence (the fire brigade). Formerly, the Russians could operate by local defence in Central Asia; in the future it seems likely that disturbances will require the equivalent of the fire brigade. The result is that whereas in the past disputes could be snuffed out before they became significant, they are now increasingly likely to become the subject of political dispute at republican level. One could imagine, in the future, a dispute arising out of proposed changes in the school curriculum in which Uzbeks asserted a requirement for more Middle Eastern or Muslim history in their schools. If such a demand rose to republic level, it could become the type of issue around which national feeling could gather. A dispute over the division of resources could have a similar effect, although not the same symbolic importance.

It does not seem, therefore, that it is going beyond the bounds of reasonable speculation to foresee that disputes within the Soviet system may increase in consequence of the increased assertiveness of Soviet Muslims, operating at first within a secular framework and presenting demands which are defensible within Soviet terms. At a later stage, and under certain conditions, such demands could acquire a distinctly Muslim character. The development of such a situation may be accelerated or postponed not only by decisions within the Soviet Union but by the progress of events beyond the borders. It is difficult to believe that Soviet Muslims, with their higher standard of living, would find much that they wished to copy in the present condition of Iran and Afghanistan. Nevertheless, the spectacle of resistance to the USSR and the possibility of alternative modes of development can only foster ambitions in the minds of Soviet Muslims and bring nearer the time when cracks emerge in the Soviet system.

How, by its policy towards the Northern Tier states, can the USSR diminish the possibility of disputes arising with Muslims within the Soviet Union? The answer seems to be by the demonstration that there is no genuine alternative model of development displayed within the Northern Tier, that the Northern Tier countries are lagging behind on the great journey through history, and that Soviet Muslims should put aside whatever fantasies they might have, and should resolve to accept the inevitable with good grace and to become good Soviet citizens. This demonstration is to be achieved through ideology and prestige.

The role of ideology
The role of ideology in Soviet policy towards the Northern Tier countries and the Middle East generally is not an easy one to assess.[17] It has two aspects: in relation to the countries of the area, and in relation to the USSR. With regard to the first, there can be no doubt that ideology does shape Soviet perceptions of the area. It is assumed that the Kremlin has two quite separate perceptions: one, designed for public consumption, of an imaginary world

progressing inexorably towards the communist paradise; and the other, for the purposes of decision-making, of the real world. In practice, however, such a bifocal system cannot exist. All information fed to the Kremlin has to be coloured by ideological orthodoxy in order to protect the position of the supplier. Only utterly erroneous information mixed with ideological claptrap can explain the course of Soviet policy towards Afghanistan. Recently, a Soviet reviewer remarked that Soviet commentators have underestimated the importance of tribal divisions in South Yemen.[18] Indeed, the commentators had ignored it, for ideology had said it was irrelevant. Soviet commentators also ignore the existence of tribalism in Central Asia. Ideology is a grievous handicap to Soviet policy-makers in attempting to elucidate the significance of events in the Northern Tier or elsewhere.

The purpose of these remarks about the role of ideology is not to show that ideology is a weakness in Soviet policy-making, but merely to argue that it is an important factor. It is often claimed that the readiness of the USSR to write off local communist parties in the region in favour of good relations with the states which persecute the communists shows how small a part ideology plays in Soviet thinking, and that Soviet policy is essentially pragmatic and dictated by the interests of the Soviet Union. The claim would appear to rest upon an inadequate analysis, however. The decision to defend bourgeois nationalist regimes is justified by reference to necessary stages of evolution, and local communists who aspire to power too early may be abandoned because their policy was adventurist and not in accordance with what are described as the objective realities of the situation. Once the movement has been made to a new, so-called higher stage, however, backtracking becomes very difficult. The movement of history is irreversible – on that proposition the legitimacy of the Soviet regime is staked. No doubt, in certain cases, it is possible to explain a movement backwards, as in Chile, but if belief in the validity of the proposition of irreversibility is shaken, the prestige of the Soviet regime would be greatly weakened within and outside the Soviet Union. From the point of view of the USSR, it is not necessary that the countries of the Northern Tier should follow the socialist road, but once they have set their feet on that road they must not turn back, for that would be to admit that history has other possible directions and would open the possibility that the Soviet Union might itself move in a different direction. In principle the same argument applies to Cambodia and Madagascar, but in practice countries on the borders of the Soviet Union are of greater importance. Of course imperialist conspiracies may be blamed for minor setbacks, but if there are major reverses, people may begin to suppose that imperialism is actually winning.

Conclusion: Soviet policy since 1978

It remains to glance briefly at events in the Northern Tier since 1978 to see how these factors have operated on Soviet policy. As remarked previously, the USSR neither planned nor wanted the April 1978 revolution in Afghanistan; but when that revolution took place, it was obliged to support the new regime, both because Afghanistan was a border country and because the revolution claimed to be an ideological step in the direction prescribed by history. When opposition to the People's Democratic Party's ridiculous programme developed, the Soviet Union called for a moderation in keeping with its analysis of the position of Afghanistan. When that call had insufficient effect, the USSR first tried to murder the leader of the radical faction, and then, when that attempt failed, invaded Afghanistan in order to replace him with a man whom theory suggested was more likely to restore stability, but who was wholly unsuitable. The obvious course was to get out of Afghanistan, but border security and ideology excluded that course. The Soviet Muslim question now also came to play a part. It would not seem that the position of Soviet Muslims had played any significant part in the decision to invade Afghanistan, but as resistance to the Soviet forces continued, it began to appear that some Soviet Muslims identified not with the Soviet forces but with the Afghan resistance. Prestige now demanded that the Afghan resistance should be defeated so that it could not be claimed that the USSR had been obliged to withdraw by a movement which, however inaccurately, could be labelled Muslim. The problems which induced the Soviet Union to intervene in Afghanistan have become worse as a result of that intervention, but the same problems make it more difficult for the Soviet Union to retreat.

The Islamic revolution in Iran took the USSR by surprise, but it was quicker than the USA to detect the strength of the wind of change and to switch its support from the Shah to the revolutionaries. Its fear, suspicion and lack of comprehension of the new regime, combined with its desire to remain on good terms with any government in Iran so long as it was possible, are revealed by the almost deafening absence of any serious analysis of the revolution in the Soviet press and by the often obsequious Soviet attitude towards Ayatollah Khomeini. The revolution is described as anti-Shah and anti-imperialist, but there appears to be no idea of what it is actually for. Theory demanded that the regime of the Shah should have been replaced by a national liberation movement of bourgeois nationalists and the left, but the Soviet Union observes instead a bewildering array of religious fundamentalists, religious radicals, middle-class nationalists and army officers, among which the still small voice of the left is lost in a cacophony of discussion which is totally meaningless in the Soviet Union. The expulsion of the USA is a solid gain, but whether it is worth the presence of a load of deliquescent gelignite on the borders of the Soviet Union is another matter. So far, the moment of confrontation has been postponed, first by the hostage episode and subsequently by the Iran–Iraq war and the fall of President Bani Sadr, who espoused a strong anti-Soviet line; but it cannot be avoided indefinitely. Particularly puzzling to the Soviet Union is what it describes as the fratricidal Iran–Iraq war.[19] Plainly, the war serves no direct Soviet purpose, whatever its beneficial side-effects, and it decidedly embarrasses Soviet relations with the two countries. So the USSR is driven to conclude that the conflict must help the USA, and from that conclusion makes the easy transition to the supposition that the USA encourages the war. The mode of argument is foolish, but it is not peculiar to Soviet commentators.

Finally, it may be noted that since 1978 Soviet-Turkish relations have lost some of their previous warmth. The long Soviet courtship of Turkey began to have increasing success during the 1970s in the form of economic agreements, cultural exchanges and border settlements, culminating in the 1978 political agreement. The Turkish inclination towards the USSR must be partly set down to a degree of dissatisfaction with the fruits of its Western alliance, in particular with the level of economic and military aid and with the lack of sympathy for Turkish policy in Cyprus. The Afghan and Iranian revolutions, however, have wonderfully contrived to concentrate the minds of Western statesmen and to enhance the value of Turkey in their eyes. Economic and military aid have been forthcoming in much greater abundance and Greek complaints against Turkey have carried less weight. In turn, the closer Turkish ties with the West have led to a more critical attitude towards Turkey in the Soviet press. But it should not be supposed that this new situation will continue indefinitely. If Western concern for Turkey is not maintained, Turkey may well incline once more towards the USSR. If the West espouses the Greek cause in the Cyprus and Aegean disputes, Turkey may again look to the Soviet Union for support. And if the European Economic Community does not make the considerable effort required to accommodate Turkey in some form, Turkey may feel impelled to seek an alternative economic shelter within the CMEA, where market forces are strictly controlled and Turkey's agricultural produce and the products of its hothouse industries might find acceptance. The pre-1978 Soviet policy towards Turkey may yet prove to have a good deal of mileage left in it.

The contention of this chapter has been that the policy of the Soviet Union towards Turkey, Iran and Afghanistan has been dictated primarily by regard for border security and for ideology and that the two impulses have not always worked in harmony. The events of 1978–81 in these countries have obliged the USSR to devise a new policy to replace that which obtained since 1953. The new policy is not uniform. It appears to be a series of *ad hoc* responses: business as usual in Turkey; wait and see in Iran; ideology and intervention in Afghanistan. It is a policy as fluid as the situation itself, and the strategic position and the great resources of the USSR give that power a wide range of options for the future. The error committed by the Soviet Union in involving itself militarily in Afghanistan, and its inability so far to retrieve that error, does not inspire great confidence in the wisdom with which the USSR will make its choice of options. In many ways these are options which the Soviet Union would rather not have had. The new policy serves Soviet purposes much less well than did its predecessor. The situation on the Middle Eastern frontier of the Soviet Union has changed materially for the worse from the Soviet point of view. Whereas in the past border security and ideology/prestige could move roughly in tandem, in the future they may move in opposite directions. The USSR, thus, may have to trade off prestige against border security.

Notes

[1] See M.E. Yapp, 'The Soviet Union and the Middle East', *Asian Affairs,* February 1976, pp. 7–18.
[2] On nineteenth-century Russian interest, see D. Hopwood, *The Russian Presence in Syria and Palestine 1843–1914* (London, Oxford University Press, 1969).
[3] On Soviet policy in Egypt, see A.Z. Rubinstein, *Red Star on the Nile* (Princeton, N.J., Princeton University Press, 1977); R.O. Freedman, *Soviet Policy in the Middle East Since 1970* (New York, Praeger, 1975); and Hélène Carrère d'Encausse, *La Politique soviétique au Moyen-Orient* (Paris, Presse de la FNSP, 1975).
[4] On the history of Soviet relations with the region, the following are of particular interest: A.B. Ulam, *Expansion and Coexistence: The History of Soviet Foreign Policy, 1917–67* (New York, Praeger, 1968); H. Kapur, *Soviet Russia in Asia, 1917–27: A Study of Soviet Policy Towards Turkey, Iran and Afghanistan* (London, Michael Joseph, 1966); and B.R. Kuniholm, *The Origins of the Cold War in the Near East* (Princeton, N.J., Princeton University Press, 1980).

[5] V. Shoniya, 'An Important Landmark in Soviet–Turkish Relations', *International Affairs* (Moscow), September 1978, pp. 75–8.

[6] 'Colossus or Humbug? The Soviet Union and its Southern Neighbours', paper presented at a conference on the Soviet Union and the Third World, held in London in April 1979 (in press).

[7] In 1977 Soviet trade with Turkey, Iran and Afghanistan, despite a substantial increase in the previous decade, represented only 3 per cent of total Soviet foreign trade.

[8] The theory of a Soviet oil shortage derived from the Central Intelligence Agency report: *Prospects for Soviet Oil Production: A Supplemental Analysis* (July 1977). The CIA estimates were strongly criticized and were confounded by Soviet statistics; they have recently been heavily revised.

[9] On Soviet naval policy in the Indian Ocean, see G. Jukes, *The Soviet Union in Asia* (Sydney, Angus and Robertson, 1973), and *The Indian Ocean in Soviet Naval Policy*, Adelphi Paper No. 87 (London, International Institute for Strategic Studies, 1972); Michael MccGwire (ed.), *Soviet Naval Development* (New York, Praeger, 1973); M. MccGwire, K. Booth and J. McDonnell (eds.), *Soviet Naval Policy* (New York, Praeger, 1975); A. Yodfat and M. Abir, *In the Direction of the Persian Gulf* (London, Frank Cass, 1977); and S. Kozlov, 'The Indian Ocean: Myth and Reality', *Soviet Review*, October 1971.

[10] H.C. Hinton, 'The Soviet Campaign for Collective Security in Asia', *Pacific Commentary*, vol. 7 (1976), pp. 147–61; V. Vorontsov and D. Kapustin, 'Collective Security in Asia (1930s–1970s)', *Far Eastern Affairs*, 1976, pp. 37–49.

[11] On Soviet policy towards India, see R.H. Donaldson, *Soviet Policy Towards India; Ideology and Strategy*, (Cambridge, Mass., Harvard University Press, 1974); H. Kapur, *The Soviet Union and the Emerging Nations: A Case Study of Soviet Policy Towards India* (London, Michael Joseph, 1972); and Bimal Prasad, *Indo-Soviet Relations 1947–72: A Documentary History* (Bombay, Allied Publishers, 1973).

[12] See *International Affairs* (Moscow), May 1981, p. 27.

[13] On the Straits question, see H.N. Howard, *The Straits and US Policy* (Baltimore, Johns Hopkins University Press, 1974); and Feridun Cemal Erkin, *Les Relations Turco-Soviétiques et la question des Détroits* (Ankara, 1968; no publisher given).

[14] On the Muslim question in the USSR, see G. Wheeler, *The Modern History of Soviet Central Asia* (London, Weidenfeld & Nicolson, 1964); A. Bennigsen and C. Lemercier Quelquejay, *Islam in the Soviet Union* (London, Pall Mall Press, 1967); E. Goldhagen (ed.), *Ethnic Minorities in the Soviet Union* (New York, Praeger, 1968); E. Allworth (ed.), *Soviet Nationality Problems* (New York, Columbia University Press, 1971), and *The Nationality Question in Soviet Central Asia* (New York, Praeger, 1973); R.A. Lewis, R.H. Rowland and R.S. Clem, *Nationality and Population Change in Russia and the USSR* (New York, Praeger, 1976); R.A. Lewis and R.H. Rowland, *Population Redistribution in the USSR: Its Impact on Society 1897–1977* (New York, Praeger, 1979); Hélène Carrère d'Encausse, *L'Empire éclaté* (Paris, Flammarion, 1978); J.R. Azrael, *Soviet Nationality Policies and Practices* (New York, Praeger, 1978); B.R. Bociurkiv and J.

Strong (eds.), *Religion and Atheism in the USSR and Eastern Europe* (Toronto, Toronto University Press, 1975); and G.W. Simmonds (ed.), *Nationalism in the USSR and Eastern Europe in the Era of Brezhnev and Kosygin* (Detroit, Mich., University of Detroit, 1977). Both for information and for the opportunity to formulate opinions on this topic, I am greatly indebted to members of the seminar on Soviet Central Asia sponsored by the Foreign and Commonwealth Office in April 1981.

[15] The point is discussed in Malcolm Yapp, 'Language, Religion and Political Identity: A General Framework', in D. Taylor and M. Yapp (eds.), *Political Identity in South Asia* (London, Curzon Press, 1979), pp. 1–33.

[16] For an exposition of this view of the Islamic Revival, see M.E. Yapp, 'Contemporary Islamic Revival', *Asian Affairs*, June 1980, pp. 178–95.

[17] For the influence of ideology on Soviet policy, see R.H. Donaldson, op. cit., note 10; and E.P. Hoffman and F.J. Fleron (eds.), *The Conduct of Soviet Foreign Policy* (London, Butterworths, 1971), part 3.

[18] M. Kapitsa, *International Affairs* (Moscow), February 1981, p. 124.

[19] On the Iran–Iraq War, see Karen Dawisha, 'Moscow and the Gulf War', *The World Today*, January 1981.

4 Ideology, Soviet Policy and Realignment in the Horn
Robert Patman

When the large contingent of Soviet military advisers were expelled from Somalia on 13 November 1977, the Soviet reaction was one of thinly veiled anger. Georgiy Samsonov, the ambassador to Somalia, warned that the Soviet Union 'will teach the Somalis a lesson they won't forget. We will bring them to their knees.'[1] Today, four years on, this prediction has become a grim reality. The rot started with the collapse of the Somali attempt to annex the Ogaden in March 1978. The Ethiopian success, which had earlier looked impossible, was due almost entirely to a massive infusion of Soviet military assistance and Cuban combat troops. In the guerrilla war that followed, that pattern has repeated itself. The Somali-backed WSLF (Western Somali Liberation Front) has been gradually overwhelmed by an Ethiopian military machine which, thanks to Soviet support, has become the best in Black Africa. Ironically, these reverses have qualified Somalia for defensive military equipment from the United States. Such assistance however, cannot be expected to offset the terrible costs to President Siad Barre's policy: the influx of over a million war refugees, a devastated economy, rising political opposition and virtual diplomatic isolation.[2] Recognizing this, Barre has belatedly launched a new initiative, based on a peaceful solution to the disputed Ogaden region.

Clearly, the Soviet switch to Ethiopia in 1977 has had profound consequences, and it forms, along with the events that led up to it, the main subject of this chapter. The somersault raised a host of questions, some old, some new, about Soviet motives. Had Soviet policy entered a new phase? Was it a clear example of what Kissinger has called Soviet geopolitical momentum? If so, why did the Soviet Union antagonize Somalia, an ally of considerable strategic value? Or was it simply driven by the internationalism of Marxism–Leninism? But what, then, was the motivation for Soviet policy in the period preceding Marxist–Leninist regimes on the Horn?

*The author is grateful to the Social Science Research Council for assistance provided during the preparation of this chapter.

Does one have to look beyond explanations that are either ideologically or geopolitically based in order to understand Soviet
behaviour on the Horn?

The Soviet connection with the Horn

The Soviet Union first established a foothold in the region in
October 1963, when it outbid three Western countries, the USA,
Italy and West Germany, by offering Somalia military assistance
worth $30 million. This agreement envisaged the expansion of the
Somali army – from 2,000 to 10,000 – and included an assortment of
MiG-15 aircraft and T-34 tanks. Although the commitment was a
modest one by Soviet standards, it was a significant one in local
terms. For it was made, without conditions, to a state dedicated to
the creation of a Greater Somalia through the absorption of territories, occupied by ethnic Somalis, in neighbouring states. The
territories were the Ogaden area, the North-East Province in
Kenya and the then French colony of the Land of the Afars and
Issas (later to become independent Djibouti).

   The Soviets, however, remained ambivalent on the specific question of supporting Somalia's irredentist objectives. This was just as
well, for the majority of Black African states rejected such claims,
and instead endorsed an OAU resolution recognizing the immutability of boundaries established at a state's independence. Consequently, during the brief border war of 1964 between Ethiopia and
Somalia, the Kremlin maintained a position of strict neutrality,
with Khrushchev even offering to mediate between the two sides.

   In the years from 1964 until 1969, the USSR remained the chief
external supplier of arms to Mogadishu. Relations were friendly
but hardly intimate. This, however, significantly changed with the
ascension of Siad Barre to power on 21 October 1969 (via a military
coup). Barre, who rose to the rank of general in the Soviet-trained
army, promised to end the endemic corruption and to rule the
country along the lines of 'scientific socialism'. Within six months, a
major reorganization of the economy resulted in the nationalization
of all foreign banks, oil companies and import-export firms. In
addition, private education was abolished, and various self-help
projects and cooperatives were set up.

   The Soviet government apparently was impressed. This was, in
part, related to the change in the Soviet attitude towards military
regimes in the Third World. In the late 1960s, the old Leninist
notion that national armies were either progressive or reactionary
by virtue of the dominant class interests of the state gave way to a
new position. This emphasized the independent revolutionary
potential of national armies in developing countries. Thus a

spokesman for the main political administration of the Soviet armed forces argued that in contrast to the past, when military coups as a rule 'possessed an openly expressed anti-popular bent', in the current time they could 'serve the purposes of the struggle against reactionary regimes.'[3] Barre was seen in this light. In October 1970, the Kremlin described him as an 'outstanding leader and devoted patriot'.[4] Military and economic assistance was greatly expanded. Over the next four years, the number of Soviet personnel in Somalia increased from about 300 to 2,500, the majority of whom were military advisers. About a tenth of the entire Somali army went to the USSR for its training. Furthermore, extensive modernization made the army one of the best equipped in Black Africa; its inventory included 150 T-35 and 100 T-54 tanks, 300 armoured personnel carriers, 200 coastal batteries and about 50 MiGs (including MiG-15s, MiG-17s and some MiG-19s and MiG-21s). In this way, the army was transformed from a rag-bag band of 10,000 into a finely honed force of 20,000. In return, the Soviet Union was permitted to develop naval facilities at Berbera, and similar facilities at the ports of Kismayo and Birikao.

The growing ties between Somalia and Moscow developed against what was a deteriorating Ethiopian–Somali relationship in 1973. The brief détente, highlighted by the restoration of diplomatic relations in 1969, was cut short by the discovery of small oil and gas deposits in the Ogaden in December 1972. Almost immediately afterwards there were reports of small-scale skirmishes in the area.

Within this context, Ethiopia viewed the budding 'Marxist-Leninist alliance' with considerable foreboding. By tradition, its own relations with Moscow had been friendly but always correct. From the Soviet standpoint, Haile Selassie's regime was tainted by a close association with the United States. In 1953, the USA obtained a 25-year lease on the Kagnew communications facility in Asmara as part of a *quid pro quo* for American diplomatic support in the UN for Ethiopian trusteeship over Eritrea. During the next two decades, the Kagnew station served as an important link in the wordwide network of US military communications which stretched from the Philippines through Ethiopia and Morocco to Arlington, Virginia. Thus, Ethiopia was regarded in Washington as the principal buffer against communism in Black Africa. Between 1953 and 1970, Haile Selassie's government received 20 per cent of all US economic aid ($350 million), and 50 per cent of all US military aid ($278.6 million), that went to Black Africa.[5]

By the early 1970s, however, the importance for Washington of Ethiopia began to diminish. The need for the Kagnew station was obviated by rapid advances in satellite communications technology. And so when a harried Haile Selaissie, already faced with rumblings of domestic political discontent, visited Washington and requested additional military aid to counter the Soviet-backed Somali threat, he got a cool hearing.

The reluctance of the United States to get further involved reflected domestic political concerns, rather than an appreciation of the limitations of Soviet influence over Somalia. Yet such limitations clearly existed before 1974. In the first instance, President Barre solicited assistance from a variety of sources. One of these was Moscow's ideological rival, China. The granting of a large $110-million loan in 1971 meant that Chinese economic assistance overtook that of the Soviet Union. And whilst Chinese-backed projects – the building of a 650-mile road as well as factory and irrigation schemes – did not threaten Moscow's position as the main military supplier, their success was probably a source of considerable anxiety. Not only did the Somali government at times criticize Soviet-supported projects; it also paid public tribute to the 'profound basis' of Somali-Chinese friendship.[6] In addition, on 15 February 1974, Somalia joined the Arab League, and was rewarded by $36 million worth of aid from Saudi Arabia, Kuwait and Abu Dhabi. Secondly, while Barre supported the Soviet stand on certain international issues – Vietnam, the Middle East, recognition of the German Democratic Republic – he emphasized the independent, non-aligned nature of Somali foreign policy, one which he described as 'positive neutrality'. Thirdly, his brand of 'scientific socialism' remained a locally adapted doctrine. It attempted to straddle both Muhammad and Marx by stressing the need for self-help projects without displacing the entrenched Muslim religion. Indeed, Barre showed a marked sensitivity towards Somalia's independence of thought when he publicly rebuked Somali students for returning home with foreign ideas such as Maoism, Leninism, and Christianity by declaring that 'the imposition and introduction of foreign doctrines in our country will not be tolerated'.[7]

The shift in Soviet policy
On 11 July 1974, the Soviet Union codified its relationship with Somalia by concluding a Treaty of Friendship and Cooperation. The agreement included a provision for strengthening Somalia's defence potential and coincided with a new influx of MiG-21s, Ilyushin-28 bombers and T-54 tanks. The treaty was widely interpreted as a formal endorsement of Somali territorial ambitions. But the event that served as the main catalyst in the eventual realignment of forces on the Horn was the toppling of Haile

Selassie's feudal regime. The 'creeping coup' began in February 1974 when a group of military officers presented a list of grievances to the Emperor. Although Selassie tried to placate their demands, it was the perennial problem of too little too late. On 12 September 1974, the Emperor was formally deposed and replaced by a revolutionary military government, the Provisional Military Administrative Council (PMAC), otherwise known as the Dergue. By 1976, the increasingly pro-Soviet, anti-Western stance of the Dergue, combined with its repressive policies and large requirements for arms to fight the Eritrean secessionist movements, made it difficult for the US government to justify its support for Ethiopia. In 1975 the Ford Administration demonstrated its dissatisfaction by granting $7 million in military aid instead of the $30 million requested.[8]

However, as Washington's interest faded, Moscow's grew. Confident that the 'correlation of forces' had begun to shift in its favour, the USSR signed a secret $100-million arms deal in December 1976. This came at a time when the USA had cancelled its military grant assistance programme to Ethiopia (the Ethiopians were still allowed to continue purchasing US arms). It was a limited agreement, however, whereby Ethiopia received mostly dated equipment. It was not until the emergence of Lt. Col. Mengistu Haile Mariam as the new leader of the Dergue on 3 February 1977 that prospects for Soviet influence increased.

Soviet interest in Ethiopia began to complicate its relations with Mogadishu. The desire to unite all Somalis under one flag had remained the core objective of Somali foreign policy. The year 1977, moreover, seemed to present a historic opportunity in the Ogaden as the upheavals of the Ethiopian revolution added to the hydra-headed revolts that engulfed the old empire. Not only were leftist movements in Eritrea forcefully asserting their right to independence, but other guerrilla groups – representing various ethnic people (Gallas, Afars, Tigrians, etc.), conservative landowners and radical city dwellers – were also active. Ethiopia was on the verge of disintegration. Thus, the Soviet support for the Dergue brought it into direct conflict with Somalia.

Yet the Soviet leadership did not see the problem as insurmountable. In February 1977, the month the pro-Soviet Mengistu became the Dergue's new chairman, the Kremlin proposed a Marxist-Leninist confederation of Ethiopia, Somalia, Djibouti and South Yemen. It also promised to back the scheme economically and militarily. Within a month, President Fidel Castro of Cuba presented the proposal to both Mengistu and Barre in Aden. His efforts met with disappointment. Barre argued that there could be no room for international solutions until Somalia's national problem was solved. Accusing Mengistu of having a colonial mentality, Barre rejected the proposal. But the Somalis, according to Castro, promised 'that they would never invade Ethiopia, that they would never carry out a military attack'.[9] The Soviet leaders remained concerned. A month after the abortive talks, the then Soviet President, Nikolai Podgorny, visited Mogadishu and urged Barre to be patient.

Meanwhile, the USSR completed its displacement of the United States in Ethiopia. In April 1977, the Dergue announced the closure of the Kagnew Communications Station and other US facilities. And although this action followed new criticisms by the Carter Administration about the absence of human rights in Ethiopia, it was unlikely that this step would have been taken without the assurance of an alternative supply of arms.

On 5 May 1977, Mengistu was received with full honours in Moscow, where he signed a declaration on the 'foundations for friendship and cooperation'. If the form of the agreement showed a Soviet concern for Somali sensitivities – a declaration was still a level lower than the Soviet-Somali Treaty of Friendship – its substance certainly did not. As well as technical and economic agreements, the Soviets concluded a major arms package with the Ethiopians worth $400 million. This included 48 MiG-21 intercepters, up to 200 T-54 and T-55 tanks, an unknown number of SAM-3 and SAM-7 anti-aircraft missile batteries and Sagger anti-tank missiles.

The arms agreement represented a turning-point in Soviet-Somali relations. Barre described the delivery of arms to Addis Ababa as a 'danger'[10] and openly questioned Soviet advice to be patient: 'Who can guarantee us that once his regime is consolidated and his army strengthened, Mengistu will consent to negotiate the territorial conflict between us so as to find a solution that complies with the wishes of the Somali people in the Ogaden.'[11]

Barre now began to exercise his Arab option. Earlier, in March (after the meeting with Castro), he attended a meeting in Taiz, North Yemen, with representatives of the Sudan and both North and South Yemen. The purpose of the meeting was to discuss Red Sea security, or what the Soviets derisively called an 'Arab lake' scheme designed to exclude Moscow and Tel Aviv from the Red Sea. Barre publicly declared his support for this scheme, and Saudi Arabia renewed a long-standing offer to grant Mogadishu $300 million if they expelled the Soviets. Barre's leanings towards the Arab world were probably encouraged by the events of 19 May 1977, when President Numeiry of Sudan expelled all 90 of the Soviet military advisers and drastically cut Soviet diplomatic representation in Khartoum.

Furthermore, the Somalis sought weapons from the West. At first, the United States was agreeable, since it gave the West an opportunity, in Carter's words, 'aggressively' to challenge Soviet influence in the area, and also to improve its relations with moderate Arab states. But although Washington, along with France and Britain, agreed to supply light 'defensive' weapons, the offer was promptly rescinded in July 1977 after Somali regular forces joined the Somali-backed guerrillas, the WSLF, fighting in the Ogaden.

The Soviet Union was surprised by the Somali invasion. Initially, it maintained an even-handed position and continued to arm both sides. It interpreted the conflict between its allies as a classic case of 'imperialist' intrigue. The news agency Tass noted that attempts were being made 'to separate Somalia and Ethiopia from their natural allies',[12] while *Izvestia* observed that 'the United States uses all methods of neo-colonialism – instigating nationalism and separatism to discredit progressive African regimes and to slander their ties with the Soviet Union and other socialist countries'.[13]

And, although Moscow did not abandon the class-based interpretation, it became increasingly obvious that Somalia had become the 'pawn of the imperialists'.[14] On 6 August 1977, the Soviet Afro-Asian Solidarity Committee appealed for a cease-fire and reaffirmed its support for Article 3 of the OAU charter regarding the territorial integrity of each state: 'Practice has confirmed that violation of these principles and attempts to use force in recarving the existing frontiers, no matter what justification is made, damage the anti-imperialist unity of the African peoples and only assist the imperialist forces.'[15] The Soviet stand also placed it in direct opposition to the leftist liberation movements in Eritrea. This must have been embarrassing for the Kremlin because its allies, Cuba and Bulgaria, had provided armed support for the Eritrean liberation movements since the late 1960s. However, as in the Somali case, the Soviets reversed themselves. In May 1976, they endorsed the Dergue's plan for Eritrean 'administrative' autonomy. The guerrilla groups rejected the plan and said they would accept nothing short of self-determination for the province. By mid-1977, the guerrillas controlled a large part of Eritrea. But at this stage the Soviet Union was reluctant to back a military solution for Eritrea.

The Somali problem, however, could not be deferred. Moscow wanted to preserve its links with Mogadishu and, as a palliative, signed an economic agreement in August with Barre's government. At the same time, Moscow was unwilling to withdraw its support for Ethiopia. The success of the Somali invasion, though, forced its hand. Under pressure from Mengistu, who had been assured that Somalia could be restrained, the Soviet leaders publicly committed themselves. On 17 August 1977 *Izvestia* condemned Somalia's 'armed intervention' and asked Barre to withdraw his troops from the Ogaden.[16] In an attempt to patch things up, Barre visited Moscow at the end of the month. He was not received by either Brezhnev or Gromyko, and left without any agreement.

The USSR now increased its support for Addis Ababa. On 14 September 1977, Somalia captured Jijiga, Ethiopia's main tank and radar base. Defeat in the Ogaden appeared imminent, but Soviet assistance soon made a decisive impact. MiG-21s, 'Stalin Organs' (batteries of 40 122mm rockets mounted on lorries) and new units of T-55 tanks found their way into the front-line towns of Harer and Dire Dawa by mid-October. This equipment, along with a growing presence of Soviet and Cuban military advisers, played an important part in denying these towns to the Somalis.

The Soviet bloc also provided help for the Dergue against its internal enemies. During 1977, Addis Ababa and most of the major Ethiopian towns were in a virtual state of anarchy as the Dergue and its arch rival, EPRP (the Ethiopian People's Revolutionary Party), waged urban guerrilla warfare. In September 1977, Mengistu's campaign against the 'counter-revolutionaries' was boosted by advisers from the German Democratic Republic.[17] They were given responsibility for organizing the internal security apparatus and instructing the 'People's Militia'.

In addition, the Soviet Union reduced its support for Somalia. Fuel shipments ceased. Arms deliveries were, by September 1977, confined to spare parts and light arms. Delivery of heavy weapons ceased altogether. Nevertheless the Dergue remained uneasy about what remained of the Soviet-Somali connection. On 18 September 1977, Mengistu warned Moscow that 'if socialist countries are still supplying arms to Somalia, then this is not only violating one's principles, but also tantamount to complicity with the reactionary Mogadishu regime'.[18] A month later, on 20 October 1977, Anatoly Ratanov, the Soviet ambassador to Ethiopia, publicly announced the cessation of all arms deliveries to Somalia.

By November 1977, the Somali offensive had lost momentum. The initial thrust had yielded large gains, but the Somalis failed to capture any of the major towns, other than Jijiga. Without assistance from the West, the Somalis' need for arms became desperate. Secure supplies of arms were prerequisites for the continuation of the Somali campaign in the Ogaden. Friends like Saudi Arabia provided light arms and fuel but not the heavy weapons Mogadishu required. Only the Western countries could do that. In an attempt to rally Western support, Barre warned that a Soviet-inspired Cuban-Ethiopian invasion of Somalia was likely: 'We are sure that Ethiopia with their friends are planning to attack Somalia. We are expecting it and are prepared. But will they stop at Somalia? I don't think so.'[19]

On 10 November 1977, Mr Abdul Barre, the Somali foreign minister, made Somalia's position clear: 'We are ready to accept every assistance we can get from any country because the Soviet Union has stopped arms shipments to Somalia.'[20] Finally, on 13 November 1977, in what some commentators saw as a desperate gamble to enlist Western aid (a narrow interpretation, given the mounting domestic political pressure to do something and the apparent availability of American arms through the Shah of Iran), Barre abrogated the 1974 Soviet-Somali Treaty of Friendship and Cooperation, expelled Soviet advisers, revoked Soviet use of military facilities, reduced diplomatic representation in Mogadishu and severed relations with Cuba. Thus Soviet-Somali relations had gone full circle.

But Barre had played his final card. His action simply pushed the Soviets whole-heartedly behind the Ethiopians. Previous aid to Addis Ababa, effective though it was, paled in comparison with what was to follow. On 26 November 1977, the Soviets launched a massive airlift that was to last for over a month. The operation involved 225 giant Antonov transport planes (about 12 per cent of the entire Soviet transport fleet) in flights from Soviet Central Asia to Addis Ababa, sometimes via staging posts in Aden and Maputo in Mozambique. This was backed up by a huge sealift involving scores of Soviet merchant ships. And to coordinate and control the whole exercise, the Soviets launched a military reconnaissance satellite, Cosmos 964. Overall, the USSR ferried in over $1 billion worth of armaments and 17,000 Cuban combat troops, as well as General Vasily Ivanovich Petrov, Deputy Commander-in-Chief of Soviet General Forces, to direct the war against the Somalis.

Apart from the impressive technical merits of the airlift, its sheer size suggests that the effort was not strictly tailored to the Ogaden war, for it far exceeded Ethiopia's immediate requirements. Indeed, some of the Antonovs were reported to have been empty. This suggests that the Soviets wanted to demonstrate, along with the Cubans – a combination effectively forged in Angola – that they could sustain friendly governments. Presumably, the point was not lost on Somalia. From the moment that the Ethiopian-Cuban counter-offensive was launched in January 1978, the Ogaden conflict became a predictable end game. Moreover, with its greatly increased stake in Ethiopia, Moscow's attitude (and, to a lesser degree, Cuba's) began to harden towards the Eritrean guerrillas. Within a year, Soviet tank crews were participating in the Dergue's offensive in the province.

Soviet policy: an assessment

Any assessment of Soviet policy must start with the observation that the Soviet interest pre-dated the establishment of any self-proclaimed Marxist-Leninist regimes in the Horn. As intimated, the USSR enjoyed good relations with the pre-1969 Somali governments. The early Soviet interest, therefore, could not be said to be ideological except in the most indirect, long-term sense.

Rather, the initial Soviet concern was linked to the general geopolitical significance of the Horn. Since 1968, the Soviet navy has maintained a continuous presence in the Indian Ocean with a naval squadron of approximately eighteen ships, about one-third of which are combatants. This presence has given the USSR the capability to threaten the Persian Gulf oil 'lifeline'. It is argued that in the advent of a general war, oil tankers would be targeted by Soviet ships in the area, whilst in peacetime the Soviet presence is a potential instrument of political blackmail. Secondly, the Soviet naval presence has been depicted as a defence against submarines which can strike Soviet territory. Thirdly, it is claimed that the dramatic expansion of the soviet merchant fleet and diminishing Soviet oil reserves has heightened the need to preserve what is the shortest sea route open all year round between the USSR's European and Pacific ports.

Whatever the reasons for the Soviet naval presence, it has had one manifest requirement – namely, the need for shore-based support. The Soviet-Somali relationship reflected that need. Soviet returns for military and economic assistance were largely strategic in nature. In 1972, Somalia became only the second Third World country, after Egypt, to grant the USSR access to extensive facilities ashore. Soviet access privileges included the exclusive use of a long-range communications station at Berbera and the rights to stage periodic maritime reconnaissance flights from Somali airfields. And had it not been for Somalia's strong desire for arms, which only the USSR was prepared to satisfy, it is unlikely that the Soviets would have obtained those shore-based facilities even then.

The rather permissive Soviet definition of Somalia as an 'anti-imperialist' state was misleading. For there were formidable limitations on Soviet influence in that country. In the first place, there was Islam. The Somalis are very devout Muslims. In domestic political terms, there were very real limits to how far Barre could implement Soviet preferences. This was underlined in the early part of 1975, when Barre aroused considerable hostility by executing ten Muslim leaders, who had refused to comply with new equal inheritance laws on the grounds that they contradicted the Koran's teachings. On the day of the execution, two Soviet MiGs collided in mid-air in what was widely seen locally as a case of divine retribution. It was difficult, therefore, for the Russians to have much contact with the Somali people. Known as the 'Godless' ones, Soviet advisers were often subject to popular abuse, and, as a precaution, were taken off the streets in times of tension.

The second obstacle to Soviet penetration was Barre's personalized style of government. Like many other developing countries, Somalia's government was dominated by the personality of its leader. Using a combination of patronage along tribal lines and nepotism, Barre managed to concentrate an enormous amount of power in his own hands. He had all his 'own men' in the top jobs. Barre himself was President, Prime Minister and Secretary-General of the SSRP (Somali Socialist Revolutionary Party); his son-in-law, General Ahmed Suleiman, was leader of the dreaded National Security Service (NSS); his nephew, General Omar Hagi Masala, was commander of the Army; and Masala's brother, Colonel Abdullah Haji Masala, was No. 2 man in the party.

Under these circumstances, there were few channels for Soviet influence other than through Barre. One holder of office, Ali Samantar, member of the bureau of the Central Committee of the SSRP, Vice-President and Defence Minister, was identified by the Western press as being pro-Soviet. This, however, was disputed by an opposition group called Somali Democratic Action Front (SODAF), based abroad, who argued that Samantar was 'totally dependent on Siad for his political existence'.[21] That point has subsequently been confirmed. President Barre has recently dismissed Ali Samantar (Observer Foreign News Service, 21 May 1981.)

A third problem for the Soviets was Barre's pragmatism. Although Barre often flattered Moscow by lacing his comments with Marxist rhetoric, he remained essentially a pragmatist. He always sought the maximum advantage for Somalia by playing off one side against the other. For example, during the Berbera 'missile crises' of July 1975, he invited Western journalists and delegations from the US Senate and Congress to inspect the facilities. The visit did nothing to refute Schlesinger's allegations about storage facilities for Soviet missiles. Nevertheless, Barre used his new-found audience to call for closer relations with Washington and repeat an earlier offer of naval facilities. Whilst his words did not endear him to the Kremlin, they had positive benefits for Somalia. Within months, the Ford Administration gave Somalia some assistance for drought-stricken refugees.

Fourthly, Moscow's economic assistance did not live up to Barre's expectations. Despite six years of close relations with Moscow, Somalia remained in the bottom 25 poorest countries in the world. In was not until 1975 that Soviet economic assistance matched that of the Chinese. Barre's dissatisfaction was heightened by the knowledge that his country would have attracted more economic aid if it had not been for the Soviet connection. Conservative Arab states like Saudi Arabia suggested as much. Barre probably had this in mind when he told an audience of US senators that 'the man who is drowning does not question those who extend a helping hand'.[22]

Taken together, these factors retarded the growth of institutional linkages between Moscow and Mogadishu. For the first seven years of its existence, Barre's regime was essentially a radical military junta. There were no party-to-party relations until July 1976, when Barre announced the formation of a one-party state. Moreoover, where linkages did exist, they seemed to be oriented towards merely keeping Barre in power. The role of the KGB in the organization of the Somali NSS is a case in point. The close liaison between the two organizations was not in doubt. But the presence of the KGB did more than improve the performance of the NSS, and thereby strengthened Barre's domestic position. It also provided additional information otherwise not available. For example, Mohamed Heikal has related how Brezhnev warned Barre in June 1970 about an imminent coup attempt.[23]

On balance, therefore, the relationship between Somalia and the USSR was not so strong as it seemed. Yet the Soviets remained confident that they could maintain close relations with both Somalia and its traditional adversary, Ethiopia. They persisted in this attitude even after the failure of the Federation scheme.

The Soviet attempt to ride both horses indicated a naivety that was ideologically induced. A Third World scholar, Mohammed Ayoob, described the Marxist-Leninist confederation scheme as 'preposterous'; the implication being that the Soviet initiative was totally insensitive both to the historical nature of the conflict on the Horn, and to the forces of nationalism in the region. President Numeiry of the Sudan was equally scathing. Soviet policy, he argued, reflected the fact that it was 'based on inaccurate information'.[24] Anatoly Gromyko, head of Moscow's Institute of Africa and son of the Soviet foreign minister, put the Soviet position in the following way: 'In spite of the historical contradictions between Somalia and Ethiopia, there are progressive forces in both able to sort out their social political and economic problems. Here we are optimists: we think it is possible to have a Marxist-Leninist confederation in the Horn of Africa.'[25]

Such optimism, however, was finally crushed by the Somali invasion. Few options were left for Moscow. With Ethiopia's existence as a state in jeopardy, the prospects for a Somali victory in the Ogaden looked good. Why, then, did the USSR risk good solid naval facilities in Somalia and throw its lot in with a state widely perceived as a loser? The Soviet leaders may have calculated that in return for support, they would obtain eventual access to the Ethiopian ports of Assab and Massawa. But even in normal times these Red Sea ports are congested in comparison with Berbera. And by the spring of 1977, if not earlier, it was clear that such access depended on the cessation of the Eritrean rebellion.

Thus, while all risks by definition involve some degree of uncertainty, the Soviet tilt towards Ethiopia seemed excessive in that there were few or no elements objectively indicating the probability of success. Indeed most US officials who left Ethiopia in April 1977 (after the closing of the US military mission) felt that the Soviet Union had made a grave miscalculation.

The Soviets, however, were not short of explanations for the switch. One commentator noted: 'The Soviet Union, for its part, did everything possible to avert an armed conflict between Ethiopia and Somalia. However, when the leaders of the latter country, despite common sense and the efforts of the true friends of the Somali people, began in the summer of 1977 military operations against Ethiopia and Somali troops invaded its territory, the Soviet Union, as always in such situations, came out on the side of the victim of aggression: at the request of the Ethiopian government the Soviet Union rendered Ethiopia material aid to repulse the attack.'[26]

They also apparently believed that, in Podgorny's words, 'social processes in Ethiopia create favourable prerequisites for substantial headway in bilateral cooperation'.[27] It is true that the political programme enunciated by the Dergue in April 1976 was a radical one. The Dergue introduced some fundamental changes, such as a major land redistribution programme, nationalization of all industry and the prohibition of ownership of more than one house. What is less clear is why the Kremlin regarded the Dergue as a potential vanguard party rather than the civilian Marxist–Leninist EPRP which it repressed. In fact, on the very weekend Podgorny made his speech celebrating Ethiopia's 'National Democratic Revolution', nearly 500 students, most of whom were EPRP members, were slaughtered following a demonstration.

The Kremlin's attachment to the Dergue may be more plausibly explained in terms of its foreign policy stance. Unlike Barre, who pledged a policy of strict neutrality between the superpowers, the Dergue asserted that 'anti-imperialism' was the foundation of the non-aligned movement.[28] In other words, Ethiopia's position with respect to the non-aligned movement was like that of Castro's. This must have been gratifying for the USSR, which had long since regarded China as part of the 'imperialist camp'.

There were, of course, some potentially good reasons for backing Ethiopia after the Somali invasion. With the second largest population in Black Africa (ten times larger than that of Somalia), with resources sufficient to justify reasonable hopes for long-term economic development – providing they kept the Ogaden – and with its capital and headquarters of the OAU, thanks largely to its independent tradition, Ethiopia was both an important African country and the key state in the Horn. Thus, the otherwise ironic statement by the Soviet ambassador to Somalia that 'the Ethiopian revolution will succeed at all costs' takes on a clearer significance.[29]

Furthermore, although it was going to be costly, the attempt to put the Ethiopian humpty-dumpty back together again had a fundamental political appeal. It placed the main class enemy in a 'no-win' situation. The United States could not contemplate counter-intervention on the side of the Somalis without antagonizing its main partner in the Middle East, arousing the wrath of the majority of Black African states or flaunting the OAU stand on the principle concerning the inviolability of territorial borders at independence.

And while the USSR could not count on US non-involvement, the alternative of sitting on the sidelines and picking up the pieces was not attractive either. The prospect of a satisfied, victorious Somalia, with a new range of needs, closely allied with 'reactionary' Arab states, did not augur well for the Soviet Union's future in the area.

Thus, the Soviet intervention on Ethiopia's behalf must be considered a success in the most fundamental sense. Ethiopia survived. But the fact that the intervention was necessary revealed the limitations of Soviet diplomacy in a part of the world where zero-sum perceptions prevail. External parties were (and still are) assessed according to their position with regard to the dominant, local conflict. Ideological entanglements with outsiders are acceptable in so far as they converge with the local states' definition of needs. In the case of Somalia (and Ethiopia, too), this was arms. Consequently, when the Soviets started arming Ethiopia, Barre responded by accusing them of rank disloyalty because 'they're arming our worst enemies'.[30] As far as Mogadishu was concerned, the relationship had lost its *raison d'être* and was therefore terminated.

Certainly, Barre had no ideological illusions about the Soviet Union. 'Russia is no different from other major powers who are foreigners in the area pursuing what they perceive to be their own interests.'[31] And with regard to the switch to Ethiopia, he remained equally pragmatic: 'When the US was evicted from Ethiopia, a vacuum was created and the Soviet Union filled it.'[32]

It seems, therefore, that Soviet involvement in the Horn (between the overthrow of Haile Selassie and the split with Somalia) was motivated by a blend of state interests and ideology. One cannot be divorced from the other, particularly since the Soviet definition of what constitutes an anti-imperialist state has become increasingly broad. This has been the result of the need to accommodate the diminishing appeal of Soviet Marxism in the Third World, and the steady increase of the military component in Soviet policy. Thus it is instructive that both Somalia and Ethiopia acquired 'scientific socialism' fundamentally via Soviet weapons. This new tendency on Moscow's part to grant 'progressive' status (and all that it entails) to certain Third World military establishments has been criticized within the Soviet Union by, amongst others, Professor Georgiy Mirskiy, a leading Soviet specialist on the Middle East. He has argued that 'to consider the army as the leading force of the anti-capitalist revolution and as the leader of society in the socialist-oriented countries would be a serious error', since 'the corporate interests of the privileged military elite will make it an opponent of radical trends'. Only a vanguard party committed to 'scientific socialism', Mirskiy contends, will safeguard the path to 'democratic, progressive development'.[33]

The realignment on the Horn supports Mirskiy's thesis. Having failed to maintain its influence in Somalia, the USSR has not been able to institutionalize its position as political patron to Addis Ababa either. Mengistu's willingness to make arrangements to strengthen the security of his regime – he signed a Treaty of Friendship with Moscow in November 1978 and concluded a regional agreement with Libya and the People's Democratic Republic of Yemen in August 1981 – contrasts with his reluctance to change the regime itself. Indeed, Mengistu has long resisted Soviet pressure to form a ruling political organization. Not until June 1980 did he accede to the establishment of a Commission for the Organization of the Ethiopian Workers Party (COPWE). However, the Commission, consisting of Mengistu and six standing members of the ruling Dergue, has not met regularly since it was formed. The signs are, then, that the authority of the Ethiopian military, Mengistu's power base, is not going to be sacrificed by him for the sake of international goodwill. Nor is this the only case of such independence from Moscow. In Eritrea, Mengistu's penchant for a military solution has prevailed despite Soviet and Cuban misgivings. And if, as it seems, Soviet policy is based on strategic considerations, there has been little by way of returns. In March 1981, the Soviet attempt to obtain base facilities at Massawa (in addition to existing anchorage facilities in the Dahlak Islands) apparently failed.[34] Moreover, relations have been further strained by Moscow's unrelenting insistence for arms repayment in hard currency or coffee, Ethiopia's only major cash crop.[35] Such demands are likely to cause even further crises in the already fragile Ethiopian economy.

These tensions in the Soviet-Ethiopian relationship suggest that the process of realignment on the Horn may not yet be complete. Moscow's position in Ethiopia is less secure than is generally assumed. Its influence remains a hostage to the dynamics of the local situation. Should Mengistu ever reach an accommodation with a new, weakened Somalia, and he has not ruled it out, the Soviets may find themselves, once again, in the position of guests who have outstayed their welcome.

Notes

[1]   Quoted in K. Weiss, *The Soviet Involvement in the Ogaden*, Professional Paper 269 (Arlington, Va., Centre for Naval Analysis, February 1980), p. 25.
[2]   The OAU 'Good Offices' Committee, first set up in 1973 to resolve the Ethiopian–Somali dispute, issued a resolution effectively recognizing Ogaden as an integral part of Ethiopia. See *Africa Research Bulletin*, 1–31 August 1980, p. 5762.
[3]   Quoted in C. G. Petersen, *Third World Military Elites in Soviet Perspective*, Professional Paper 262 (Arlington, Va., Centre for Naval Analysis, November 1979), p. 20.
[4]   *Soviet News*, 27 October 1970.
[5]   M. Ayoob, *The Horn of Africa: Regional Conflict and Superpower Involvement*, Canberra Papers on Strategy and Defence, no. 18 (Canberra, Australian National University, 1978) p. 11.
[6]   Hsinhua News Agency (HNA), 15 February 1974.
[7]   Quoted in *The New York Times*, 6 September 1970.
[8]   J. Bowyer Bell, 'Strategic Implications of the Soviet Presence in Somalia', *Orbis*, Summer 1975, p. 405.
[9]   Quoted in K. Weiss, *The Soviet Involvement*, p. 5.
[10] Quoted in *The Guardian*, 17 May 1977.
[11] Quoted in K. Weiss, *The Soviet Involvement*, p. 6.
[12] *Soviet News*, 16 August 1977.
[13] Quoted in *International Herald Tribune*, 2 August 1977.
[14] *Izvestia*, quoted in *The Times*, 17 August 1977.
[15] *Soviet News*, 9 August 1977.
[16] Quoted in *The Times*, 17 August 1977.

[17] *International Herald Tribune*, 5 September 1977.
[18] Quoted in *The Washington Post*, 27 September 1977.
[19] Quoted in *The Daily Telegraph*, 3 November 1977.
[20] Quoted in *The Guardian*, 10 November 1977.
[21] *International Herald Tribune*, 31 August 1977.
[22] Quoted in *The Guardian*, 11 July 1975.
[23] M. Heikal, *The Road to Ramadan* (London, Collins, 1975), p. 92.
[24] Quoted in *The Guardian*, 2 June 1977.
[25] Quoted in K. Weiss, *The Soviet Involvement*, p. 22.
[26] V. Vorabyov, 'Colonialists' Policies in Africa', *International Affairs* (Moscow), no. 9, 1978, p. 42.
[27] Quoted in *The Egyptian Gazette*, 6 May 1977.
[28] See joint communiqué issued at the end of the visit by Captain Moges Wolde Mikael, *Soviet News*, 20 July 1976.
[29] Quoted in *The Observer*, 14 August 1977.
[30] Quoted in *the Sunday Times*, 22 May 1977.
[31] Quoted in *International Herald Tribune*, 21 June 1977.
[32] Ibid.
[33] G. I. Mirskiy, *'Tretiy Mir': obshchestovo, vlast', armiya* (Moscow, Izdatel'stvo 'Nauka', 1976), p. 378.
[34] *The Guardian*, 31 March 1981.
[35] Observer Foreign News Service, 28 May 1981.

5 The East Europeans and the Cubans in the Middle East: Surrogates or Allies?
Edwina Moreton

There can be little argument that several of the Soviet Union's allies have become directly and extensively involved in the conduct of Soviet foreign policy in the Third World. Analysts do disagree, however, over the motives for this involvement and its implications for Soviet–East European and Soviet–Cuban relations in the future.

The tangle of argument stretches back to the post-war beginnings of Soviet policy towards the countries of the Near and Middle East. Active Soviet involvement in Middle Eastern affairs, for example, is usually dated from the 'Czech arms deal' of September 1955. This supply of armaments to Nasser's Egypt, using Czechoslovakia as intermediary, was the first occasion that the Soviet Union had engaged openly in the sale of arms to a non-communist state in the region. It was soon followed by others: during 1955–6 weapons were supplied through similar channels to Afghanistan, Syria and Yemen.[1]

But, as the name implies, the Czech arms deal also signifies the close coordination between the East European states and the Soviet Union in all aspects of military affairs, and in arms sales in particular. The Warsaw Pact had been set up in May 1955. The Czech arms deal preceded the Pact's drive for modernization and standardization in the late 1950s and 1960s. Yet at this early stage the Soviet Union was assumed to be in control. Since the 1950s, independent armaments industries in Eastern Europe have largely been wound up. With the exception of some trucks, small arms and ammunition, all Eastern Europe's weapons have been either supplied by the Soviet Union or else built under licence – and ultimately Soviet control – in Eastern Europe. As far as sales of these weapons are concerned, it is fair to assume that arms transfers to Third World states require at least Soviet approval.

Yet even as far back as 1955, Czechoslovakia was not wholly a newcomer to the arms trade in the Middle East. The Czechs had provided Israel with weapons to support Israeli independence in the late 1940s.[2] The original agreement to do so, in November 1947, preceded the February 1948 coup which brought the Czechoslovak Communist Party openly to power (although the arms did not start arriving until July 1948), and it is not clear whether the weapons were transferred exclusively at Czech initiative. Soviet writers are inclined now to overlook the episode. However, that is no reliable guide to the Soviet Union's role at the time.

The Israeli deal does push back the date of Czech involvement in the region and suggests at least a tentative hypothesis: that there is more to East European (and, later, Cuban) involvement in the area than can be explained by reference simply to Soviet foreign policy drives. At the risk of spoiling the story, it will be one of the conclusions here – and perhaps the only reliable one – that in the more recent period, and despite the undeniably close coordination between the Soviet Union and its allies, East European and Cuban involvement in the Third World is not the result of simple Soviet fiat.

An assessment of the extent of East European and Cuban involvement in the region will be followed by a more detailed examination of possible motives. On this basis, some concluding thoughts will be offered on: (1) the extent to which their participation has been 'directed' by the Soviet Union; (2) whether the Soviet Union and its more active allies are pursuing parallel or divergent interests; (3) the practical and political problems the smaller allies face as a result of their involvement in Soviet foreign policy; (4) the extent to which the precise nature of their involvement has changed over time; and (5) the nature of their influence, if any, on the conduct or objectives of Soviet foreign policy.

Cuban and East European involvement

Military personnel. Since the Czech arms deal of 1955, both the extent and the nature of the East European, and later Cuban, involvement in the Near and Middle East have changed. This is illustrated most graphically by the figures for the number of communist military personnel engaged in Third World activities. Despite a tentative start in the mid-1950s,[3] by 1979 there were 51,000 communist military personnel scattered through the officially 'non-communist' Third World: fully two-thirds of those – or 34,185 – were Cubans. Between 1965 and 1979, the Soviet and East European contingent had more than quadrupled. Prior to the Soviet intervention in Afghanistan in December 1979, three-quarters of the total number of communist military personnel were stationed in sub-Saharan Africa, with 32,000 Cuban troops stationed in Angola and Ethiopia. The leap in numbers came in three basic stages: after the 1967 Arab-Israeli conflict, but particularly after 1970, when large numbers of Soviet advisers were moved into Egypt; in 1975, when large numbers of Cubans were deployed in Angola; and again in 1978, following the large-scale commitment to Ethiopia. Since then as many as 80,000 Soviet troops have occupied Afghanistan.[4] (See Table 5.1.)

These same figures for communist military personnel are also usually the 'proof' cited for the involvement of the Cubans and East Europeans as 'proxies' in the conduct of Soviet foreign policy.[5] Undoubtedly, aside from the large numbers of Cubans in Angola, the highest concentration of both Cubans and East Europeans is in countries of importance for Soviet foreign policy: Afghanistan, Ethiopia, Syria, South Yemen, Iraq, Algeria and Libya (and, previously, Egypt and Somalia). Unfortunately, the habit on the part of those who regularly publish the figures of lumping together the Soviet and East European personnel in the same category both obscures the precise numerical contribution of each country and implies the conclusion that there is no point in making any distinction between them. The Cubans are treated with more reverence, presumably because of their numbers and because, unlike the East Europeans, they are not formally members of the Warsaw Pact.

Table 5.1   Communist military technicians in the Middle East, 1979 (number of persons)

	Total	USSR and Eastern Europe	Cuba
Algeria	1,030	1,015	15
Libya	1,820	1,820	—
Ethiopia	14,250	1,250	13,000
Iraq	1,065	1,065	—
Kuwait	5	5	—
North Yemen	130	130	—
South Yemen	2,100	1,100	1,000
Syria	2,480	2,480	—
Afghanistan	4,000	4,000*	—
LDCs	50,555	15,865	34,315

* Excluding Soviet troops.

Source: NFAC, CIA, *Communist Aid Activities in Non-Communist Less Developed Countries, 1979 and 1954–1979*, ER 80–10318U, October 1980, p. 15.

Although all the East European states have been involved to some minimal extent in the region (e.g. arms shipments, aid, training facilities), some distinct patterns have emerged. In particular, the deployment of military personnel in the Third World appears to be governed by a bilaterally negotiated division of labour. The general provision of military aid or arms is presumably discussed at Pact meetings (in the committee of defence ministers or of foreign ministers or, where major foreign policy decisions are at stake, the Political Consultative Committee), but the pattern of activity suggests that a decision was taken at some point to make the active commitment of military advisers the subject of bilateral negotiation between the donor state and the Soviet Union. That is, some members of the Warsaw Pact have opted out, some have opted in.

Since East European involvement has been stepped up, the GDR, and to a lesser extent Bulgaria and Czechoslovakia, have been more happy to commit their nationals to military activity in the Third World than Poland or Hungary. Romania has often been actively involved politically – but not necessarily on the same side or on the same terms as the rest. Notorious for its stubbornly autonomous line in foreign policy, it is something of a maverick. It refused to toe the line and break off diplomatic relations with Israel after the June 1967 war. And during the Angolan civil war it supported all three guerrilla movements – the position advocated by the OAU – rather than support the Soviet Union's favourite, the MPLA. But it prefers to keep its troops at home.

Arms sales. Not surprisingly, in view of their own dependence on Soviet supplies of military equipment, in quantitative terms the East Europeans have played only a relatively minor role in arms transfers: their total military aid to the Third World amounts to a combined total of $4 billion in the period since 1954, compared with $47 billion for the Soviet Union.[6] Some would argue the East Europeans have themselves suffered as a result of the Soviet Union's eagerness to transfer arms to important clients. After the June 1967 Arab-Israeli war, arms destined for Eastern Europe were diverted instead to the Middle East. And the most modern Soviet equipment has had a habit of turning up in the arsenals of Third World clients before it reaches Eastern Europe. After the expulsion of Soviet advisers from Egypt, the Romanians apparently supplied spares for Soviet-built equipment in Egypt – although most likely with Soviet acquiescence.

Military training. Like the Soviet Union but on a smaller scale, the East Europeans and the Cubans have all played some role in providing military training for Third World nationals in their own countries. Again, the available figures do not differentiate between the East European states, but the Poles and Czechs have a long record in this field. The East Germans were important latecomers. Recently, information has been rediscovered concerning the operation of guerrilla training camps located, it is alleged, throughout the Soviet Union, Eastern Europe, Cuba and the Near and Middle East (Table 5.2).

Table 5.2   Communist training of Middle East military personnel in communist countries, 1955–79 (number of persons)

	Total	USSR	Eastern Europe
Algeria	2,401	2,195	200
Libya	1,595	1,370	285
Ethiopia	1,790	1,290	500
Somalia	2,585	2,395	160
Sudan	550	330	20
Egypt	6,250	5,665	585
Iran	315	315	—
Iraq	4,400	3,710	690
North Yemen	1,360	1,360	—
South Yemen	1,095	1,075	20
Syria	5,455	4,245	1,210
Afghanistan	4,010	3,725*	285

* Excluding Soviet troops.
Source: NFAC, *Communist Aid Activities*, p. 16.

Economic and technical assistance. The provision of economic aid by both the Soviet Union and Eastern Europe also suggests some interesting patterns. In both cases the trend in recent years has been to concentrate on two countries, Cuba and Vietnam, both of whom are members of the CMEA. In 1978, 96 per cent of the CMEA's net aid disbursements ($3,800 million) was swallowed up by these two.[7] Most of this aid took the form of preferential pricing arrangements for intra-CMEA trade in sugar, nickel and oil. A slim $223 million of net disbursements was left over (and if interest and amortization on previous loans is allowed for, the non-CMEA developing countries, according to these figures, received only $14 million between them). Much of the remainder of Soviet aid was concentrated on 'socialist' countries such as Laos, Cambodia, North Korea and strategically important Near and Middle Eastern countries (Iran, Iraq, Syria and Turkey). By the same calculation, developing countries in Africa are now paying back more in past loans than they are receiving in new disbursements, with the pattern of commitments showing little change for the future.

The pattern for East European non-military aid is similar. Although proportionally the East Europeans have not reduced the level of their aid to Africa as dramatically as the Soviet Union, the bulk of their non-CMEA aid is now also channelled increasingly to the Middle East (Iran, Iraq and Syria). The East Europeans have also reduced the number of non-CMEA countries to whom they make commitments: from thirteen in 1972, to eight in 1978 and two in 1979.[8] Further evidence of the close coordination between the Soviet Union and the East European states is the fact that eight of the largest Soviet recipients of aid between 1955 and 1979, accounting for 75 per cent of the USSR's aid commitments, also received one half of Eastern Europe's commitments. And in many cases, the two sets of credits were extended within twelve months of each other.[9]

The gross figures for East European aid are not large, but, like the Soviet Union, the East Europeans have tended to concentrate on specific projects, such as the oil industry in Iraq, oil refineries, a phosphate plant, land reclamation, the power industry and transport in Syria, electrification and diesel equipment in Egypt.[10] In the early period, the East Europeans also subcontracted goods and services for Soviet aid projects, especially in the Middle East. The practice still continues, especially where a particular East European country specializes in the equipment needed for a project.

Economic technicians and advisers. Particularly since the start of the 1970s, both Eastern Europe and Cuba have supplied large numbers of economic technicians. In this category the overall numbers come closest to balancing out the Soviet effort.[11] Economic assistance would seem to be a far less troublesome issue – even for those East European states which 'opted out' of military entanglement. Again the main targets are the Middle East, North Africa and Afghanistan. According to CIA figures, as many as half these communist technicians are working on commercial contracts, which includes 23,500 East Europeans and Soviets in Libya alone who are engaged on various public works projects and agriculture. Indeed, it is estimated that in 1979 half the East Europeans so employed were working in Libya.

Trade. The total figures for East European trade with the region are not large, but are roughly on a par with the Soviet Union. Trade covers some basic raw materials and oil, both of which are lacking in large quantities in Eastern Europe, but otherwise agricultural products seem to account for much of Eastern Europe's import trade throughout the Third World.

Two basic conclusions emerge from this round-up of East European and Cuban involvement in the Near and Middle East: first, the East Europeans, and now increasingly the Cubans, have directed the main thrust of both their military and their non-military aid effort towards those countries that are of prime concern also for Soviet foreign policy. Second, this complementary and parallel pattern does not of itself confirm the 'proxy' theory. A 'proxy' state is presumably one that acts only as directed by a third power. This would be a misleading designation of Soviet-East European relations on issues much closer to home. It is doubtful whether it should be applied to any aspect of the relationship. For a broader discussion of the 'proxy' versus 'ally' issue, it is necessary to turn to a consideration of motive.

Cuba

Cuba's involvement in Africa and the Middle East dates back to within a matter of months of Castro's coming to power in December 1959. By 1961 Cuba was reportedly operating a guerrilla training base in Ghana. Between 1963 and 1965 small numbers of Cuban combat troops were sent to Algeria to aid the regime in its border conflict with Morocco. And during 1965 and 1966 Che Guevara, before meeting a sticky end in the jungles of Bolivia, led a contingent of guerrillas operating in Zaire and then Congo-Brazzaville, where Cuba had installed a large military mission. In 1966 Cuba's military assistance to Guinea included soldiers to staff the presidential bodyguard. Although much of this activity was confined to strategically less important states in Black Africa, during the 1960s Cubans are also said to have acted as advisers to al-Fatah in Jordan. Although Cuba's overseas activity appears to have declined somewhat in the late 1960s, it was to pick up again in the 1970s.[12]

The main purpose in drawing up this list is to make the point that Cuban involvement outside Latin America, while not extensive in numbers compared with the present, was persistent, and that it continued despite the ups and downs of Cuba's relationship with Moscow. Since 1961 Cuban combat troops have reportedly been deployed at least four times: in Algeria in 1963; in Syria in 1973 (although in this case there are no reports of Cubans actually engaged in the war); in Angola in 1975; and in Ethiopia in 1978. What has changed is the scale of the involvement in the two last-mentioned cases.

By 1975 Cuba was estimated to have 5,000 military personnel of one sort or another in ten countries, including in the early 1970s 600–700 in South Yemen (Cuban pilots are said to have flown some sorties for the South Yemenis during the Dhofari rebellion against the British-backed Sultan Qabbous), and 500–750 tank troops in Syria.[13] In 1974 Cuba opened a military mission in Somalia, to add to its mission in Algeria. According to Cuban sources, in 1980 Cuba had some 15,000 military personnel stationed overseas,[14] the vast majority of whom were in Angola and Ethiopia.

The dramatic change in numbers has also brought with it a change in the nature of Cuban involvement. The Cuban commitment to Angola in 1975, following a request for assistance from the MPLA, had begun along similar lines to Cuba's previous limited deployments of combat troops. The final decision to send Cuban troops to Angola in increasing numbers was taken in either late August or early September 1975. The troops were ferried in Cuban ships and aeroplanes initially. The heavy weaponry was supplied by the Soviet Union, to be picked up by the Cubans on arrival. The subsequent threat to Cuban forces and the Cuban-backed MPLA, in particular from South African forces moving into Angola from the south, was later met by concerted Soviet assistance to airlift in more troops.[15] According to Castro, at the peak of the 1975–6 war, there were some 36,000 Cubans in Angola.[16] By 1977 Western sources put the figure at 19,000–20,000 Cuban troops still in Angola to shore up the Neto regime and the MPLA.[17] Whatever the figures, the point about the Cuban intervention is that it was decisive in the civil war and that it preceded any major Soviet commitment to Angola. The victory of the MPLA with Cuban and Soviet help was later portrayed as the result of an internationalist alliance. The Cubans were seen as the pivot. Cuban initiative led eventually to a 'joint' victory.

Cuban involvement in the Horn of Africa appears to have been a less straightforward affair. After the establishment of a military mission in Somalia in 1974, Cuban instructors helped train Somali guerrillas to fight in the Ogaden.[18] In December 1976 the Soviet Union is reported to have signed a secret accord to supply arms to Ethiopia. Although it is not clear what role the Cubans played in the decision to lend initial support to the new Ethiopian regime, in November 1977, in response to Western and Somali claims, Cuba denied any involvement in Ethiopia – a claim confirmed by the Ethiopians in January 1978. However, the transfer of troops, when it happened, was swift: 2,000–2,500 Cuban troops were in Ethiopia by February 1978; 15,000 by April; and 17,000 by May.[19] There were also reports that Cubans flew MiG-17s and MiG–21s in support of the Ethiopians against the Somali invasion of the Ogaden, although the main body of troops was brought in only after the Somali attack had been turned.

Again, the lending of Cuban support was probably decisive in deterring further Somali incursions. But this time the theme of internationalism had been toned down considerably. One reason has been Cuban discomfort with the policy of the Ethiopian government towards the Eritrean secessionists. The Cubans have been unhappy at the violent suppression of what they see as a national liberation struggle in Eritrea. On 26 February 1978 the Cuban Vice-President, Carlos Rodriguez, a former head of the pro-Moscow communist party in Cuba in earlier years, stated publicly that Cuban troops would not be used in Eritrea,[20] although the Soviet Union's advisers have played a role.

This refusal to allow Cuban troops to be used in Eritrea suggests a degree of Cuban control incompatible with the role of Soviet 'proxy'. The Soviet Union has apparently tried to persuade the Ethiopian government to reach a political settlement with the Eritrean secessionists. This may indicate that the Cuban argument was primarily with the Ethiopian regime rather than the Soviet generals. But either way, the Cubans had made their point.

There is, however, a second uncomfortable aspect to the Ethiopian adventure: whereas in Angola the Cubans seem to have forced the pace and persuaded Moscow – if only by the prospect of imminent defeat – to provide the extra logistical support, in Ethiopia Cuban troops, where they have been used, appear to have operated under much more direct Soviet command.[21] The whole operation in the Ogaden appeared to place the Cubans in a more subordinate role than had appeared to be the case in Angola. Most recently the Cubans have adopted a much lower profile, although by 1979 there were still an estimated 11,000–12,000 troops in the country.[22]

The various military roles played by the Cubans in Africa have been summarized as follows: (1) training and advising revolutionary movements, including training Third World personnel in Cuba itself; (2) assisting 'progressive' left-wing governments; (3) providing pilots (e.g. training Algerian pilots, providing advisers for the Syrian air force, and flying combat missions for such countries as Ethiopia and South Yemen); (4) delivering arms to both guerrilla organizations and states (although in close coordination with the Soviet Union in countries where the Soviet Union is also committed); and (5) providing Cuban combat troops (including tank crews in Algeria in 1963 and Syria in 1973).[23]

Cuba's involvement in countries of the Near and Middle East has increased in recent years but the basic pattern has remained the same. Thus, according to one view, Cuba's involvement in Angola – the first major jump in the numbers of Cuban troops – represented merely the acceleration of an already evident trend, rather than a radically new change of course.[24]

Motives

There are several schools of thought as to Cuba's motives for its foreign adventures, although they are by no means mutually exclusive. The first assumes that Cuba's foreign adventures are indeed directed by the Soviet Union. Cuba is obliged to undertake the tasks allotted to it for any one of several reasons – its financial indebtedness to Moscow, its increasingly close integration in the Soviet orbit (witness the adoption even of the Soviet model for Cuba's political institutions). A second school puts the emphasis on Cuba's ideology of revolution. It sees Cuba more as an autonomous, revolutionary actor committed to national liberation around the globe, rather along the lines of Cuba's activities in Latin America in the 1960s. Rather than a 'proxy', in this case Cuba could be seen either as an ally of the Soviet Union or possibly as an 'opponent', where revolutionary ideology runs up against great-power diplomacy. Fidel Castro appears to be the main proponent of this argument.

By contrast, a third possible motive is economics: the need for the resources with which the Third World is liberally endowed. This has also been used as an argument to explain the occasional softening of Cuban hostility towards the 'Yankee imperialists' in the United States. If this latter point is correct, why jeopardize good relations with a rich neighbour by global activism for a lesser reward?

A fourth argument relies on an analysis of Cuba's internal politics. According to this school, Cuba's global activism has been the result of the interaction of three groups in the leadership: the pragmatists, who emphasize expansion of trade links; the revolutionaries, who include Fidel himself, and put their emphasis on the struggle against imperialism as a means of gaining leverage in world affairs; and those of a military tendency, including Raul Castro, who emphasize the external mission of the Cuban armed forces. Of these three groups, the last two were seen to be in the ascendancy following the intervention in Angola. The success of the venture reinforced their arguments. The Angola operation was responsible for a breakdown in Cuban-American talks in 1975. However, as a result of Cuba's active role, the country received increasing amounts of aid and weapons from the Soviet Union (trade was due to increase 250 per cent from 1976 to 1980; and another 50 per cent between 1981 and 1985 – and, given the terms of trade, in Cuba's case more trade means more aid). Thus, in the end, the result of the Angolan operation must have pleased all three groups.[25]

A further motive might be domestic weakness. According to this theory, Cuba's overseas activity, and the internationalist propaganda it generates, has been needed to maintain revolutionary *élan* in the face of mounting domestic economic and political problems (some of which, paradoxically, have presumably been caused by the overseas activity). It has led to the creation of a new set of myths for a new generation. This 'return of the slaves' is really, then, an expression of Cuban nationalism.[26]

Costs and benefits

Whether or not Castro's Cuba has acted as the Soviet Union's 'adjutant' in the Third World, it has earned tangible reward from its foreign adventures. But on top of the material benefits, Castro appeared for a time not only to enjoy privileged status within the Soviet camp, but to have successfully projected himself as a Third World statesman, and thereby to have earned a degree of immortality in the non-aligned movement. In this, Castro appeared to see himself as an ally, even a sponsor, of the Soviet Union. He underlined the point during his two African tours in spring 1977 and summer 1978.[27] And he seemed to bask happily in the international and 'revolutionary' limelight. However, his increasing ability to ship his soldiers to distant wars cannot be explained simply by a happy coincidence of circumstances, plus a dash of international fervour.

The Cuban economy remains totally dependent on Soviet sugar subsidies and cheap oil. Since roughly 1975, when the prices of Soviet oil and other commodities in CMEA trade were raised substantially, the Soviet Union has taken it upon itself – and persuaded the East Europeans also – to cushion Cuba from the price shock: unlike the European CMEA members, Cuba seems to get as much oil as it needs; and when the price of CMEA oil goes up, so does the price the Soviet Union pays for Cuba's sugar crop. Such subsidies now amount to over 40 per cent of Cuba's GNP. Increased aid commitments and trade may be a reward for internationalist behaviour but they are also a strong string in the hands of the Soviet leadership. There is no evidence that Cuban troops were committed against Castro's wishes – and to that extent the term 'proxy' is inappropriate. On the other hand, whether it was the Cubans themselves who first saw their chance in Angola, or indeed elsewhere, it is ultimately the Soviet Union which controls the purse, the flow of arms and most of the aircraft and ships to ferry the troops.

Nor has the economic benefit necessarily offset the political problems caused by foreign wars. It has been estimated that, in proportion to its population, Cuba by 1979 was using twice as many soldiers as the Americans did in Vietnam and suffering proportionately four times as many casualties.[28] The sustained impact of a faltering economy and this loss of young Cuban lives no doubt played a large role in encouraging as many as 125,000 Cubans to flee to the United States when given half a chance in spring 1980. The spectacle drew little sympathy for the Cubans elsewhere in the communist movement. The following is an excerpt from *The People's Daily,* Peking:

Question: 'What's the largest country in the world?'
Answer: 'Cuba. Its heart is in Havana. Its government is in Moscow. Its graveyards are in Angola and Ethiopia; and its people are in Miami.'[29]

Although the Cuban leadership appeared reasonably pleased with the results of their Angolan adventure, their attempts to build on this base have run into snags. In an attempt to head off open war between Somalia and Ethiopia over the Ogaden, Castro arranged in March 1977 a secret meeting between Mengistu and Siad Barre in South Yemen.[30] But the Cuban proposal of some kind of federation between the two regimes foundered on the very unrevolutionary rock of local nationalism. War subsequently broke out in July, and the Somalis broke diplomatic relations with the Cubans in November 1977. The Cubans were apparently left somewhat disappointed by the entire episode. Somalia also abrogated its Treaty of Friendship with the Soviet Union but stopped short of a final break. The size of the Soviet embassy staff in Mogadishu was reduced drastically.

A second problem concerns the nature of Soviet-Cuban cooperation. For as long as Soviet and Cuban interests were running parallel, it mattered little that Cuba was almost entirely dependent on the Soviet Union for much of the logistical support to promote their jointly held revolutionary aims. However, if it is to maintain its credibility in the Third World and the non-aligned movement, Cuba has to be seen to be able to act independently. At times this has reportedly put a strain on relations. In May 1977 Castro had allowed Agostinho Neto in Angola to use Cuban troops to help suppress an attempted coup by an extremist 'pro-Soviet' faction. It is not clear that the Soviet Union was actively behind the plotters, since at the time Angola was of less strategic interest to the Soviet Union. But the incident does point to divergent interests. Later Cuba was happy to aid the Ethiopian government in its fight against Somali infiltration in the Ogaden – a position which squared with the principles of the OAU, among others. But when the Ethiopians, with Soviet assistance, attempted the violent repression of the Eritrean secessionist movements, that posed a different problem. The Cubans resolved it by declining to become involved in the internal conflict. Ethiopia is a target of greater strategic value to the Soviet Union than was Angola and, as some outside observers have noted, this has meant that the Cubans have anyway played a more subsidiary role – even, some argue, to the point of direct subordination.[31] Yet this overdraws the political point. The Cubans do appear to have had less of a free hand in Ethiopia. They have not, however, been forced into compromising their basic ideological principles. And they do appear to be there at their own initiative.

A harder and more recent blow to Cuba's prestige was the Soviet invasion of Afghanistan. The occupation, in December 1979, of a hitherto officially non-aligned state by Soviet troops, effectively pulled the rug from under Castro's statesman-like stance in the Third World. And it scuppered his attempt, using his chairmanship of the movement, to guide the non-aligned states to a more actively pro-socialist and, indeed, pro-Soviet line. It probably also cost Cuba the support it would have needed in the General Assembly to claim the vacant Latin America seat on the UN Security Council in October 1980. Earlier, the non-aligned movement had taken the unusual step of deciding to bring forward its June 1981 meeting to January and to change its venue from Havana to New Delhi. It is a measure of Castro's high dudgeon over Afghanistan that it took him until the second congress of the Cuban Communist Party in December 1980 to add his official endorsement to the Soviet action. (The announcement followed the election of President Reagan and the signing of a new trade agreement with the Soviet Union.) There appears to have been no question of Cuba's being asked to provide troops for Afghanistan. There was no *prima facie* case for consultations either. But Cuba did suffer considerably from the political 'fall-out', and Castro made his point on this score.

East Germany
Dubbed somewhat misleadingly 'Europe's Cubans', the East Germans have played the most active role of all the East European states in the Third World. East German military advisers were first spotted in Congo-Brazzaville in 1973. The total numbers are con-

siderably less than those for the Cubans. Estimates have varied considerably from a possible 15,000 (Brookings Institution), to 4,500 (US State Department), to as low as 700.[32] Another estimate in 1980 put the number of NVA (National People's Army) personnel who were working as instructors, military advisers and signalling specialists at 2,720.[33] The precise numbers are less important. What is clear is that the distribution pattern in the Near and Middle East follows closely that of Soviet advisers in the region: clusters of East German military advisers are to be found in Syria (now reportedly in considerable numbers), Iraq, South Yemen, Ethiopia, Libya, Algeria and Afghanistan.

Like all the other East European states, East Germany also contributes to arms exports. In 1979 it was estimated that close to 50 per cent of all East European weapons shipments to Third World countries had been delivered in the preceding five years.[34] East Germany now has the most modern equipment in Eastern Europe in its inventories and, although the figures on arms shipments are not available, the East German army probably has a fair amount of obsolete equipment to sell off.

But it is East German skills that are most in demand: East German military personnel have helped train and reorganize local armies (e.g. Mozambique, Ethiopia, Libya, Angola), and have trained police forces and run intelligence operations (e.g. Iraq, South Yemen, Syria, Afghanistan). East Germany is even reported to have supplied prison guards for South Yemen. East Germans have also contributed other technical skills, particularly in agriculture, education and medical care. (Many a wounded guerrilla has no doubt been relieved to wake up in an East German, rather than a Soviet, hospital.) And by Soviet standards, the East Germans, like the Cubans, are said to be quite popular in the countries where they are based. As a mark of appreciation of East Germany's contribution to its economic development, Somalia kept East German youth brigades working on aid projects after Cuban and Soviet advisers had been expelled in November 1977.[35] Indeed, when the East German ambassador left Mogadishu in 1978, he was replaced after only a very brief interval, and the Somalis appointed a very experienced man as their ambassador in East Berlin. For a time it looked as if Somali relations with the East European countries were being conducted largely through East Berlin. The Somali case is a feather in the cap of the East Germans, a boon to the Somalis, and probably does not offend Soviet interests either.

Where regimes have taken the non-capitalist path, the East Germans have been on hand to help write new constitutions, set up political parties and organize mass movements (of trade unionists, women, youth, etc.) along the lines of East Germany's own National Front. And for those waiting impatiently on the rubbish heap of history, East Berlin makes a well-patronized rest-home familiar in the past, among others, to the PLO's Yasser Arafat and the previously exiled members of Iran's Tudeh party. It was the East German leader, Erich Honecker, who on 13 November 1979 while on a visit to Addis Ababa, laid the cornerstone for the first monument to Karl Marx in Africa.

Motives

Like Cuba, East Germany has a long history of political contacts with states and national liberation movements in Africa and the Middle East. Unlike either the Cubans or the other East Europeans, the GDR has had a very particular axe to grind, and one that is more national than international: *diplomatic recognition*. For the first twenty years following its founding as a state in 1949, the GDR was recognized only by its socialist allies. West Germany's claim to sole representation of the German nation, and its success in impressing the point on its allies in the West and on Third World states, left the GDR in diplomatic isolation. The blockade could not be broken in the West, so that East Germany's only resort was to carry the battle to a different staging-ground. The result was a struggle for influence between West Germany and East Germany in Africa, the Middle East and Asia.

A number of trade agreements were signed, beginning with Egypt in 1953, but the GDR failed to achieve any diplomatic breakthrough until 1969, when a string of states, including Iraq, the Sudan, Yemen and Egypt, followed a year later by Algeria, chose to tread on West German toes and recognize the East German state. However, their action had to do more with their annoyance at West Germany than with the political attentions of East Germany. When West Germany and Israel established diplomatic relations in 1965, Egypt, Jordan, Lebanon, Sudan, Iraq, Saudi Arabia and Yemen all broke their relations with Bonn. Yet it took another four years and a Middle East war for East Germany to achieve its long-sought-for breakthrough.

Alongside the rest of Africa, the region still offers the GDR the easiest platform to display its new international profile. Since East Germany won widespread international recognition in the 1970s, Honecker has made several highly publicized tours through Africa, and East Germany has signed friendship and cooperation treaties with Ethiopia, South Yemen and Iraq. Since 1972, when both German states were admitted as members of the United Nations, East Germany has been able to distinguish itself from its

West German sister-state by consistently voting with the developing countries and the Arab countries on all crucial issues.

This points to a second motive for East German involvement: *ideology*. Like Castro in Cuba, the East German regime has always liked to see itself as a champion of Third World interests in the struggle against imperialism (and with typical East German thoroughness has turned the whole effort into something of a science).[36] Partly for this reason, and partly because for a long time normal state-to-state contacts were hard to establish, the GDR has a long history of contacts with national liberation movements which dates back to the early 1960s. These early contacts included such later successes as Frelimo in Mozambique and the MPLA in Angola. Since the early 1970s the GDR has assiduously cultivated close contacts with the PLO.[37]

From the noble to the pragmatic: without doubt, another motive for East German involvement in the Third World in general and the Middle East and the Gulf in particular is *economic*. The developing world is not only an easier market for East German industrial goods; it is also a source of important raw materials. While levels of trade are not particularly high, like the rest of Eastern Europe, East Germany (which is 90 per cent dependent on Soviet oil and 100 per cent dependent on Soviet natural gas) is interested in finding new and preferably cheap sources of minerals and energy. No doubt with oil and gas on his mind, Honecker reportedly was planning to entertain the Shah of Iran on a visit to East Berlin when the Iranian revolution intervened and swept the King of Kings off his throne.

And then there is the *Soviet Union*. East Germany, like Cuba, has been described as a Soviet 'proxy' and worse. Its close involvement in Soviet foreign policy is undeniable. In part this follows naturally from a broadly shared political and ideological outlook – a point stressed over and over again by the East German press. But while East Germany clearly has had, and still has, its own motives for involvement in the Third World, it has also been forced by political circumstances to rely heavily on the Soviet Union for its entrée into diplomatic circles. But there is an extra dimension in East German-Soviet relations. Unlike the other national armies of Eastern Europe, the NVA is officially directly subordinated to Warsaw Pact, i.e. Soviet, command. This relic from East Germany's past means that military coordination between the Soviet Union and the GDR is far easier to achieve than between the Soviet Union and the more tetchy national armies of, say, Poland or Hungary. The distinction is more than a formality. But, whatever the true explanation, East Germany has consistently followed the Soviet lead on all major political issues: it condemned Israel after the June 1967 war, rejected the Camp David agreement, assiduously courted the members of the 'steadfastness front' (Syria, Libya, Algeria, PDRY and PLO), and gave immediate, some would say almost premature, and unstinting support to the Soviet invasion of Afghanistan.

Costs and benefits

For a number of reasons, the costs and benefits of East Germany's involvement in Soviet foreign policy are harder to measure. The occasional tantrum over West Berlin or West Germany aside, publicly the GDR regime has been the Soviet Union's most loyal ally. For reasons already mentioned – East Germany's former diplomatic isolation and its reliance on Soviet sponsorship – the GDR regime may feel it has cause to be grateful for the opportunity to ride on the Soviet bandwagon in the Middle East and Africa. It is hard to tell whether this is now in process of change following East Germany's widespread recognition. In the propaganda battle with West Germany, East Germany has no doubt been grateful to find states in the developing world which are happy to go along with its claim that West Berlin cannot be considered a part of West Germany: the point is not as arcane as it sounds, since any country trading with the EEC is obliged officially to take the opposite view.

It is hard to distinguish peculiarly East German perspectives on the Middle East or the Gulf which would clash with those of the Soviet Union. Africa may be a different story. East Germany has long cultivated its own contacts there – more often in response to West German initiative than any grand socialist design. It is at least conceivable that in the future the Soviet Union may take action in the area which could do damage to East German interests. The region has always seemed of greater importance to the Soviet Union's smaller allies than to the Soviet Union itself.

Like Cuba, East Germany is closely tied in to trade with the Soviet Union. Presumably if a serious difference of opinion were to arise, this economic dependence would be a valuable weapon in Soviet hands. Short of that, East Germany is not dependent on Soviet aid (although happy to pay CMEA prices for oil). Indeed, the point is usually put the other way round: that East Germany, as the most efficient of the CMEA economies, could better serve its own interests by switching some of its trade elsewhere. Nor is there any evidence that East Germany has benefited more from Soviet oil policy within the CMEA because of its overseas activities. (For entirely different reasons, Poland, the black sheep of the CMEA fold, seems to be doing best at present.) But any state with an eye to the future must bank on gaining some practical benefit from solidarity with the Arab cause. It is considerations such as these which presumably balance out the serious economic drain on all the East European economies resulting from fraternal aid to Cuba and Vietnam. Even the East German habit of acquiring the most sophisticated Soviet tanks, helicopters and other equipment owes more to East Germany's ability to pay – and probably through the nose at that – than any special treatment. But even though the material rewards to East Germany are less than those enjoyed in the past by the Cubans, the experience gained by the NVA in overseas operations must be invaluable to an army otherwise mostly confined to its barracks.

And whatever the balance of benefits versus costs within the CMEA, the GDR has earned itself a good reputation in the developing world. East Germans are evidently better liked – both for their manners and their technical skills – than the Russians. When the architect of East Germany's new, active Third World policy, Werner Lamberz, was killed in a helicopter crash in Libya on 6 March 1978, the entire Ethiopian military leadership went into public mourning. But the Lamberz incident also illustrates one of the hazards of Third World diplomacy: the helicopter in which he was travelling had reportedly been blown up in an assassination attempt on the life of the Libyan leader, Colonel Gaddafi.

More general problems have also arisen: the East Germans, like the Cubans, have at times had to reckon with both local nationalism and a yawning culture gap. Middle Eastern socialism is often scarcely recognizable to a European Marxist-Leninist – and vice versa. The problem has been particularly acute in Ethiopia, and before it in Somalia, where East Germany has been closely involved in moulding new political institutions. All attempts to set up a single, centralized political party in Ethiopia, the Workers' Revolutionary Party, have been frustrated by local intra-Marxist intrigue and the reluctance of the Ethiopian military regime, despite its public commitment to 'socialism', to contemplate an avowedly civilian-based political institution.

Also like Cuba, East Germany has found that its commitment to Third World activity within the broad framework of Soviet foreign policy has led it into some strange alliances. For example, the involvement with Libya has reportedly led to active support for the Libyan incursion into Chad which, by offending the OAU, may in future dent the shiny internationalist image the GDR has earned for itself. Moreover, as a defender of the narrower interests of the Soviet camp, East Germany welcomed the Soviet invasion of Afghanistan. With no independent profile to maintain in the non-aligned movement, East Germany has suffered less than Cuba from the fall-out in the Third World. Yet at some point East

Germany, too, must begin to feel the effects of such Soviet actions. The UN votes condemning the invasion were no doubt something of an embarrassment to East Berlin.

Conclusions

In both the Cuban and the East German case, there is ample evidence to suggest that both regimes had more than sufficient reasons of their own for cultivating Third World contacts in the first place. In doing so, to a large extent they have pursued interests which converge with or run parallel to those of the Soviet Union. On the other hand, it is easy to conceive of actions, such as the invasion of Afghanistan or some shift in Soviet priorities in Africa, where the interests of the smaller allies diverge. As a superpower, with a claim to involvement in all major international issues, the Soviet Union is apt to view problems from the perspective of grand strategy, rather than local particularism. Not surprisingly, the East Germans and the Cubans (and indeed the Romanians and the rest) have been left to their own devices more in Africa south of the Horn than in the Near and Middle East.

Even for those reluctant to commit military advisers, solidarity with any Third World state imposes a price. In economic terms, the burden is now almost exclusively the sum of aid to the two CMEA allies, Cuba and Vietnam (both active in different parts of the globe), and, increasingly, Afghanistan. Whether simply disgruntled at the size of the burden or at the way it hamstrings aid policy in the rest of the developing world, all the East European states, but Czechoslovakia and Romania in particular, have reportedly made clear their discomfort. And as, under the delayed impact of world recession, the Soviet Union and Eastern Europe face their own energy crunch (increased prices for Soviet oil and the need for the East Europeans to find more of their increasing oil requirements from outside the CMEA, on the even more expensive world market), the problem will become even more acute. It is burdens such as these, to be borne politically at home, that can be expected to govern East European commitment to new foreign ventures.

There have also been other political problems. Both Cuba and East Germany have encountered difficulties in dealing with local cultures and the force of nationalism. In the Middle East, atheistic Marxism-Leninism is scarcely an attractive option for most regimes. This makes for alliance based on expediency and opportunism – particularly on the part of the local states. The policies of the Soviet Union, the East Europeans and the Cubans will ultimately be judged by the degree to which they advance or harm perceived local interests. Soviet strategic interests may be well wide of the mark, and ringing declarations of solidarity against the forces of 'imperialism' in the region can have a double edge.

Perhaps partly in response to these and other frustrations, the pattern of involvement in Ethiopia and South Yemen (and Afghanistan) has been different. It remains to be seen whether it has been effective. Pouring local particularism into a recognizable Marxist-Leninist mould may make the job of arranging political and economic cooperation temporarily easier. But in the end its only value may be to prove the irrelevance of European Marxism-Leninism to the developing world. Such a conclusion could also have repercussions both in Eastern Europe and in Cuba.

Nor have some of the other East European states shown the requisite degree of enthusiasm over the defence of the revolution in Afghanistan. While East Germany, Czechoslovakia and Bulgaria welcomed the Soviet intervention, Poland and Hungary for a long time remained reprovingly silent; and Romania called openly for a withdrawal of all Soviet troops. To some extent, all are now suffering the effects of the post-Afghan hangover on East-West relations. And lesser interruptions have occurred in the past: the break in Soviet-Egyptian relations also harmed the economic ties of both Czechoslovakia and Bulgaria, although not East Germany and the rest.

But it is the Cuban experience which offers most food for thought. The success of the Angolan adventure would not have been possible without Soviet help, but at the time it was still possible to portray it at least as a 'joint' achievement. The same cannot be said so simply of Ethiopia. The problems facing outside powers in the Horn are greater than those in Angola. At the same time, having once taken the decision to intervene in one place with large numbers of troops, it is presumably that much harder to turn down a second request for assistance. Whether for that reason or simply because the region is of such strategic importance to the Soviet Union, the once triumphant internationalist lustre of the Cubans appears to have been tarnished, first by the dust of a Soviet-commanded desert war and then by the Soviet invasion of Afghanistan.

To point to overall Soviet command is not to confirm the 'proxy' thesis, if those commanded are there because they want to be. On the other hand, voluntary self-assignment to the Soviet cause does not amount to partnership if, when push comes to shove, the junior allies are unable to make their influence felt in Moscow. For Cuba the crunch came first in Eritrea and subsequently in Afghanistan. Castro was able to resist any pressure to use his troops in Eritrea but was powerless to influence the course of events in Afghanistan, save by withholding his public support and causing Moscow further embarrassment. Presumably, in the future, Cuba could again refuse to commit troops to a particular war, but always at the risk of biting the hand that feeds it. Much will depend on the importance of the issue at stake.

The East Europeans are themselves equally powerless to reverse a chosen course of action by the Soviet Union once it has begun. Over the years the Warsaw Pact has developed more of the trappings of an alliance than it had in 1955. There have been times when East European resistance has thwarted intended Soviet action (e.g. over the extension of alliance commitments to the Sino-Soviet border, closer military integration, etc.), but only when the policy at issue required direct East European acquiescence and participation. None of the East European states can be considered a mere 'proxy' in Soviet policy in the Near and Middle East. The decision to organize East European involvement on a bilateral basis would seem to indicate a desire to avoid conflict over the issue. It represents a clear example of how bilateral agreement can circumvent the otherwise cumbersome process of multilateral consensus-building. And in the particular cases cited in this chapter, there is, as yet, no sign that either East Germany or Cuba are contemplating any major changes in their now international roles.

Notes

[1]   Roger F. Pajak, 'The Effectiveness of Soviet Arms Aid Diplomacy in the Third World', in Robert H. Donaldson (ed.), *The Soviet Union and the Third World: Successes and Failures* (Boulder, Colo., Westview Press, 1981), p. 391; and Stephen S. Kaplan, *Diplomacy and Power* (Washington, D.C., The Brookings Institution, 1981), p. 153. It must be noted, however, that arms had been shipped to Guatemala in 1954.

[2]   Ibid.

[3]   Ibid., pp. 154–5.

[4]   National Foreign Assessment Center, CIA, *Communist Aid Activities in Non-Communist Less Developed Countries,1979 and 1954–79*, ER 80–1031U, October 1980. This source has been used consistently for serial figures throughout the chapter. Other sources differ considerably, but no other similar set of figures exists for the period since 1954.

[5]   For example, G. G. Ra'anan, 'The Evolution of the Soviet Use of Surrogates in Military Relations with the Third World, with Particular Emphasis on Cuban Participation in Africa', Rand Paper Series P-6420, December 1979.

[6]   *Communist Aid Activities*, p. 13.

[7]   The Foreign and Commonwealth Office, *Soviet, East European and*

DAC Aid 1970–78, Foreign Policy Document No. 49, 1980. Afghanistan has also received considerable economic aid in comparison to the relatively low level of Soviet and East European disbursements to the developing world. In 1980, Afghanistan received $276 million from the Soviet Union and a further $110.3 million from the rest of Eastern Europe combined.

[8] Ibid, p. 4.
[9] *Communist Aid Activities,* p. 9, and table, p. 18.
[10] Ibid, pp. 30–33.
[11] Ibid., table 5, p. 10.
[12] A.M. Kapcia, 'Cuba's African Involvement: A New Perspective', *Survey,* Spring 1979, p. 150.
[13] William J. Durch, 'The Cuban Military in Africa and the Middle East', *Studies in Comparative Communism,* Spring/Summer 1978. The presence of Cuban troops in Syria has been disputed. The primary source of the reports is obscure but, such as they are, they are summarized in Ra'anan,'The Evolution of the Soviet Use of Surrogates', pp. 36–7.
[14] Jorge I. Dominguez, 'Cuba in the 1980s', *Problems of Communism,* March/April 1981, p. 48.
[15] The sequence of events is covered in detail in A. J. Klinghoffer, *The Angolan War: A Study in Soviet Policy in the Third World* (Boulder, Colo., Westview Press, 1980), pp. 110–14. The case for Cuba's logistical 'independence' in the Angolan operation is put in G. G. Marquez, 'Operation Carlota: Cuba's Role in Angolan Victory', *Venceremos,* vol. 4, no. 5 (1977) – and is partly criticized by Klinghoffer.
[16] Dominguez, 'Cuba in the 1980s', p. 48.
[17] E. Gonzalez, 'Cuba, the Soviet Union and Africa', in David E. Albright (ed.), *Africa and International Communism* (London, Macmillan, 1981), p. 153.
[18] Kapcia, 'Cuba's African Involvement'.
[19] Ibid.
[20] Ibid; and Gonzalez, 'Cuba, the Soviet Union and Africa', p. 156.
[21] Jiri Valenta, 'The Soviet-Cuban Alliance in Africa and the Caribbean', *The World Today,* February 1981.
[22] 'Impact of Cuban-Soviet Ties in the Western Hemisphere, Spring 1979', *Hearings, Subcommittee on Inter-American Affairs of Committee of Foreign Affairs of the House,* 96th Congress, First Session, April 25–26, 1979, p. 11.
[23] Summary in Klinghoffer, *The Angolan War,* ch. 9.
[24] Ibid.
[25] Point 4 is argued by E. Gonzalez, 'The Complexities of Cuban Foreign Policy', *Problems of Communism,* November/December 1977. Points 1–3 are included in the same article as summaries of arguments by Durch in his article, 'The Cuban Military in Africa and the Middle East'.
[26] Kapcia, 'Cuba's African Involvement', p. 157.
[27] Gonzalez, 'Cuba, the Soviet Union and Africa', p. 155. Castro is described as a 'paladin'.
[28] 'The Cost of Castro', *The Economist,* 19 January 1980.

[29]   Quoted in *Foreign Report*, 3 September 1980.
[30]   Gonzalez, 'The Complexities of Cuban Foreign Policy', p. 12.
[31]   Valenta, 'The Soviet-Cuban Alliance', p. 48.
[32]   All figures quoted in *The Economist*, 24 February 1979, p. 49.
[33]   *Der Spiegal*, no. 10, 1980. However, the *SIPRI Yearbook 1980* put the number of NVA military advisers in Africa alone at between 3,500 and 5,500.
[34]   William F. Robinson, 'Eastern Europe's Presence in Black Africa', *Radio Free Europe, RAD Background Report*, 21 June 1979.
[35]   *Neues Deutschland*, 9 August 1979.
[36]   Documented in Bernard von Plate, 'Aspekte der SED-Parteibeziehungen in Afrika und der arabischen Region', *Deutschland Archiv*, no. 2, 1979.
[37]   Hans-Adolf Jacobsen *et al.* (eds.), *Drei Jahrzehnte Aussenpolitik der DDR* (Munich, Oldenbourg Verlag, 1979) part 5, chs. 3 and 4.

6 Energy as a Factor in Soviet Relations with the Middle East
*Anthony Stacpoole**

This chapter will set out the basic energy data which influence Soviet policy in the Middle East and outline the controversies arising from those facts. It is not intended to stoke the fires of those controversies, but rather to facilitate a discussion of the scope for action in the area by the principal powers concerned.

Oil is, of course, the dominating factor because of its abundant presence in the Middle East. The chapter therefore concentrates on examining the energy balance of the Soviet bloc, with the aim of establishing whether there is any present, or likely, need to acquire important quantities of oil.

Before we look at the Soviet energy balance, it is as well to acknowledge that, like everything else in this vast region, it is so big as to defy comprehension. This should engage our sympathy for those who try to manage it. Surprise is often expressed at the fact that there is no Energy Ministry in Moscow, though it may be doubted whether the US Department of Energy has much improved the energy scene in the USA, the only comparable complex in the world today.[1] This absence of centralization is especially striking in a society in which belief in the beneficence of central direction is axiomatic, and in which the miner and the power station are immutably the twin symbols of industrial vigour. Gosplan and other state committees do not excercise executive powers appropriate to bridge the gaps.

Statistics, ever imperfect guides to understanding, are particu-

*The author warmly acknowledges much help in the preparation of this chapter from colleagues and members of the Chatham House Study Group; thanks also, to Dr Philip Hanson of CREES, Birmingham University, for his comments and invaluable identification of sources. These views and interpretations, however, are purely personal, and most of them were formed in the period prior to the presentation of the paper in April 1981. The facts and figures adduced are, where possible, referenced and were believed to be correct at the time when the text was finalized.

Table 6.1 *Soviet production of energy (million tonnes oil equivalent)*

	1979	%	1980	%	1981	%	1985 Min.	%	Max.	%	
Oil	586	44	603	44	610	42	620	39	645	38	(620–645 mt)
Gas	338	25	361	26	380	26	498	31	531	31	(600–640 bcm)
Coal	336	25	335	24	345	24	360	23	374	22	(770–800 mt)
Other fuels	35	3	38	3	40	3	36	2	48	3	(52– 68 mt SFE)
Nuclear	11	1	14	1	20	1	40	3	54	3	(30– 40 GW)
Hydro	38	3	42	3	44	3	49	3	59	3	(35– 42 GW)
TOTAL	1,341	101	1,393	101	1,439	99	1,603	101	1,711	100	

Note: For conversion factors, see special note, p. 102 below.

Sources: (a) *Oil, gas, coal*: 1979/80 USSR, *Central Statistical Board*; 1981 *Ekonomicheskaya Gazeta (EkGaz)*, no. 44, October 1980, Supplement, p. 4; 1985 as note 2, p. 101 below. (b) *Other fuels*: 1979 *Narkhoz 1979*, p. 170; other years estimated. (c) *Nuclear*: London Uranium Institute estimates, and see note 6, p. 101 below. (d) *Hydro*: 1979 *Narkhoz 1979*, p. 57; 1985 as note 2, p. 101 below; 1980/81 interpolated.

larly unhelpful in this case. Glance, for instance, at Table 6.1 at the figure for 'Other fuels' – 35 million tonnes (mt) of oil equivalent. The actual weight of fuel represented by this was about 173 mt, an immense field of activity spreading across the land, which the cypher at our disposal can do little more than imply. In peat alone, output increased in 1979 by over 10 mt and has still not reached the levels of the early 1970s. As with this category, so it is, in one way or another, with all the others. Such are the imponderables which stand in the way of any attempt at objective assessment of the USSR's energy potential and its development. Even so, this chapter will look briefly at production, trade and consumption, in that order, and then suggest some tentative conclusions.

Production
On the production side (Table 6.1), the outlook is believed to be gloomy for oil and coal, rosy for gas and nuclear power, and satisfactory for hydroelectric power. Gigantic as they are, the rest don't really count at this level of inspection: wood, peat, shale, sun, wind, geothermal, magneto-hydrodynamics, etc., all together are unlikely to account in 1985 for more than the current level of under 3 per cent of total supply.

Soviet oil supply is one of the great enigmas which students of global economics and strategy love to study. Recently published Soviet plans suggest that they are indeed allowing for production to plateau in the period to 1985.[2] It must, however, also be noted that, month by month, output continues to grow at an annual rate of over 2 per cent, and Petrostudies and others (recently rather discreetly) expect continued growth. Opposing forecasts, however, do exist: the CIA and others stick by their prediction of decline to maxima of 535 mt in 1985 and 450 in 1990.[3] Given this divergence, it seems safest to assume that the lower Soviet target (620) for 1985 will be met, and that all bets thereafter are open; but, in any case, significant growth to 1990 is improbable.

Similar problems have been encountered in oil and coal production. Throughout the 1960s and 1970s, rich fields (Volga/Urals for oil, and Donbass for coal) of both fuels were in full production, not too far from the centre. Both regions have now peaked. In the case of oil, the USSR (using long-distance pipelines) had bridged the gap from western Siberia, where it has carried out operations in some respects comparable in difficulty to the North Sea on a very similar time-scale but roughly three times the size.

They have been less successful with coal, where the transport problems from Central Asia and Siberia continue to perplex them. Persistent efforts to improve the long-distance transmission of electricity (from power generated at the mines), or the rail-carrying capacity, have so far failed. Both the quantity of coal delivered and its energy value, having been virtually static since 1975, actually declined in 1979 and 1980.[4] There is no dispute as to the immense reserves of coal in the USSR. The main problem is to deliver coal-energy economically into consumption; the additional effort needed for this tends to drain resources urgently required elsewhere in the economy. Here again Soviet forecasts are pessimistic, aiming for about $2\frac{1}{2}$ per cent growth in 1981, and no more than 11 per cent in all to 1985. It seems unlikely that the lower target of 770 mt will be exceeded in that year, an overall growth of little more than 1 per cent pa (1980 production fell short of the original target by no less than 89 mt).

To turn now to the bright side of the coin, Soviet gas reserves at about 35 per cent of the published proved total, are the largest in the world, larger than the Middle East's 29 per cent.[5] It is clear that ample reserves have been established to cover the 1985 production target. Doubts have, however, been expressed about the gas industry's ability to provide/procure the requisite pipes, compressors, etc. One might conjecture that the difference between the figures 600 and 640 billion cubic metres (bcm) in 1985 is represented by exports to Western Europe now under negotiation but not finally planned, though similar ranges are standard in the Plans.

Some of the gas reserves are also more conveniently sited than the oil and coal. The considerable accumulations in the central/southern regions (notably at Orenburg) have replaced the earlier reliance on the Ukrainian fields. The great mass of the reserves, however, has been discovered in the far north of western Siberia, and it is in the accelerated development of these deposits that the main future growth in output will be sought. The problem with gas supply, however, is in its transmission by pipeline, which is much more costly than piping oil. In this case, prodigious quantities and distances are involved, including a significant permafrost problem, although this is not so serious as it would be with oil. The Soviet authorities have claimed that, with their own resources, they could boost production by about 30 bcm pa in the period, rather less than the target total. It is clear that, in effect, by trading western equipment for gas, they hope not only to increase their foreign earnings but also to fortify the whole gas production network.

As regards nuclear energy, it seems that natural wealth is being effectively exploited to serve the neon-lit world of physicists, econometricians and futurists. There is of course the gigantic plant at Volgodonsk-Atommash – a production line for nuclear reactors. The first unit, already two years late, was due to be rolled out during the 26th Party Congress on 26 February 1981. It is impossible to resist the Orwellian reference: as the Windmill was to *Animal Farm*, so is Atommash to the USSR today. In any case, the Plan provides very precisely that nuclear power shall supply 14 per cent of total electricity generated in 1985. Today the figure is nearer to 6 per cent, having apparently grown from 4 per cent over the last twelve months. So, on the face of it, the 1985 target seems not unreasonable.

When one looks at the post-1985 period, the increase in nuclear capacity is striking. The 1980 nuclear-generating capacity was reported as 12 gigawatt (GW) – say, an average of 10 GW operating during that year.[6] Atommash is designed to add 3 GW pa initially, rising to 8 by 1990 – say, over 100 GW by 2000. Capacities of 130 to 165 GW are spoken of for 2000; these would thus appear to be feasible, given satisfactory operation of the Atommash and other facilities. The doubt resides in the nature of the expansion envisaged, which can be likened to turning up deliberately the vertical slope of a growth-curve. This, of course, has often been done before: for instance, in the West, with ships, bombers, cars, sewing machines and electric toasters; in the USSR, with tanks, oil and gas, to name but three. Can they do it again? We cannot say for sure but, smarting from decades of assault by the foes of our own atoms (both human and material), it is only prudent to allow for the possibility that it might not go as fast we might all wish.

While planned growth in hydro is unspectacular, overall energy supply is planned to grow between 2 per cent and 4 per cent pa in 1981–5. With some improvement accruing in the quality of the mix, that ought to be enough for the USSR alone.

Trade
According to Soviet statistics, out of a total energy supply in 1979 of 2,110 tonnes standard fuel equivalent (SFE), 314 were exported, about 15 per cent. Export growth diminished during the late 1970s to $2\frac{1}{2}$ per cent in 1978–9. From 1975, imports were steady at about 35 mt SFE, but slumped to 26 in 1979, principally from loss of Iranian gas.

Table 6.2 shows estimated breakdowns of Soviet energy trade. The fact that completed deliveries can only be estimated must in itself be a source of uneasiness. Until the end of 1976, accurate figures were made available fairly promptly by the communist authorities.[7] In 1978, the year following the CIA's wide proclamation of their suspicions of Soviet oil potential, the USSR stopped publishing detailed volume figures describing Soviet fuel trade. An outline picture of these movements can be obtained from

Table 6.2   Soviet energy trade

	Exports			Imports			Net
	mt OE	mt SFE		mt OE	mt SFE		mt OE
1979							
Oil	163 mt	163	233	7 mt	7	10	156
Gas	45 bcm	37	54	8 bcm	6	9	31
Solids	30 mt	17	24	10 mt	7	8	9
Electricity	12 bkWh	3	4	—			3
TOTAL		220	315		21	25	199
1985							
Oil	120 mt	120	172	10 mt	10	14	110
Gas	90 bcm	76	108	14 bcm	12	17	64
Coal, etc.	30 mt	17	24	10 mt	7	8	9
Electricity	24 bkWh	6	9				6
TOTAL		219	313		30	39	189

Source: For total exports and imports 1979, see note 12, p. 101 below. Split between fuels estimated. 1985 figures estimated, assuming developments favourable to USSR.

financial, as well as other, information still available. The net effect of this change, however, has been to obscure the movements; in particular, it becomes almost impossible to plot the trends. Attempts have been made to justify this action on technical grounds, and it does also apply to some other materials. A reasonable view, however, must take into account the probability that the intention is to conceal. It is possible to postulate commercial motives for this concealment; other motives are also imputed.

Not so long ago, the West feared the Soviet potential to swamp the continent with oil. Cheap Russian oil, flooding Western markets, was to 'undermine the economies of the vigorous but struggling democracies and destroy their will to be free'. In the event, Soviet oil exports rose by the 1970s to a total of about 3 million barrels per day (bpd), comparable to Iraq in a good year. Of this total, not much more than 1 million has come West, less if you cut out bridge countries like Finland and Yugoslavia. Indeed, looking back to their pre-1972 Western oil trade, the Russians might well return some rueful answers to the question of who was doing what to whom, and wish that they had kept that oil to sell today.

For over a decade Russian oil sales have provided the bulk of Soviet hard-currency earnings; latterly, this feature has become so marked that cynics have spoken of the USSR as a 'one-crop economy'. Over sixty years after the Revolution, such reliance on raw material exports is certainly a striking spectacle. What of the future? There might very well be a decline in oil exports, which is consistent with the view of a production plateau and slow growth in consumption. Of course, the feuding forecasters clash venomously when they reach this critical margin: one side proclaims an imminent vast Soviet import requirement, with dire consequences for world oil prices; the other urbanely promises continued growth of Soviet oil exports.

The other two-thirds of Soviet oil exports go to the communist world. There, the Russians have also jacked their prices heavily, but on a system which appears to keep them lagging far behind the world market: the conduits carrying energy from the USSR to Eastern Europe comprise important strands of what some liken to an umbilical cord. And the Russians have undertaken to maintain oil supply to their allies at around prevailing levels for the next five years.[8] In all circumstances, it seems safest to assume that efforts will be made to hold supplies to the 'West' as near as possible to 1 million bpd. In this they will get some help from 'imports'. It is important to note that these are acquisitions which are retraded. The Russians repeatedly tell foreigners that they have no facilities physically to import crude oil. They tried it once, they say, and it was a classic muddle. What is certain is that, to date, they have not imported crude. The oil accrues to them in return for material and services which they supply to the producer nations. In 1973, from Iraq, they got 11 mt this way. When, in 1974, the price revolution resulted in the quantity being cut to four, they were dismayed. There is no evidence, however, that the acquisition of large volumes of Middle East oil ranks high in prevailing Soviet priorities. If they were to favour this option, they would presumably seek to trade at terms advantageous in comparison with their own marginal production costs. High as the latter are, it is not suggested that they come up to the prices ruling on the world oil market. Accordingly, the Soviets seem to prefer trying to improve their own costs, for instance, by importing Western equipment.

The pledging of assets in brisk demand, nevertheless, is essential for the Russians to acquire the hardware they need from the West. If oil supply dwindles, where will they turn? Luckily another good crop is coming on fast – gas. In the early 1970s, no countries wanted to increase the exposure that resulted from buying Russian oils by also getting hooked on to a Soviet gas pipe. With customary patience and persistence, the Russians made offers which could not be refused, and supplies (now going to many West European countries) built up to a total of about 25 bcm in 1980:[9] in energy equivalent, comparable to half the 1 million bpd oil supply. The prices for this gas now seem to the Soviets too low and they are trying hard to raise them, the prospect of increased supply being their best lever for this purpose.[10] Their success, however, will depend largely on the global energy market, in which oil price trends may have been seen by them as a happy augury; coal and uranium price trends, however, must have seemed less encouraging. Such are the commercial questions to be resolved before an increase in gas supply can be agreed. It still appears possible that the new deal will go ahead.

There are already two pipes which carry fuel from the Middle East to the USSR. A small short line crosses the border into Tajikistan from Afghanistan, carrying up to 4 bcm per annum of gas from a Soviet-developed field. In a more substantial operation, the Iranians have supplied up to 10 bcm pa of associated gas from oilfields close to the Gulf (IGAT 1; see below, p. 99). These are long-standing transactions; in fact, as late as 1974, when the USSR was already producing over 250 bcm pa, it was still a net gas importer. In those days the price of gas was very low and Russian industrial aid was adequate to finance the trade. In the case of Iran, the anchor project was the Isfahan steelworks. Times change, so do faces: the new regime in Iran denounced the low gas price. Some have seen irony in the Russian struggle to stabilize the IGAT gas price whilst, in Europe, their efforts are exerted in the opposite direction.

Pressure cannot be maintained in the IGAT line if Iranian oil output remains at present levels, and throughout the last two years there have been serious shortfalls in deliveries, which at times have ceased entirely. The gas is consumed in the Transcaucasus region and must be replaced from elsewhere in the Soviet system. Ten bcm pa equates, for instance, to about 20 per cent of total Soviet oil exports to the West. Though the first interruption coincided with one of the coldest winters in memory, Soviet reaction was remarkably unruffled. Further, IGAT II, a larger operation involving natural gas, had long been agreed and had largely been equipped. This involved the supply of about 15 bcm pa additional gas to the USSR which, in its turn, would increase supply to Western countries. The Iranians have suspended work on IGAT II. The Russian response has been to indicate that the extra westward pipe facility, already allocated for that purpose, would be used to carry a portion of the additional Russian supply now under negotiation.

Of the remaining energy export categories, electricity is of some curiosity interest. The first Soviet long-term economic plan was called GOELRO. It was unveiled at the Bolshoi Theatre and, when the model was illuminated, the lights in the surrounding district flickered in reaction to the extra load. To this day Moscow generating stations are emblazoned with Lenin's rubric, 'Communism = Soviet Power + Electricity', and, from that beginning, the development of generating capacity has remained firmly installed at the head of the central planner's list of priorities. Thus, in the USSR, every nerve is strained to optimize the power grid by improving conversion-efficiency and, in particular, increasing transmission power. The six East European CMEA countries (the Six) have for many years been closely linked together (with control in Prague), and with the USSR, in arrangements known as the MIR (peace) grid. A much publicized feature of the CMEA nuclear programme for the 1980s is to build capacity in the USSR to transmit an additional 4 billion Kilowatt-hours (bkWh) pa to the Six. In seeking a pan-European energy conference, the USSR apparently accords high priority to boosting exchanges of power across East-West borders, thus improving efficiency on both sides. Exciting though such prospects are, it seems unlikely that their real energy yield could be much more than marginal in the foreseeable future, even in the most benign political ambience.[11]

Total Soviet coal exports are in the region of 25 mt pa, declining. Outside the CMEA the most significant movement is of around 3 mt pa to Japan in an east Siberian compensation deal. There are imports of around 10 mt pa from Poland and Czechoslovakia.

Consumption

Table 6.3 outlines the possible development of Soviet consumption, fuel by fuel and overall. Past overall trends are published annually in Soviet statistics.[12] Reasonably accurate past figures are available for gas, but oil and coal trade can only be estimated. For 1980, production figures are near actuals; for 1985, minimum production targets are used for oil, gas and coal; *ad hoc* low estimates are entered for the rest. These low estimates support the view that the USSR should have enough energy for its own needs in 1985. Such predictions appear to allow for consumption to increase by 18 per cent in the period, compared with a 21 per cent increase in 1975–80. The pressure on energy resources will be reduced by the following factors: (*a*) lower economic growth; (*b*) improved fuel-mix – proportionately less solid fuel and more piped fuel and primary electricity, solids accounting for only 27 per cent in 1985

Table 6.3 *Soviet consumption of energy (million tonnes oil equivalent)*

Fuel	1980				1985			
	Prod.	Trade	Cons.	80/75	Prod.	Trade	Cons.	85/80
Oil	603	156	447	22%	620	110	510	14%
Gas	361	31	330	41%	498	64	434	32%
Coal	335	9	326	2%	360	9	351	8%
Other fuels	38	—	38	0%	36	—	36	—
Nuclear	14			300%	40			300%
Hydro	42	3	53	40%	49	6	83	17%
TOTAL	1393	199	1194	20%	1603	189	1414	18%

Sources: *Production*: 1980 as Table 6.1; 1985 as note 2, p. 101 below (minima when applicable). *Trade*: Net trade 1979 (Table 7.2) used as indication for 1980. *Consumption*: Difference between production and trade. *Percentage change*: 1975 base in L. Dienes and T. Shabad, *The Soviet Energy System* (Washington, D.C., V. H. Winston, 1978), p. 34.

compared with 30 per cent in 1980; and (c) fuel conservation.

In the East, as in the West, the first factor is overwhelmingly the most important. Cooler economies use less heat. In the East, of course, a scaling down of economic ambitions is politically more acceptable in a period of prolonged Western recession. Slow but steady Eastern growth can be presented as superior, and Eastern audiences are comforted by exaggeration of Western chaos. The Polish recession, however, has proved politically disastrous and one must ask how low a growth rate will be tolerable even in the USSR. Both Brezhnev and Tikhonov have spoken of the 1980s as the period in which the intensification of the economy is finally to be achieved.[13] This, however, would require a major shift, which is not apparent in the new Plan, of resources from heavy to light industry. Such a fundamental change of policy is inhibited by non-energy factors (political, military and economic), and the resultant Plan appears to leave room for manoeuvre in the energy field.

Soviet energy conservation prospects call for further comment. The need to save energy has been added to the list of slogans for the new Five-Year Plan. Western analysts point to the egregious waste on the production side of centrally planned economies (CPEs), averring that therein lies a wealth of conservation potential. Indeed, the production-waste in CPEs may well be comparable to our own consumption-waste, but it seems likely to prove even more elusive of treatment. A group returning from a high-level in-depth study of Soviet energy had been much impressed by their hosts' intellectual mastery of energy problems and their evident vigour and ability. When it came to seeing how things worked out in practice, it was another story. One visitor to a large plant reported: 'I stood by the hearth and observed their operations. In the course of discussion, I inquired about regulations to conserve fuel and protect the environment. "Here we are already overful-filling our output plan by more than 5 per cent," was the proud reply. I could see what they meant.'

Conventional wisdom has it that effective energy conservation is dependent on the rate of renewal of capital stock, in which high-energy plant will be replaced by energy-efficient machinery. This seems very close to the truth. The present stumbling-block is that stock-renewal must await resumption of economic growth, which in its turn is inhibited by energy prices. That is the problem with which the West has hardly begun to grapple. Meanwhile, the USSR may be in a position to keep pace within the scope of its existing energy reserves. If the West does find a way out of its impasse, however, the USSR will have to face its own more difficult options.

Table 6.4 Estimated CMEA energy consumption, 1980 (million tonnes oil equivalent)

	GDR	Poland	Czecho-slovakia	Hungary	Bulgaria	Romania	Total EE6	1980 (%)	1975 (%)
Oil	20	20	20	11	13	16	100	24	23
Gas	8	11	8	8	5	25	65	16	14
Solids	55	98	45	8	10	15	231	56	60
Electricity (Primary & imports)	2	1	4	2	4	3	16	4	3
TOTAL	85	130	77	29	32	59	412	100	100

Source: Estimated. Bases in NFAC ER 79–10624, December 1979. Estimate for a full current year in Poland, ignoring political interruptions.

At that point, energy may become a key restraint.

One can now turn to the rest of the bloc – the GDR, Poland, Czechoslovakia, Hungary, Bulgaria (Five) and Romania (Six). Their 1980 energy position is sketched in Table 6.4. It is appropriate to look at them in the context of Soviet energy consumption because their import requirements (of the Five at least) have become almost an extension of Soviet internal demand. After the war, the Five subsisted on domestic coal. Subsequently they began to convert to oil, importing almost entirely from the USSR. In the late 1960s they planned accelerated conversion, using cheap Middle East oil. The soaring price of oil in the early 1970s disappointed these hopes, and the Six (with the accession of Romania, whose own oil production has gone into decline) have been thrown back on to a rigid mix. The Russians have undertaken no more than to maintain oil supplies, with some increase of gas and electricity; for the rest, the Six must rely on their own coal and primary electricity. What is certain is that the readiest means of improving their mix is now denied to them – they lack the financial power to import significant quantities of hard-currency oil. Economists tend to congratulate the Six on this condition, observing that we must all tend towards it whereas they have already achieved it without the pangs of decline. It seems, however, fairer to observe that the Five are stranded in the first coal age with no sure hope of ever extricating themselves.

Conclusions

Many of the tentative conclusions promised at the outset of this chapter have, in fact, already been implied: oil supplies are in some doubt, gas should continue to flow strongly, nuclear expectations may be exaggerated, there may be some room for manoeuvre on consumption and so forth. Though these things all influence the Soviet–Middle East stance, they move on a long time-base and there is nothing much that the West can do to affect their movement.

In one area, however, there is apparent scope for Western concern. On a number of occasions in 1980 the Soviet authorities referred to the need for more even-handed access to Middle East oil supplies.[14] They meant that they would like more of it to go in their direction, amongst others. As outlined in the body of this chapter, they do not seem to be in a position to use much of it themselves, and it is a reasonable guess that they have in mind particularly supply to the Six. This in turn, however, would clearly ease their own energy strains, enabling them to reduce production investment, postpone reform, spend more on defence – a number of options which the West might prefer to deny them.

On the other hand, it is arguable that access to Middle East oil would be a visible contribution to enabling the Six to leave the coal age behind them, to modernize their economies and, hence, to expand the European market, thus contributing to the wealth of all, and even perhaps to their own political evolution. The additional acquisition of 22 mt of oil pa by 1985 would enable the Six to increase from 25 per cent to 30 per cent the proportion of oil in their mix. This represents under 2 per cent of oil currently traded on hard-currency markets. Small though the proportion may be, it is nevertheless a large quantity, worth about $5 billion pa at current prices. Lack of finance at present makes acquisition on this scale impracticable. Though Western economists may ascribe this to the endemic incapacity of CPEs, a glance at our own side of the hill is less reassuring. The Bank of England recorded that, at the end of 1979, oil producers' cash balances totalled about $240 billion.[15] This is a measure of the funds which institutions attempt to recycle in order to maintain financial confidence in the teeth of the reversal of energy values. At 1980 prices, $240 billion would have bought 1,200 mt of oil, or rather more than total Middle East exports in 1979. In 1981, this surplus was growing, a trend which can give producer governments little satisfaction.

The theory of recycling appears to provide that producers' funds will be put to work for them until they are ready to absorb them. In the event, these producers can have been little encouraged by the apparent effect of the total absorption achieved by the Shah's Iran. They must also notice that, each time they raise oil prices in an attempt to combat inflation-erosion, they thereby (in oil terms) reduce the value of the cash surplus.

In attempting to resolve the triangle of forces labelled (for convenience) Bloc/the Middle East/West, oil analysts have long been intrigued by the oil-thirst of the Six, which existing systems appear unable to accommodate. Few non-oil commentators have spared much attention to such an apparently marginal demand. It may be that the time has come to turn a more powerful spotlight on this problem.

APPENDIX: Notes on Soviet Activity in the Energy Sectors of Iran, Iraq, Turkey and the PDRY

Iran

In the petroleum industry, Soviet activity in Iran has been almost entirely concentrated in the gas sector. In the early 1960s, political pressure to reduce the waste by gas-flaring in the southern fields led to a study of the feasibility of gathering associated gas and piping it to the population centres.[16] This project was combined with plans to distribute gas to the central cities from the small central gasfield of Sarajeh. During the planning period, the Shah visited Moscow, and in 1965 an agreement was made to extend the line to the USSR and double its capacity. First gas flowed in 1970, and soon afterwards full capacity of 17 bcm pa was reached, over 9 bcm going to the USSR. The pipe was of high quality and none of it was supplied from the Soviet bloc. The USSR, however, laid about half the line and equipped 8 of the 10 main-line compressor stations. It seems that the pipe could be fairly readily converted to convey crude oil.

This first Iranian Gas Trunkline (IGAT I) operated until 1979 to the satisfaction of both the Iranians and the Russians. Since, however, it transmitted mainly associated gas, it was impossible to maintain pressure in the line in periods of drastic reduction of oil output. Supplies to the USSR were consequently interrupted when oil production was choked back. When it was temporarily resumed (before the Iran–Iraq war), gas supply started again at reduced volume. In 1981, however, the Iranians were holding out for a big increase in price before they would consider full-scale resumption of the contract.

In the later 1970s, satisfactory experience with IGAT I led to the agreement of a more ambitious project. This was to provide for about 16 bcm pa natural gas from Iranian gasfields to the USSR via a new trunkline. The USSR would supply about 11 bcm for Western Europe, the balance being retained in the East. Though the pipe was delivered to Iran, the line has not been laid, and no further developments are expected for the time being.

Iraq

From June 1969 onwards, the USSR provided Iraq with substantial credits to finance the purchase of Soviet and CMEA equipment and services for oil production. By June 1973 the total of the credits had reached nearly $600m.[17] The agreed interest rate was 2½ per cent, with repayment in crude oil. Among the unusual aspects reported were apparent Soviet reluctance to take payment in oil and the agreement, initially, of a low price for the oil. The Iraqis thus obtained a new source of expertise and equipment at a time when relations were strained with established Western operators. By making (initially large) sales of crude oil to the bloc, they showed that the West did not control absolutely the movement of their oil. These proved to be cheap and valuable advantages. At that time, Soviet oil production (though rising much more rapidly) was still not much more than half of North American production. Moscow therefore eagerly seized this opportunity to display its competence and generosity in a sector hitherto dominated by Western technology, which (according to the Soviets) had suffered from the ruthless exploitation of local resources. Western observers, of course, saw this as the economic aspect of Soviet infiltration.

Ten years on, the Russians are still there. Their technicians are still working under contract in many areas of the Iraqi oil industry, they supply a good deal of equipment for the industry and they still lift Iraqi crude oil. In all these activities, however, they (together with the East Europeans) still count for much less than Western companies. Soviet demand for Middle East oil is minimal in comparison with Western demand: only by contributing significantly to Western requirements can the Iraqis acquire the modern plant and services needed for their oil and other industries, facilities which the USSR cannot provide in either the quantity or the quality required.

Turkey

In line with its policy of seeking political (as well as financial) returns on its oil exports, the USSR recently began crude oil deliveries to Turkey, estimated at almost 3 mt pa, on apparently favourable terms. Prior to 1979 there had been virtually no oil trade between the USSR and Turkey, although the USSR had participated in the construction of Izmir Refinery.

As political problems intensified, prior to the installation of military government, the Soviet authorities agreed to provide substantial project-credits in two steps: $400 million on current work (June 1979) and a total of $4 billion on about 20 projects less closely defined. Currently, work is still in hand on the Iskenderun Steel Works expansion ($150 million), Seydisehir Aluminium Plant ($200 million) and the Izmir Refinery expansion ($56 million). The body of the new programme appears to consist of heavy industrial projects, most of which are at an early stage of study.

Whilst the scope of the Soviet credit-programme does not seriously challenge the Western orientation of the Turkish economy, it must (in conjunction with preferential crude oil supply) be seen as a significant gesture at a time of exceptional anxiety in Turkey.

The PDRY

Although the USSR is deep into politics in the area and has entered into a number of military and economic agreements, there has not yet been much joint activity in the energy field. The refinery continues under management contracted from a Western company; the operation of the refinery is entirely in local hands. The Yemenis now acquire a certain amount of crude, which they refine for local consumption in addition to undertaking throughput on behalf of Kuwait, Libya, Abu Dhabi, French companies and the Soviet Union. However, a recent agreement has been announced providing Soviet participation in local exploration for oil and minerals.

Notes

[1] See Joint Economic Committee, Congress of the United States, *Soviet Economy in a Time of Change* (Washington, D.C., US Government Printing Office, 1979), chart II (between pp. 50 and 51).

[2] 'Osnoviye Napravleniye . . .', *Izvestia*, 2 December 1980. The maximum production target for oil in 1985 (645 mt) is virtually identical to the corresponding figure for 1980 (640 mt).

[3] 'Crisis Postponed?', *The Economist*, 23 May 1981, p. 74.

[4] National Foreign Assessment Center *USSR: Coal Industry Problems and Prospects*, ER 80–10154, Washington, D.C., March 1980, p. 3.

[5] British Petroleum Company Ltd., *BP Statistical Review, 1981*, p. 4.

[6] *The Financial Times*, 28 December 1979 and 10 July 1980. The actual percentage is hard to establish.

[7] Compare *Vneshnyaya Torgovlya SSSR v 1976g* (Moscow, Statistika, 1977), pp. 63–4, with the same publication for the following year, p. 61, and also subsequent years.

[8] Boris Rachkov (Soviet analyst), *Oil and Gas Journal* (Tulsa, Okla.), 3 December 1979, p. 54. Rachkov forecasts an increase from one five-year period to the next. His figures, however, show that annual deliveries are planned to stabilize at about 1980 levels.

[9] J. V. Baranovsky, President of Soyuzgasexport (Moscow) at European Gas Conference, Oslo, May 1981.

[10] *Petroleum Intelligence Weekly*, 3 August 1981, p. 4.

[11] See, for instance, C. T. Saunders (ed.), *East and West in the Energy Squeeze* (London, Macmillan, 1980), p. 106.

[12] *Narodnoye Khozyaistvo SSSR v 1979 g* (Moscow, Statistika, 1980), p. 57 (annual).

[13] L. I. Brezhnev to CPSU Central Committee, Moscow, 21 October 1980, and N. A. Tikhonov to 26th Congress of CPSU, Moscow, 27 February 1981, published in English as a supplement to *Moscow News*, issue 10 (2946), 1981, p. 3. The speakers used identical

terms: 'In the 1980s we have to conclude the transition of the economy to the road of intensification.'

[14]   E.g. Oleg Bogomolov, *Marxist Review* (in English), vol. 23, no. 8 (1980), p. 80.
[15]   Bank of England, *Quarterly Bulletin*, June 1980, p. 158.
[16]   C. H. McMillan and J. B. Hannigan, *The Soviet–Iranian Energy Relationship* (Ottawa, Carleton University, 1979); also *Oil and Gas Journal*, 13 January 1969 and 19 July 1971.
[17]   Edith and E. F. Penrose, *Iraq* (London, Ernest Benn, 1978), p. 426.

Conversion factors for energy tables

1 metric tonne of standard fuel = 7,000 kilocalories
1 metric tonne of oil = 1.43 TSF
1 billion cubic metres natural gas = 1.19 TSF
                                      0.83 TO
1 metric tonne of coal = 0.67 TSF
                          0.468 TO

The above factors appear to have been used in *Narodnoye Khozyaistvo* (Narkhoz), 1979, p. 170. Factors for the various 'other fuels' can be deduced from the same page.

One gigawat of generating power has been assumed to replace 1.4 mTO in a full operating year. For hydro, the full 1.4 has been applied in the table. For nuclear, a lower replacement rate is applied to allow for lags in the commissioning of large numbers of new units. For both hydro and nuclear, only the maximum figures come from the published targets. The minimum figures are *ad hoc* estimates to allow for installation delays.

7 The Influence of Trade on Soviet Relations with the Middle East
Alan H. Smith

A major concern for the economist studying trade relations is to measure the size and distribution of the gains of trade between participating nations. In certain cases where comparative costs have not been accurately assessed, or where trade is practised for essentially political reasons, or involves aid, the existence of economic benefits to either partner or both partners cannot be guaranteed. It has been argued that the Soviet Union derives no pure economic benefit from its trade relations with CMEA and that its trade with the East European countries involves granting economic concessions in order to maintain its political hegemony within the bloc, while its relations with the less-developed CMEA countries involve substantial quantities of direct and indirect aid. It is possible that a similar situation occurs in Soviet trade relations with the Middle East, and the purpose of this chapter is primarily to assess whether this trade represents an economic cost or benefit to the USSR.

From this viewpoint the countries can be divided initially into two distinct groups. The first group consists of those countries that possessed observer status at the 1981 CMEA session (Afghanistan, Ethiopia and the People's Democratic Republic of the Yemen) and has been identified by some as the 'New Communist Third World'. These countries are relatively poorly endowed with natural resources, and it could be anticipated that economic flows would largely involve substantial volumes of aid and that they would currently be a net economic cost to the Soviet economy. In the case of Afghanistan the cost to the USSR would be considerably increased by the military occupation. The second category, though not forming a single homogeneous group, includes several countries of considerable strategic importance, with resource endowments which may be of some value to the USSR, but which are also of considerable importance to the West. It may be important for

Western policy in the area to determine the role of economic interests in Soviet relations with this second group, and in particular whether these economic interests outweigh the Soviet Union's political interests.

It should be noted that the primacy of political or economic interests should not be directly equated with 'hawkish' or 'dovish' attitudes, either on behalf of the Soviet leadership or as a guide to the response that would best serve Western interests in the area. One possible hypothesis (which is largely associated with the need for a 'strong' Western response) is that the Soviet Union deliberately trades economic benefits in the pursuit of long-term political objectives. These have been variously described as the pursuit of empire, the pursuit of military or strategic goals, or even the desire to weaken the industrial economies of the West by disrupting their major energy sources, either permanently or in situations of crisis. Furthermore, the uncertainty engendered by such a policy may cause the Western countries to develop high-cost alternative sources of energy.

An alternative hypothesis, which places greater emphasis on the economic importance of the area to the USSR and has partly been inspired by the CIA's prediction of Soviet oil deficits in the 1980s (a prediction now largely retracted by the CIA itself), is also frequently associated with the need for a firm Western response. The economic basis of this argument, which has been excellently described and assessed by Philip Hanson, is that the USSR will be faced by severe economic problems in the 1980s.[1] These problems will arise from the continued deceleration of Soviet economic growth, which will be aggravated by a rising capital-to-output ratio resulting from the need to undertake high-cost investment to develop new sources of energy in difficult terrain and to transport them over long distances. The development of these areas may also involve labour problems, particularly since the main anticipated source of growth of the labour force lies in the southern (Muslim) regions of the USSR, whose population may not be easily persuaded to move elsewhere. It is further argued that if the growth of defence expenditure attained in the 1970s is to be maintained in the 1980s, while economic growth declines, defence will inevitably take a growing proportion of GNP. If this occurs at the expense of investment, it would in turn lead to a further deterioration in the rate of economic growth.

On the other hand, a cut in the growth rate of consumption would also pose severe problems for Soviet economic planners, especially in view of the rising volume of savings deposits which express either voluntarily or involuntarily deferred demand. Consequently, a severe reduction in the growth of consumption, combined with the low quality of existing consumer goods and the perennial problems of agriculture, could result in domestic unrest. It is argued that, subsequently, the Soviet Union would be forced to reduce the scale of its domestic energy investment programme and would seek alternative supplies of energy, which might entail the diversion of substantial volumes of oil supplies away from Western markets towards the USSR.

Hanson[2] has questioned the economic assumptions on which this analysis is based, and most analysts do not predict a decline in oil production as severe as that anticipated by the CIA. In addition, the implications for Western policy would be considerably affected by the importance of economic factors in Soviet relations with the Middle East. If the pursuit of political aims in the Middle East involves a cost to the Soviet Union, those policies would be constrained by domestic economic problems. In this case, the West's interests in the area may be best served by policies that both raise the cost of Soviet involvement in the area and do little to alleviate domestic economic pressures.

If, on the other hand, benefits are to be obtained from Soviet relations with Middle Eastern countries, domestic economic pressures will cause them to be pursued more fully. If those interests are inimical to those of the West, the West may consider that its best policy is to raise the costs of Soviet operations in the area while simultaneously helping to alleviate domestic pressures and in particular helping the USSR to lower the costs of developing its own energy sources.

Finally, an intermediate view is that day-to-day trade relations are determined not by any Soviet grand design in which political or economic objectives are paramount, but by pragmatic considerations in which those objectives are combined. This view places greater emphasis on the differences between individual Middle Eastern countries, and on their ability to determine not only the framework in which both East and West operate, but also their own policies *vis-à-vis* the Soviet Union. Under these circumstances, it is harder to detect whether relations with specific countries are determined by economic or by political considerations, which may be either substitutes for, or complements to, one another. If they are substitutional, the pursuit of political goals will be constrained by economic costs, or will even change in response to changes in their cost. If they are complementary, the Soviet leadership itself need not necessarily determine whether political or economic objectives predominate. Under these circumstances, if economic and political benefits occur from trade with individual nations, the

Soviet Union will tend to take advantage of them on an *ad hoc* basis.

The problems of 'unspecified' trade

The measurement of the costs and benefits to the USSR of trade with the Middle East is complicated by a number of deficiencies in Soviet trade statistics, and an explanation of some of the problems involved in interpreting the data is provided further on in this chapter. There remains, however, a major problem concerning Soviet export data, which appears to be of considerable importance when analysing Soviet relations with the Middle East, and this requires separate explanation.

In recent years, Soviet official statistics have provided little or no information on either the commodity composition or the direction of a significant and growing proportion of Soviet exports to non-socialist developing countries. Most Western analysts consider that significant volumes of Soviet trade in strategic items are not directly omitted from Soviet aggregated trade statistics (e.g. total exports) but are concealed by their exclusion from the appropriate commodity or geographic category.[3] This practice gives rise to 'unspecified residuals', which occur whenever there is a discrepancy between the figure for the total trade in a particular category and the sum of the sub-groups that comprise that category. These residuals are not random and cannot be explained by under-reporting. For the purposes of this chapter the following residuals appear to be significant (see Table 7.1):

1. The less-developed country (LDC) residual. This is the difference between the figure given for exports to developing countries as a whole and the sum obtained by aggregating exports to each individual developing country.
2. The intra-country commodity (ICC) residual. This is the difference between the figure given for exports to a specific country and the sum obtained by aggregating the commodity composition given for exports to that country.
3. The commodity residual for exports to non-socialist (CRENS) countries. This can be obtained only indirectly and is difficult to describe, but is of growing significance. It is composed of the difference between the figure given for total exports to non-socialist countries and the sum of (estimates of) the commodity components of that trade. The latter is obtained by subtracting the commodity components of exports to socialist countries (which are given in the form of percentages of exports to socialist countries) from the commodity components of total exports (which are similarly given as percentages of total exports).

The sum of the ICC residual for each individual country added to the LDC residual is greater in each year than the CRENS

Table 7.1 *Unspecified residuals in Soviet exports (billion roubles)*

	1972	1973	1974	1975	1976	1977	1978	1979	1980
CRENS residual	1.3	2.2	2.1	2.2	2.6	4.0	4.3	4.6	4.5
LDC residual	0.9	1.7	1.5	1.4	1.8	2.9	3.0	2.9	3.1
ICC residual for Middle East	0.1	0.1	0.2	0.2	0.2	0.4	0.7	0.8	0.5

Source: Calculated from *Vneshnyaya Torgovlya za SSSR*, various years. For explanations see text.

residual. In most years, this discrepancy can be explained by the ICC residual for exports to the United Kingdom, which can be shown to be composed of diamonds that have been included in specified exports to non-socialist countries in total. In years when other factors account for the discrepancy, they can be identified separately (e.g. the ICC residuals for several countries have recently been increased by the omission of figures pertaining to exports of non-ferrous metals). It can be concluded that the LDC residual and the ICC residual for exports to Middle Eastern countries are separate components of the CRENS residual, and it can be demonstrated that the ICC residual for Middle Eastern countries is a major component of the difference between the CRENS residual and the LDC residual.

Political factors and the level of trade
Soviet statistics indicate that reported trade with the Middle East countries accounts for only 3–4 per cent of the total Soviet trade turnover, and that the latter is itself a relatively insignificant proportion of GNP. In certain cases, monetary measures of trade (which reflect prices paid multiplied by quantities purchased) may be an inaccurate indication of their impact on the economy, particularly where interdependence with other resources is involved or where that impact is either regionally or structurally concentrated. More important in the Soviet case, however, is the problem of the LDC residual, which means that reported trade understates actual trade.

Soviet statistics report significant volumes of trade only with Afghanistan, Iraq, Iran, Egypt, Syria and more recently Libya, of which only Afghanistan is an observer at the CMEA (see Tables 7.2 and 7.3). It appears, therefore, that political factors do act as a constraint on trade – the absence of a pro-Soviet political orientation appears to be the best explanation of the relatively low volumes of trade recorded with Saudi Arabia, Jordan, Kuwait, Lebanon and the United Arab Emirates – but that a 'pro-Soviet' policy alone is insufficient to bring about significant volumes of trade.

In some cases, trade flows have been interrupted by political events. Deteriorations in political relations with Egypt, in 1972 and 1977, led to reductions in trade flows, and Soviet support for Ethiopia in the war with Somalia, following Somalia's invasion of the Ogaden, led to a complete cessation of trade. A sharp reduction in trade with Iran followed domestic political events in that country, although this resulted more from the impact of the revolution on the ability of the Iranian economy to absorb imports and provide exports of natural gas than from any Soviet political response to the new regime. Finally, drastic reduction in trade with Iraq was recorded in the last quarter of 1980 and the first quarter of 1981 (see Table 7.4) following the Iraq–Iran war. It is noticeable that the reduction of Soviet imports is sharper than that of Soviet exports, which suggests (unless it merely reflects a change in statistical recording) Iraq's unwillingness or inability to supply the USSR as much as Soviet unwillingness to supply Iraq.

In all these cases the initial political impetus that resulted in reduced trade flows came from the partner country, not from the USSR, while in the case of Somalia the reduction resulted partly from events in that country and partly as a result of the Soviet response to events in a third country. There is therefore little or no evidence from the figures of the absolute volume of Soviet trade to indicate the successful pursuit of a political strategy with substantial economic benefits to the USSR.

Trade with individual countries

Trade with CMEA observers
Afghanistan, Ethiopia and the People's Democratic Republic of the Yemen (PDRY) currently possess observer status at the CMEA. Iraq signed a 'multilateral cooperation agreement' with the CMEA in 1975, which is aimed principally at developing Iraq's oilfields. This is a far looser form of cooperation in a political sense, and similar agreements have been made between the CMEA and Mexico and Finland; there is little or no evidence to indicate that Iraq is proceeding to observer status.

Soviet trade volumes with the PDRY and Ethiopia have been relatively insignificant, primarily involving Soviet exports of machinery and equipment with negligible volumes of trade in the opposite direction. Ethiopia was of course a major recipient of Soviet arms during the war with Somalia, which itself had previously received Soviet arms. Although some quantities of arms supplied to Ethiopia were paid for in hard currency, the net effect of military involvement in both countries would appear to involve the USSR in economic costs rather than benefits. It also appears that current levels of reported trade with the PDRY and Ethiopia involve the USSR in a small diversion of resources from domestic uses.

Although Afghanistan, largely as a result of its contiguity to the USSR, was a major recipient of Soviet aid in the late 1950s and 1960s (which was reflected in a visible trade imbalance), the reported trade between the two countries was in balance by the mid-1970s. The Soviet Union does receive some economic benefits from its trade with Afghanistan, from which it imports natural gas which is

Table 7.2 Soviet exports to Middle Eastern countries (million roubles)

	1972	1974	Sum of 1971–75	1976	1978	1979	1980	Sum of 1976–80
CMEA observers (at 1981)								
Afghanistan	38	62	247	88	139	182	248	771
Yemen (PDR)	7	15	41	20	27	64	56	201
Ethiopia	2	3	11	4	64	45	121	256
TOTAL	47	80	299	112	230	291	425	1228
Others								
Jordan	1	2	16	4	5	7	14	36
Iraq	90	182	784	342	674	854	473	2624
Iran	96	266	920	218	433	272	259	1606
Kuwait	15	5	49	10	37	7	—	76
Yemen (N)	2	9	37	9	33	43	48	154
Saudi Arabia	5	3	22	13	8	25	31	91
Libya	9	29	80	16	52	157	163	399
Somalia	12	17	69	19			—	39
Lebanon	14	26	85	7	16	19	13	68
Egypt	266	301	1449	200	148	127	173	851
Syria	59	70	352	139	131	133	168	672
Sudan	17	4	39	5	3	2	6	20
TOTAL	586	914	3902	982	1540	1646	1348	6636

Source: *Vneshnyaya Torgovlya za SSSR*, various years.

Table 7.3 *Soviet imports from Middle Eastern countries (million roubles)*

	1972	1974	Sum of 1971–75	1976	1978	1979	1980	Sum of 1976–80
CMEA observers (at 1981)								
Afghanistan	31	61	225	67	76	140	257	617
Yemen (PDR)	—	—	—	—	1	3	5	11
Ethiopia	2	4	13	1	4	19	26	52
TOTAL	33	65	238	68	81	162	288	680
Others								
Iraq	62	271	855	373	410	328	258	1690
Iran	134	230	829	227	238	137	75	961
Libya	30	—	60	—	107	280	288	752
Somalia	3	2	12	5				8
Lebanon	4	7	29	4	3	3	4	17
Egypt	248	427	1688	331	198	198	211	1227
Syria	54	102	298	97	74	66	153	496
Sudan	1	2	58	15	16	27	12	86
TOTAL*	536	1042	3833	1052	1046	1039	1001	5238

* Including small amounts from countries listed under exports only.

Source: *Vneshnyaya Torgovlya za SSSR*, various years.

Table 7.4 Quarterly data for Soviet trade with Iran, Iraq and Afghanistan (million roubles)

Quarter	Iran		Iraq		Afghanistan	
	Exports	Imports	Exports	Imports	Exports	Imports
1978/1	162	79	92	80	32	21
2	154	74	132	160	29	24
3	64	56	273	77	37	13
4	52	29	176	93	41	18
1979/1	25	14	159	37	48	29
2	35	47	305	85	52	33
3	39	39	204	95	36	25
4	168	37	167	113	49	52
1980/1	86	35	189	84	55	74
2	79	11	126	93	73	62
3	45	8	92	70	52	49
4	49	20	65	1	68	77
1981/1	47	80	36	0	63	93

Note: 'Exports' refers to Soviet exports.

Source: Quarterly data are published in various issues of the journal *Vneshnyaya Torgovlya.*

mainly used to supply the Soviet Central Asian Republics. Although the USSR has sufficient natural gas to meet this demand from domestic sources, imports from Afghanistan reduce the transportation cost and simultaneously permit a higher volume of exports to be sold for hard currency to Western Europe, where the prevailing market price is approximately double that paid to Afghanistan. Other Soviet imports from Afghanistan have been textiles and fabrics. Although the value of Soviet imports increased significantly in the 1970s, this is due primarily to price, not volume, changes. In 1980, imports from Afghanistan grew by a further 80 per cent, exceeding levels of imports from Mongolia, Vietnam, China, Egypt and Iran. It is difficult to tell whether this increased value of imports represents a real increase in trade, since it is largely attributed to an increase in the value of natural gas, for which no volume figures are provided.

The extension of full CMEA membership to any of these countries would involve considerable additional economic costs to the USSR, since any new member would benefit from the specific CMEA measures to raise the levels of economic development of the less-developed CMEA countries. These measures were initially formulated to aid Mongolia, but have been extended to Vietnam and Cuba following their elevation to full membership. Soviet aid disbursements have recently been highly concentrated on full CMEA members and, as Edwina Moreton shows in Chapter 5, aid to Vietnam and Cuba has accounted for a considerable proportion of this amount, mainly owing to their population levels. Since 1976, however, Mongolia has been one of the largest recipients of Soviet aid measured in terms of roubles *per capita* (250–300) or as a percentage of GNP (33 per cent). This has been concentrated in major construction projects, accounting for 70 per cent of all Mongolian capital outlay since 1976 and permitting over 50 per cent of GNP to be allocated to investment in 1978.[4] Much of this investment has been concentrated in prospecting for, and developing, Mongolian mineral deposits, while much of the output of the newly constructed plants will be exported to CMEA countries. The 1981 CMEA conference underlined that Cuba, Mongolia and Vietnam will continue to receive economic and scientific/technical assistance from the European members of CMEA, including specific measures of assistance for 1981–5.[5]

What prospects are there that any of the countries under discussion will become full members and benefit from similar volumes of aid? To answer this, we may have to take note of some uncertainty concerning the future status of Mozambique. The Mozambican observer at the 1981 CMEA session is reported to have announced on his return that Mozambique would join the organization,[6] although the final communiqué to the session makes no reference to this. Similarly, President Samora Machel, on a visit to Moscow in November 1980, referred to the value in cooperation between Mozambique and the socialist countries in terms normally applied to intra-CMEA cooperation, while Brezhnev's formal reply avoided all such references.[7] There are therefore indications that Mozambique may wish to benefit from increased CMEA aid, but that the potential costs of this to the other members is causing both them and the Soviet leadership some apprehension.

Mozambique's case for membership, in terms of existing trade levels, location and resource endowments, is probably less strong .than that of any of the other observers. The granting of full membership to Mozambique could therefore invite further applications that would be difficult to reject. Although the PDRY could benefit substantially from a fairly limited volume of aid in the form of machinery and equipment, the cost of extending significant aid to Ethiopia could prove so great to existing members that it would inevitably change the relationship between the developed and the less-developed members.

The possibility of full membership should not be ignored in the case of Afghanistan, which was first granted observer status in 1980. Factors such as natural resource endowments, a common border with the USSR and the size of current trade flows indicate an economic rationale for membership as strong as that possessed by Mongolia. In particular, its supplies of natural gas would be taken into account in planning future CMEA energy balances. The political case for membership – an indication of a firm commitment to the Soviet socialist camp – is as strong as that for Vietnam and Cuba. Furthermore, extensive aid to Afghanistan may be required following the Soviet invasion, whether it becomes a member of CMEA or not. If Afghanistan is admitted to full membership, this would be, as Malcolm Yapp notes in Chapter 3, a political not an economic decision, and one that resulted largely from events originating in that country, rather than an indication of a Soviet 'grand design' in the area.

Trade with other countries
Although political factors play a considerable role in determining the size and direction of trade with Middle Eastern countries not aligned to the CMEA, economic factors are important in determining the commodity structure of trade. Twenty years ago an economist writing in *Zycie Gospodarcze* argued that the Soviet and East European interest in trade with the Third World involved the

long-term prospect of obtaining scarce raw materials cheaply in exchange for capital and consumer goods, this to be achieved mainly by selling surpluses for which there was no demand on world capitalist markets.[8] The CMEA long-term target pro- gramme for cooperation in energy, fuels and raw materials approved at the 1978 CMEA session is actively considering pro- grammes along these lines involving trade with oil-producing countries:

Measures are being worked out for the further expansion of mutually beneficial long-term cooperation of the CMEA member countries with the developing countries which would involve stable imports of oil from these countries . . . the oil-producing countries are in the process of industrialization, establishing new branches of industry and infrastructure, and have a huge market for complete installations and many goods. CMEA member countries should increase their assistance to the developing countries in establishing industrial and agrarian complexes and infrastructure.[9]

The commodity structure of Soviet trade with the Middle East clearly reflects the pursuit of this strategy, although its success has been affected by political instability in the area. The Soviet Union has remained a net exporter of oil and gas, and consequently its imports of gas from the area are substituted for domestic supplies while reported oil imports are directly shipped to third markets. The Soviet Union has therefore avoided any physical dependence on Middle East oil supplies. As long as the CMEA as a whole remains a net exporter of oil, the principal factors affecting Soviet demand will not be absorptive capacity, but the ability to secure Western markets and the relative cost and availability of domestic supplies.

Imports. The degree of detail contained in Soviet statistics on the commodity composition of imports from the Middle East has been drastically reduced since 1976. In particular, few details concern- ing imports of oil and gas are now provided. Soviet data also indicate a substantially higher volume of imports than can be discerned from partners' data (see Table 7.5). Nevertheless recon- ciliation of partners' data with Soviet data, and comparison with earlier years, may help to explain the unknown factors with some certainty.

In 1972, Soviet imports from the area were composed mainly of textiles and clothing (33 per cent), fuels (30 per cent) and industrial consumer goods (33 per cent); by 1977, textiles had fallen to 17 per cent, with fuels, ores and metals accounting for 45 per cent, while 20 per cent of imports remained unspecified. The majority of the

Table 7.5 *Differences between Soviet data and partners' data (million transferable roubles)*

	1972	1973	1974	1975	1976	1977	1978
Soviet exports to *							
Iran†	36	−36	54	159	129	221	na
Iraq	47	77	96	196	279	175	572
Egypt	167	230	138	92	55	−2	13
Syria	26	36	32	59	105	33	101
Soviet imports from							
Iran†	46	54	156	146	167	186	na
Iraq	4	128‡	268‡	321	368	319	405
Egypt	7	−39	34	6	49	−4	−10
Syria	6	8	64	29	63	38	44

Notes: Soviet figures are higher than partners' data except where negative sign is given.

* Partners' imports measured c.i.f.

† Iranian statistics cover period from March to March; Iranian imports of military goods are excluded; Iranian exports of natural gas are not identified by partner.

‡ Estimates from 1975 UN Yearbook would give alternative figures of 74 for 1974 and 13 for 1975. Iraq export figures include *estimates* for crude oil exports by country of destination.

For attempted reconciliations see the text.

Sources: All Soviet data taken from *Vneshnyaya Torgovlya za SSSR*, various years. Partners' data taken from *United Nations Yearbook of International Trade Statistics*, converted from US $ to transferable roubles according to UN conversion factors.

unspecified component is accounted for by imports from Iran, and can be quite clearly identified as comprising imports of natural gas, which prior to 1976 were included in the appropriate commodity category. Iran does not identify its exports of natural gas by country of destination, which largely explains the difference between Soviet and Iranian figures (see Table 7.5). Since 1970, Iran has supplied the USSR with 8–9 billion cubic metres of natural gas per annum through the IGAT I pipeline. Soviet secondary sources indicate that the USSR imported 73 billion cubic metres in this fashion between 1970 and 1979 to serve the Transcaucasian regions.[10] Soviet quarterly data (Table 7.4) show that imports from Iran started to fall in the second half of 1978, reaching their lowest levels in the middle of 1980. Although a significant increase can be observed in the first quarter of 1980, it is not yet possible to attribute this to price or volume changes. The contribution of natural gas to the fall in value of Soviet imports can be estimated from the unspecified residual in Soviet–Iranian trade shown in Table 7.6 and confirms Anthony Stacpoole's analysis in Chapter 6 that natural gas supplies to the USSR could not be maintained when Iranian oil production was cut back.

The failure to meet supplies through the existing IGAT I pipeline seriously questions the future of the proposed IGAT II pipeline. Under an agreement signed in 1975, the USSR (according to Soviet sources[11]) was to receive natural gas from Iran through a second pipeline in exchange for transiting Iranian natural gas through the USSR to Western and Eastern Europe. Most Western observers argue that in fact this would have involved not a direct transit of Iranian gas to Europe, but the substitution of Soviet gas from the Orenburg region, while Iranian imports would have served the Soviet south.[12] The chief benefit to the USSR would have been the savings in transportation costs entailed in meeting both areas. Although these profits would have accrued to the USSR largely as a result of the difference in price obtained for natural gas in Western Europe and that paid at the Iranian border, this is one of the few areas where the USSR planned to involve its domestic economy in any degree of physical dependence on Middle East supplies.

The cancellation or postponement of the project could cause some logistical problems resulting from the diversion of domestic supplies to the Transcaucasus. Furthermore, it appears that the USSR has contracted to meet its supply obligations to certain West European countries even in the event of Iranian supply failure.[13] Should the USSR be unable to meet contracted deliveries, it could severely damage its reputation as a safe source of energy supplies to the West.

Table 7.6   Commodity structure of major Soviet imports from Middle Eastern countries (million roubles)

	1972	1977	1978	1979	1980
Afghanistan: Natural gas	14	29	34	54	135
Iran: Natural gas	52	na	na	na	na
Cotton and textiles	20	30	28	33	18
Food	12	29	16	20	11
Consumer goods	38	26	24	9	12
Unspecified	5	175*	153*	69*	32*
Iraq: Fuels and minerals†	58	318	403	324	252
Libya: Fuels and minerals†	30	77	107	280	288
Egypt: Cotton and textiles	128	180	99	101	109
Foodstuffs	53	47	40	34	50
Industrial consumer goods	43	56	54	45	48
Syria: Cotton and textiles	33	38	25	35	33
Industrial consumer goods	7	31	13	26	78
Unspecified	11	37	36	5	42

* Identified in the text as natural gas.
†Identified in the text as crude oil.

Source: *Vneshnyaya Torgovlya*, various years.

The USSR's other principal sources of reported imports are Egypt, Iraq and more recently Libya. There is a close degree of correspondence between Soviet and Egyptian data concerning Soviet imports from Egypt, which are composed mainly of cotton and textiles. Soviet imports from Iraq and Libya have been designated under the general heading 'Fuels, mineral raw materials and metals' in Soviet statistics published since 1976. Before 1976, the corresponding figures for Iraq were designated as crude oil. The figures are confirmed by Iraqi data published at that time, but have been removed from subsequent statistical series. Soviet data do not record any imports from Libya before 1977, and Libyan data show no exports to the USSR. Anthony Stacpoole shows in Chapter 6 that the USSR does not import any crude oil directly, but does lift Iraqi crude for delivery elsewhere. Consequently the best explanation of this designation in Soviet statistics is that it is used to account for crude oil liftings that are directly re-exported. This is effectively equivalent to payment in hard currency and does not involve the Soviet domestic economy in any dependence on Middle East supplies. Crude oil liftings from Iraq and Libya appear therefore to be currently saving the Soviet Union about 600 million transferable roubles per annum in hard currency.

Exports (see Table 7.7). The analysis of the economic benefit to the USSR of exports to the Middle East is complicated by the problem of the unspecified residuals discussed earlier. Although there are considerable discrepancies between Soviet and partners' data, they do not help to provide an explanation of the residuals but tend to complicate the problems of interpretation even further.

First, partners' import data (especially for Iran, Iraq, Egypt and Syria) tend to be substantially *lower* than the corresponding Soviet figure (see Table 7.5) and cannot therefore be used to explain the 'LDC residual'. Furthermore, in the case of Iran the discrepancy is caused entirely by differences in Soviet and Iranian figures for machinery and equipment exports/imports, while in the case of Iraq the discrepancy is due to differences in reported machinery and equipment exports/imports plus a proportion of the Soviet ICC residual. It is therefore difficult to estimate the size or commodity composition of Soviet exports to the area with any confidence.

The size of the various export residuals is shown in Table 7.1, from which it can be calculated that although the growth of the LDC residual has been significant between 1976 and 1979, other components of the CRENS residual grow at a faster rate. (This cannot be attributed to statistical reclassifications, most of which

Table 7.7   *Commodity structure of Soviet exports to the Middle East*
(million roubles)

	1972		1978		1979		1980	
	(a)	(b)	(a)	(b)	(a)	(b)	(a)	(b)
CMEA observers								
Afghanistan	24	1	72	15	93	15	115	14
PDR Yemen	6	1	15	7	47	9	36	11
Ethiopia	1	—	55	9	7	37	30	88
Others: TOTAL	346	75	645	701	716	739	630	482
Of which:								
Iraq	60	20	302	367	304	541	199	271
Iran	75	4	154	245	117	133	89	112
Syria	47	3	72	40	83	39	100	50
Egypt	129	45	72	5	54	2	60	22
Libya	8	1	41	2	147	4	159	1

(a) Machinery and equipment.   (b) Unspecified (the ICC residual).
Source: Totals are calculated from *Vneshnyaya Torgovlya*, various years.

took place before 1976). In the same period, the sum of the ICC residuals for exports to Middle Eastern countries nearly quadrupled, from 216 billion roubles to 800 billion roubles, this increase being largely accounted for by unspecified exports to Iran and Iraq. Between 1976 and 1979, therefore, 68 per cent of the growth of reported Soviet exports to the Middle East cannot be specified by commodity, while the remainder is attributed mainly to the growth of exports of machinery and equipment, which in turn cannot be confirmed from partners' data. Similarly, 55 per cent of the growth of Soviet exports to the area between 1972 and 1979 is unspecified, while 95 per cent of the growth of exports to Iran and Iraq is unspecified since 1976, and 70 per cent since 1972.

As a result of Kostinsky's study in 1974 it has been widely believed that the LDC residual contains Soviet arms sales (either for cash or on credit), a considerable proportion of which will have involved deliveries to Middle Eastern countries. At the time of the study, the ICC residual for exports to Middle Eastern countries was insignificant and no explanation for it was advanced.[14] The size of this residual since the mid-1970s means that an explanation is now required, and in view of the behaviour of the Iraq ICC residual in 1980, and the reduction in the Egyptian ICC residual since 1977, it is difficult to escape the conclusion that the ICC residual for Middle Eastern countries is largely composed of exports of military goods.

The economic benefit to the USSR of arms sales may be significant. The marginal cost of Soviet arms production is low, and in many cases arms are sold from stockpiles. In cases involving arms sales to oil-producing countries, their growing hard currency surpluses will have enabled the USSR to demand payment either in hard currency or in commodities that can be sold for hard currency (crude oil and natural gas).

Conclusion

In examining the influence of trade on Soviet relations with the Middle East, we have divided the countries involved into two groups: those possessing observer status at the CMEA and those without. Soviet trade relations with the former are determined largely by political, not economic, considerations and involve the USSR in economic costs. These costs would be considerably increased if any of the countries were to achieve full-member status. This was felt to be unlikely in the near future in the case of Ethiopia and the PDRY, but could not be entirely dismissed in the case of Afghanistan. The granting of full-member status would be predominantly a political act, and economic pressures (the cost of the aid involved) act as a constraint on any political initiative.

In the case of trade with other Middle Eastern countries, clear benefits accrue to the Soviet Union, which are consistent with the formulations established in the CMEA long-term target programme for energy, and which generally take the form of hard currency earnings (or savings) and do not involve the Soviet economy in any substantial dependence on Middle Eastern imports. Soviet exports to Middle Eastern countries lacking CMEA observer status amounted to 6.6 billion roubles between 1976 and 1980, of which 3.1 billion were composed of machinery and equipment exports and 2.5 billion roubles were unspecified (probably military goods). In exchange, the Soviet Union received in the same period 5.2 billion roubles worth of commodities, of which 2.5 billion can be attributed to liftings of crude oil, which were exported to third countries and contributed directly to the Soviet Union's hard currency earnings.

In addition, natural gas to an estimated value of 580 million roubles was imported from Iran between 1976 and 1980. Imports of natural gas make a multiplied contribution to Soviet hard currency earnings owing to the difference in the selling price obtained in Western Europe and that paid to importers. In 1976–80, imports of natural gas from Afghanistan totalled 270 million roubles, half of which were delivered in 1980 and compensated for the loss of deliveries from Iran in that year. This would appear to be a favourable consequence of the Soviet occupation of Afghanistan, but is not of sufficient importance to be the cause.

Although the Soviet Union does utilize imports of natural gas for domestic consumption, thereby involving itself in some physical dependence, these supplies can be replaced by domestic sources (at some cost). In the case of crude oil, the Soviet Union acts purely as a conveyancer and trader, and may be expected to continue to do so as long as it remains a net energy exporter. While this remains the case, there is little prospect of domestic energy pressures causing the USSR to be involved in Middle Eastern adventures.

The main cause of concern to the West appears to be the economic benefit that the USSR obtains from arms sales to the Middle East for hard currency, which in turn facilitates Soviet purchases from the West.

Between 1972 and 1975, the value of CRENS residual (which includes the sale of diamonds) came to 7.5 billion roubles, while the value of Soviet imports of machinery and equipment from the West amounted to 8.1 billion roubles. Between 1976 and 1980, the CRENS residual had grown to 20 billion roubles, while imports of machinery and equipment from the West amounted to 22.9 billion roubles. More significantly, however, over the same period the LDC residual (a substantial proportion of which involves exports to the Middle East) grew from 5.5 billion roubles to 13.7 billion, while the ICC residual to the (non-CMEA) Middle East increased from 0.5 billion to 2.5 billion roubles and was exactly offset by the value of Soviet crude oil liftings. It appears, therefore, that the LDC residual and the ICC residual both make a significant contribution to the ability of the Soviet Union to import from the West. Moreover the value of the Soviet Union's other major hard currency earner, oil, is also closely connected with Middle Eastern developments.

Soviet trade with the West appears to be clearly related to developments in the Middle East. Furthermore, as a result of its trade with Middle Eastern countries, considerable benefits accrue to the USSR which are consistent with a stated economic strategy. There are, however, signs that these benefits are side-effects rather than determinants of Soviet policy in the area, and that trade flows are to a considerable extent determined by partners' responses and by political factors. Furthermore, the Soviet Union has not been entirely successful in the pursuit of economic gain. On several occasions, apparently beneficial trade has been interrupted by political considerations (the most recent example being the interruption in trade with Iraq following the outbreak of the Iran–Iraq war). It is also an irony that although the USSR has successfully avoided physical dependence on Middle East energy supplies in all trade other than natural gas, it has been these supplies that have been directly affected by political instability in the area.

Notes

[1] Philip Hanson, 'Economic Constraints on Soviet Policies in the 1980s', *International Affairs*, Winter 1980/81.
[2] Ibid.
[3] Barry L. Kostinsky, *Description and Analysis of Soviet Foreign Trade Statistics* (Washington, D.C., US Department of Commerce, 1974).
[4] Alan Smith and Adi Schnytzer, 'Mongolia in the New Communist Third World', in P. J. D. Wiles (ed.), *The New Communist Third World* (London, Croom Helm, 1981).
[5] *Pravda*, 7 July 1981.
[6] *The Guardian*, 14 July 1981.
[7] *Pravda*, December 1980.
[8] *Zycie Gospodarcze*, 12 March 1961, cited by Radio Free Europe.
[9] P. Bagudin, *Vneshnyaya Torgovlya*, 1980, no. 10.
[10] V. Ivanenko, *Vneshnyaya Torgovlya*, 1980, no. 11.

[11] *Vneshnyaya Torgovlya SSSR, Itogi Devyatoi Pyatiletki i Perspektivi* (Moscow, 1977), p. 159.

[12] See, for example, M. Goldman, *The Enigma of Soviet Petroleum* (London, Allen & Unwin, 1980), p. 158.

[13] Ibid., p. 158.

[14] Kostinsky, op. cit.

8   Soviet–American Rivalry in the Middle East: The Political Dimension
Shahram Chubin

The Middle East has become the focal point for intensified competition between the East and West in the 1980s. This is particularly true for the Persian Gulf/Arabian peninsula area. The reasons for this are not hard to fathom: the interests of both superpowers overlap in the region, and neither the local states nor a substitute can assure the superpowers that their interests will be guaranteed. The magnitude of the stakes for the OECD countries, combined with severe apprehensions regarding Soviet intentions, has resulted in a renewed Western interest in taking a *direct* role in assuring the security of the region. Persian Gulf oil is a prize by any definition of the term, comprising a revenue valued at $200 billion a year, and the lowest-cost source of energy in the world. Western interests do not focus solely on the security of oil supplies, but also on the possibility that they may be manipulated for political ends. Some distinction has therefore to be made between threats to the economies and threats to the alliance; between interruptions which may be manageable and takeover by a hostile power which may not. The growth of the Soviet Union's military power, combined with a seeming willingness to involve itself in areas of the Third World, and its claims to political predominance over its periphery have underscored its traditional emphasis on the states contiguous to it.

The superpowers
The overlapping interests and capabilities of the two superpowers in the Gulf region, which, unlike the rest of the Middle East, has been largely uncharted in terms of crisis management, add to the indigenous sources of instability. This competition feeds into, and reflects, already existing differences in orientation and priority. The result is a potential for a coupling of local instability with superpower rivalry (and possibly confrontation), a situation

avoided in the period of British paramountcy, and in the decade of the twin-pillar policy, with its emphasis on the regimes of Saudi Arabia and Iran under the Shah.

Superpower rivalry in the Middle East/Persian Gulf, 'the third strategic zone', is but one theatre of a more generalized competition for influence. Any discussion of it must place it in the context of overall relations and preceding events. Three facts govern any consideration of the respective positions of the two superpowers: Western vulnerability, Soviet contiguity, and regional volatility. The first poses a problem of how to devise a political-military strategy that will reflect the magnitude of its stake and offset the disadvantages under which it labours. The second gives Moscow a plausible 'legitimate interest' and confers on her manifold advantages in competition with the West. The third provides the environment within which this competition takes place. Whatever one's interpretation of Soviet intentions in the Gulf, it is clear that the *stakes* involved have risen sharply in the 1980s, and that this has been paralleled by growing Soviet military *capabilities* (across the spectrum, including power projection) and a political environment of turmoil more conducive to Soviet *opportunities* for the extension of political influence.

It would be imprudent to assume that the growth in the USSR's military power – to strategic parity and to local conventional superiority[1] – will not affect its propensity to challenge the West in crises in the region.[2] It would be equally imprudent to assume that military capabilities do not influence intentions, or that a military balance itself does not affect the political calculation of states nearby. The first order of business for the West has therefore been to seek to redress the imbalance in military power that has been allowed to grow. The Carter Doctrine and the Rapid Deployment Force (RDF) reflect a recognition that the military balance of power in the region will affect Western politics. While the search for ground facilities will create problems for regional states, the alternative of leaving the region exposed to dominant Soviet power, or trying to achieve a credible deterrent 'on the cheap' through vertical or horizontal[3] escalation, is equally unattractive.

The Soviet Union's contiguity to the Gulf does not make its military preponderance inevitable. The removal of barriers to its overflights and the erosion of Western access, transit rights and basing points have brought this about. The emphasis on redressing the military balance which casts its shadow on everyday affairs does not mean that the actual use of Soviet armed might is the most likely contingency. Contiguity magnifies Soviet interests and increases the instruments at the disposal of the Kremlin. These range from agreements in the economic field, transit, and joint energy planning, through to subversion and assistance to dissident forces and propaganda campaigns. Adjacency allows for covert activity and the subtle exercise of pressure – to persuade or inhibit – in ways denied the distant power.

US interests in the Persian Gulf have until the recent past been relatively secure. Nuclear superiority, unconstrained access to the region, the existence of regional friends and alliance structures, the British presence, and relatively little dependence on Gulf oil made for a relaxed approach to the region. The USA's interests in the independence of the region (measured in terms of its denial to the USSR and assured access), the security of Israel, the security of the oil supply, growing interest in containing a regional arms race and the necessity of accommodating Arab economic power, all remained fairly static and discontinuous in the post-war period. By the 1980s they were often in tension. Slowly and inexorably in the 1970s the centre of gravity in the Middle East shifted eastwards towards the Arabian peninsula and Persian Gulf. As it did so the politics of the Gulf and Arab–Israeli sectors became intermeshed, conducting, as it were, Soviet influence from one region to the other. The West, which had with considerable success decoupled the two regions, was no longer able to do so by 1976. The dominant regional issue – Palestine – thus threatened to jeopardize other Western interests in the region, necessitating a more comprehensive policy for the area as a whole.

A major factor, exacerbating *inter alia* the problem of Palestine and questions relating to the security of the Gulf, has been the inability of the superpowers to regulate their competition. 'Equal security' has been interpreted by the USSR as equal status, nuclear parity, a right to a say in any major issue in international relations, and the continued right to support national liberation struggles in the unremitting quest for unilateral advantage in third areas. Rather than regulating competition through a code of conduct, détente, in this view, does no more than stabilize the superpower relationship in the Central Front (and in strategic weaponry). There is no agreement on the *status quo*, and little likelihood that technology, credits or grain will spin a web of interdependence sufficient to induce Soviet restraint in contested areas.

With the failure of both détente and linkage as sufficient answers to Soviet power and activism in the Third World, there has been a return in the West to an emphasis on military power as an instrument both for deterring Soviet use of force, and for creating a new basis for regulating the superpower relationship. It is not seriously argued that the Soviet Union *only* understands military power, but rather that without it the West would be less persuasive in arguing the case for Soviet restraint. Nor is it alleged that instability in the Middle East is principally (or even largely) the result of Soviet policies, but rather that when married to Soviet power they become transformed into major threats. It may well be that a return to a pattern of containment may not be an appropriate strategy for the West and that only an active role that inflicts reverses on the Soviet Union, for the purpose of reducing its influence, makes sense.[4] Be that as it may, it is clear that in an era of intensified superpower rivalry the prerequisite for any regulation of that rivalry, formally or not, requires a military balance of power.[5] An imbalance may encourage risk-taking, induce paralysis among local states, and fragment the Western alliance as its members seek competitive arrangements unilaterally. Even in regional disputes the military balance will count. Any settlement of the Palestine question is likely to need security assurances to the parties concerned. To be credible, they must be backed both by a military capability and by a perception of durable resolve and commitment on the part of the guarantor.

The regional environment
The argument so far has been concentrated on the superpowers, their rivalry, their relative assets and vulnerabilities, and the utility of military power as it relates both to their relationship and to the defence of their interests in the region. The emphasis on the general relationship is critical to an understanding or interpretation of their intentions and their policies in the Gulf region. This in turn influences politics in the region while being affected by developments therein.

As has been argued, the Soviet Union, because of its contiguity and growing power, seeks as its legitimate right a position of political preponderance in the Gulf region. Its goal of becoming the principal security manager of the region includes the right to exclude Western military power from the area and to obtain a right of veto over the policies of states immediately adjacent to it. In the short term it may not include preferential access to the region's resources, though this cannot be excluded later on. The Soviet leadership throughout 1980 and 1981 has been at considerable pains to assure the West that its co-management of the Gulf would be benign – and that Western interests in access to, and in the flow of, oil are recognized. It has implied that without its participation the region's instability and the dangers of confrontation threaten Western interests in more calamitous ways.

The regional environment is in many ways conducive to the

realization of Soviet interests. The Palestine issue, it is generally recognized, has provided the USSR with an entry point into the region, strengthening Moscow's argument that it supports the Arabs' interests. Attempts to focus on the Soviet presence, which in an important sense has been occasioned by the Palestinian issue, have been branded as 'diversionary'.

The historical transformation of the Gulf region, spurred by oil wealth and rapid, disorientating social change leading to political upheavals and abrupt changes in the *status quo*, favours the revisionist power. No matter that the changes may affect the interests of both superpowers, such changes *objectively* favour the USSR because they hurt the West more, and they are likely to continue. It may be that the USSR – despite its 'atheism', which is in contradiction to the current Islamic revival – is likely to be the beneficiary of movements against the *status quo*, particularly since the populations in most of those states are young and likely to be radicalized.

The nature of inter-Arab politics, and the tendency of the 'moderate' Arab states to clutch at the security blanket of the Arab consensus, makes these states susceptible to pressure from within the Arab world. The inevitable emphasis on regime-security makes most Arab states susceptible both to the threat of terrorism and to the blandishment of guarantees. Soviet assistance to liberation movements and groups disposed to violence can be traced from the Iranian revolution through, allegedly, to the seizure of the Grand Mosque in Mecca in November 1979. No wonder that Kuwait prefers an 'alliance' of protection with the Palestinian groups and the USSR. Similarly, frustration on the Palestine issue breeds extremism that could influence the Palestinians in the Gulf – a factor governments must consider in their policies.

Finally, the region is characterized by multiple cleavages – sectarian, ethnic, tribal, linguistic and ideological. Few states are immune to the prospect of secessionist movements or to the agitation of disaffected minorities. As sources of pressure these may be used by the USSR to induce sensitivity to its interests in Gulf states. Western interests are not so easy to defend in such an environment. Lacking contiguity, or even proximity, Western policies have tended to be erratic. Nor can the regional states count on the West as a countervailing power, let alone military presence, in the longer run.

Support for a dynamic *status quo*, for orderly change, is inherently difficult and is likely to be even more so in a region where the pace of change is rapid and where the West is likely to be identified as the protector of the preceding regime, the intrusive cultural force, and the colonial power. Even with its attractions of technology and education (which the USSR may lack), the difficulties for the West in forging close links with such culturally different states appear formidable. Perceptually, the tendency to judge these states exclusively as suppliers of oil, or as pro- or anti-Soviet, is self-defeating. Reference will have to be made to their priorities and concerns, ranging from the issue of Palestine to the guarantees on their investments abroad. Yet in the West the tendency is towards a short-range strategy that is instrumental rather than genuinely concerned.

The West is disadvantaged further by its reluctance to deal with the facts as they exist: to accept the reality of Soviet-assisted subversion and to counter it, and to recognize that the threats to the region will not come neatly labelled or at convenient times. The interaction of local instabilities, regional conflicts, and the East–West competition are clear enough to see since 1979. False distinctions between 'political' versus 'military' problems, and between 'external' and 'internal' threats, seem to provide only alibis for inaction; they do not have much bearing on the problems.

Many of the challenges in the region – of peaceful change, national integration and the synthesis of cultures, of economic development and diversification, of political identification and participation, of moral renewal, of institutionalization, of regional cooperation and the management and sharing of resources more equitably in the Arab world – all these and related issues will persist for a long time to come, longer perhaps than the West's oil vulnerability and dependence. By their nature most of these challenges will provide fertile avenues for exploitation but will be resistant to influence by outside powers. None in itself will be a major problem for the West. But, combined with Soviet involvement and exploitation, they can be.

The argument for resisting Soviet inroads into the region, first by restoring the military balance and then by addressing the principal regional opportunities facilitating its influence, is clear. Contrary to conclusions reached elsewhere in this book, it is this chapter's contention that regional politics will always provide opportunities for Soviet exploitation; these can be reduced with great effort but not eliminated. A military imbalance, however, may tempt the USSR to something more reckless. In the first place, the region itself is so valuable that as a stake it may encourage risk-taking. Second, in a crisis elsewhere Soviet preponderance in the Middle East could be used as a pressure-point on the West. Assiduously stacked up, these chips then would be cashed in. Third, the USSR could be sucked into the region. This could happen incrementally – as in Afghanistan – as the Soviet leaders talk themselves into a position of non-reversibility or convince themselves of Moscow's legitimate rights in the area.

Allied relations and Middle East crises

US and European attitudes towards both the Arab-Israeli dispute and threats to the Persian Gulf region have, in the past, been somewhat divergent. This was a product both of differential vulnerabilities to interruptions of oil supplies and of differing emphases in approaches to how threats should be handled. The United States's immediate reaction to the revolution in Iran and the Soviet invasion of Afghanistan was to emphasize the potential Soviet threat to the region and the need for a new military balance therein. The Europeans persisted with their emphasis on the regional problems, notably Palestine, arguing that nimble diplomacy could reduce Soviet influence in the region. Over the past two years these approaches have converged, revealing an essential consensus on both the range of threats to Western interests and on the necessity for a broad-gauged policy to deal with them.

In this regard the Europeans' potential contribution is significant. Being more 'independent', it is more politically acceptable to the regional states than is the assistance of a superpower, and also less polarizing in its effects. European positions sympathetic to the Palestinian cause – as in the Venice Declaration of 1980 – can be helpful in softening the effect of America's ties with Israel and can act as a bridge for periods of diplomatic inactivity caused by elections. Such initiatives are helpful if they are seen as adjuncts to a *total* Western diplomacy that is seeking to defuse the crisis, but not if they are seen as alternatives designed to appease the Arab states with the hope of preferential terms in return. Provided alliance relations are in healthy repair, European activism on behalf of the Arab states can help to soften the pressures on moderate Arab states oriented towards the West that need to be able to show progress on the Palestine issue. But if European suggestions emanate from a distrust of the United States and are designed to secure a 'better deal' from the Arabs, it is obvious that they will be counter-productive – both for the Arabs and for the Europeans. The former cannot expect results without US help and Israeli concessions, and the Europeans will dissipate their diplomatic strength with little assurance regarding oil supplies.

The European states can also be useful in meeting threats to the Gulf directly. It is most unlikely that this will include a formal arrangement under NATO auspices. More likely it will consist of individual contributions to specific tasks (or specific countries) on a bilateral basis. These arrangements may be informally coordinated and yet have the same effect as an 'alliance policy'. For example, a Franco-British naval presence in and around the Gulf, together with Britain's training and advisory missions in Oman and Kuwait, and the US facility in Oman are assets which could be coordinated during crises. Similarly, the economic assistance programme provided by the Federal Republic of Germany (FRG) to Turkey is a useful contribution to an important state with a potentially important role in the area to the north of the Arabian peninsula.

Alliance members' contributions to maintaining a military balance in the Middle East/Gulf region will certainly require some military component. Not all alliance members are able to allocate naval vessels or even military units to the defence of the region, but it will be important that those who can do so should participate, even in a minimal sense, for two principal reasons: first, to serve notice on the USSR that access to oil is not a superpower or a bilateral issue but rather an international and a multilateral issue; and, second, to demonstrate to the United States, by even a symbolic military involvement, that the European states (and Japan) are prepared to share the risks and the costs of the defence of the Gulf.

Arms control and crisis-management
The Indian Ocean/Gulf/Horn of Africa region has been the object of various arms-control proposals in recent years. One suggestion, by the non-aligned, has been for the exclusion of the navies of the non-littoral states from the Indian Ocean and the dismantling of bases 'conceived in the context of great power rivalry'. This 'zone of peace' proposal has been too general to be very meaningful, but it was followed in 1976–7 by attempts between the United States and the USSR to negotiate limits on their naval presence in the general region. The attempts ended with the Ethiopia–Somalia war. After the Soviet invasion of Afghanistan, there were renewed efforts by the USSR to sponsor negotiations on the neutralization of the Persian Gulf. Sometimes this was linked with the possibility of a Soviet troop withdrawal from Afghanistan and discussions among the regional states, Pakistan and Iran, for the neutralization of the three states.

The primary obstacle to any progress on these proposals is the distrust pervading East–West relations and the relative military advantages of the USSR. Of course the definition of 'bases' is not clear (does this include military advisers?), but fundamentally the problem with naval limitations is that while it would constrain the West's ability to protect its interests, it would do nothing to offset the Soviet military presence on land, i.e. in the southern USSR. An agreement to dismantle Soviet bases in the People's Democratic Republic of Yemen (PDRY) and Ethiopia, in exchange for dismantling US bases in Oman and Diego Garcia, would still leave Soviet aircraft in the southern military districts of the USSR in a position to respond rapidly to developments in the Gulf. Indeed, this would remain true even if Afghanistan were also 'neutralized'. The same problem attends neutralization proposals. It would be difficult to fashion an arrangement which would not leave the USSR as the preponderant power.

While the impulse to limit and regulate superpower competition in a zone of overlapping interests is commendable, no neat formula as yet has been devised to balance the weight of Western interests, which need a commensurate military underpinning, against the lesser Soviet interest with its asymmetrical military advantages. To prevent inadvertent confrontation and the risk of escalation, dialogue will be needed. But ill-conceived notions of negotiations as a substitute for a military balance will do little to limit the crisis potential of the region. A great-power condominium, or the delimitation of spheres of influence, or even a 'hands-off' agreement, which are all potentially tempting for the outside power confronting an unstable and dangerous area, will not be self-enforcing. They will not be substitutes for military power, but in fact will be its product. Finally, it will be important to remember that in the late twentieth century such great-power arrangements are unlikely to prove manageable if the local powers oppose them.

The Soviet Union's foothold
A remarkable feature of Soviet influence in the Middle East is its intangible quality. Within the Gulf itself, Moscow has diplomatic relations with only Iran, Kuwait and Iraq – in the last case these are strained, and with Iran they are scarcely solid. Soviet aid and trade (excluding the military component) is not extensive or likely to become so. The USSR has tended to be most successful in states which are poor or peripheral: the Yemens, Somalia and later Ethiopia. The emphasis on the periphery of the Gulf after the initial burst of post-war interest in the Northern Tier, followed in the mid-1950s by involvement in the Arab–Israeli sector, is a natural consequence of the persistent Soviet quest for influence in the entire region of the Middle East, Indian Ocean and Horn of Africa. That this influence has proved to be evanescent and even illusory has not dulled the urgency of that quest. Indeed, it may have encouraged the search for more stable influence through control – by involvement with regimes that have one-party Marxist systems of government, as in the PDRY and Ethiopia. The Soviet

Union, through East Germany and Cuba, is also in a position to guarantee regimes by the provision of security assistance and of praetorian guards to protect their leadership.

The strategic importance of these countries, linked militarily by Soviet naval facilities in the Dahlak Archipelago, with an access to a port and airfield in the PDRY and the territory and airfields of Afghanistan, is obvious. They allow Soviet maritime reconnaissance of the Indian Ocean and facilitate its power projection in the southern Gulf. Perhaps equally important is the political utility of the relationship for the USSR. The PDRY is in a position to pressure its conservative northern neighbour, the Yemen Arab Republic (YAR), and through it Saudi Arabia and Oman. To date the USSR has been cautious and averse to taking risks in using its local allies. But with strategic nuclear parity and conventional military superiority, it may feel less constrained in undertaking probes or underwriting *irridenta*.

To conclude, it is true that in *peacetime*, all things being *equal*, the attractions of the West for *the Arab states in general* may outshine those of the USSR, which is limited to providing arms for hard currency, exploiting the peripheral states, and seizing on local discontent as a means of bolstering its evanescent influence. But it is also true that the interaction of Soviet power and proximity, the vulnerability of the West and the prevalence of sources of instability cast doubt on whether one can realistically make such *ceteribus paribus* assumptions in the Middle East generally and in the Gulf region particularly.

Notes

[1] This is generally recognized by now, but for a detailed discussion see Albert Wohlstetter, 'Meeting the Threat in the Persian Gulf', *Survey*, Spring 1980, pp. 128–88.

[2] Already in 1973 the USSR was prepared to threaten the dispatch of airborne troops to Egypt.

[3] I.e. an exposed Soviet asset of equal value in another region.

[4] See William E. Odom, 'Whither the Soviet Union?', *The Washington Quarterly*, vol. 4 no. 2 (1981).

[5] This refers both to a possible 'hands-off' agreement by the superpowers and to a 'spheres of influence' (or condominium) approach.

9 Soviet–American Rivalry in the Middle East: The Military Dimension
Jonathan Alford

If it is taken as given that Soviet-American rivalry exists in the Middle East, we should, at least for the present, describe that rivalry as political in the sense that each is attempting to secure influence at the expense of the other – or, at the least, desires to exclude the influence of the other. We should then go on to note, in a rather abstract way, that one – but only one – component of a political balance consists in the threatened use of military power, whether to preserve or to change the *status quo*.

It is a notoriously difficult and even futile exercise to attempt to measure military balances – whether statistically or dynamically – for reasons which will shortly be explained, but it will be assumed for the purposes of this paper that the perceptions both of regional states and of the superpowers themselves will be shaped at least in part by objective military realities. Given the articulated attitudes of the Reagan Administration, the capability of the Soviet Union and the United States to project their military power into the Gulf region is likely to be a matter of extreme concern in Washington. Whether wisely or unwisely, the new administration appears to believe that if the United States can restore its military relationship with the Soviet Union, most international problems (including those relating to the Gulf) would be solved. That this will not prove easy is the theme of this chapter. Before examining the reasons for such a conclusion, we need to take a rather general look at the role and utility of military power in the Gulf and adjacent territories.

The role of military power
In terms of regional perceptions, a *sense* of relative military power is likely to matter. In Hobbes's words: 'Reputation for power is power.' If the Soviet Union is seen as proximate, militarily powerful and ruthless (and if, as seems to be the case, it misses no opportunity to parade that power) while the United States is seen

as half a world away, weak, confused and uncertain of its commitment, it seems reasonable to presume that the weak and inherently very insecure regional states will tend to defer to the Soviet Union in their political calculations. When, in addition, the United States has the albatross of Israel around its neck, the Arab and Islamic Middle Eastern states will each in their different ways be reluctant first to admit the need for, and then to take any steps to facilitate, American protection. Nevertheless, one may suppose, whatever the rhetoric and the dictates of intra-Arab and Middle Eastern politics, that all the smaller oil-producing states, together with Saudi Arabia, do admit – at least in their secret councils – the need ultimately for American military power to offset Soviet power in order, at the least, to permit them to maintain an independent existence and some freedom of manoeuvre between East and West. In a very real sense, one suspects that such states do view the United States *ultimately* as their protector. Yet if confidence is diminished in the ability of the United States to extend effective military protection on request, the weak have an alternative, namely to reinsure themselves with the Soviet Union. Moreover, if there is a tradition of deference to the powerful for the sake of a quiet life and limited sovereignty (as an alternative to no sovereignty at all), it could well be the case that Soviet influence will come permanently to penetrate the region by default of the West. It is therefore necessary to recreate what could best be described as an *aura* of American military power, both as a deterrent (in a strictly military sense) to Soviet territorial ambitions if they should emerge and to convince regional states that there is some kind of overall political balance in the region between East and West. It may even be preferable to fall back on Marxist-Leninist idiom and speak of the correlation of forces or trends rather than of political balances, since the former makes more explicit reference to military relationships and the part that they can come to play in transformation.

When states examine the range of contingent threats that they face, they may well conclude that, with respect to a considerable range of those threats, some kind of regional security cooperation and the purchase of arms is more appropriate than alliance – whether formal or informal – with an external power. They may even conclude that military assistance from West European states is acceptable and preferable to American assistance in terms of training and security advice. The United Kingdom is active in the UAE and Oman; France was clearly an acceptable friend to Saudi Arabia at the time of the seizure of the Grand Mosque in Mecca; and there are persistent reports that Saudi Arabia seeks security links with the Federal Republic of Germany. Nevertheless, none could have confidence that individually or collectively they could beat off a determined superpower challenge. Clearly Afghanistan has served as a reminder that Moscow's definition of Soviet security tends to be preclusive and that the Gulf falls within one of the inner rings (if not within the innermost ring) of the Soviet security perimeter. Hobbes's view of war encapsulates nicely what seems to be the prevailing opinion among the rulers of the Gulf states: the nature of war, according to him, consists 'not in actual fighting but in the known disposition thereto during all the time there is no assurance to the contrary'. The Soviet Union is presenting no assurance to the contrary; rather, in all too recent memory it has shown a disposition for 'actual fighting'.

The third general introductory remark is that the refinement of scenarios for the introduction of American military power may, in at least one sense, prove to be an irrelevant and sterile exercise, which is likely, in the event that military power is invoked, to be seen to have been based on wrong assumptions. The tendency is for military planners to be called to account very precisely to their political masters for their plans. Failure to do this results in the denial of funds or resources on the grounds that, if the military cannot convincingly demonstrate clinically and with considerable precision what kind of intervention is intended, and what politically desirable outcome can be achieved by force, the forces are not 'cost-effective'. The precise delineation of scenarios will always lay their authors open to criticisms of unreality, the but-what-if' syndrome, of over-use of imagination, or conversely of under-use of imagination. What has so often been lost sight of in recent years is the virtue of military flexibility. Of course this lays the military authorities open to the charge of planning for the worst case or the greater-than-expected threat, but in prudence one must make allowance for the unexpected and acknowledge the value of being in a position to respond to military challenges that nobody had catered for. In this context, however, I would argue that it is indeed the *aura* of American power, and a very generalized definition of capability, that is politically required, rather than a deep inquiry into the precise circumstances of its introduction into the region. It is often best to keep things fuzzy, saying in effect with King Lear: 'I will do such things, what they are yet I know not, but they shall be the terror of the earth.'[1] In terms of certainties and uncertainties, it would be best to have it certain that the United States could intervene decisively, leaving uncertain the circumstances in which it would do so or the precise form the intervention would take. In effect this means attending carefully to logistic planning and inter-theatre movement while providing a range of force levels to be drawn on.

To return briefly to Soviet concerns, there is as yet very little evidence of the possible sound of Soviet boots marching purposefully towards the Gulf even though, in a purely military context, there is at present very little to stop them doing so. Consequently, one can dismiss the 'stepping-stone theory', based as it is on the invasion of Afghanistan, which still seems to have been driven much more by defensive (and, in a sense, ideological) impulses than by dreams of conquest. Yet the nagging doubts cannot be dispelled. As Sir John Malcolm remarked to Lord Ellenborough in 1828, 'They [the Russians] will be compelled, as we were in India, to make new conquests to secure those already made.'[2] Or, as Gorchakov, then Imperial Russian Chancellor, said in 1864, 'Ambition plays a smaller role than imperious necessity, and the greatest difficulty is knowing where to stop.'[3] Furthermore, it would be unwise to underestimate Soviet concerns at the possible encroachment of American power into regions close to the vulnerable southern parts of the USSR. Soviet leaders are likely to misinterpret American efforts to secure Western energy sources as a threat to Russia's own security. With Soviet–American dialogue at a standstill, it is hard not to find an echo of G. D. Clayton's perceptive summary that 'the lasting hostility between Britain and Russia was based on a quite unreal fear of each other's supposed aggressive intentions'.[4] Moreover it is necessary to admit the military advantages accruing to the Soviet Union through the possession of Afghanistan – whether to open a new front against Iran, to pressure Pakistan, to project land-based airpower into the Indian Ocean or to facilitate the routing of military transport aircraft to the Arabian peninsula. Although currently a liability, Afghanistan could prove in the longer term a valuable military asset.

It would also seem prudent to be concerned about Soviet intentions with respect to Iran. It is easy to remember the Soviet move into Azerbaijan in 1946 and the fact that the Soviet Union would not acknowledge the Shah's unilateral renunciation of the 1921 Treaty of Friendship, which gave the USSR the right to send troops into Iran should a third party intervene militarily there or use Iranian territory as a base for an attack on Soviet territory.[5] If the Kremlin was seeking a legitimation of an intervention in Iran, not only does the legal pretext exist, but the temptation arising from a left-wing takeover in Tehran might be too great to resist. It is not hard to imagine a self-styled liberation movement with a tenuous hold on power calling for Soviet military support. In any circumstances in which American military power descended on

Iranian territory, it must be assumed that the Soviet reaction would be likely to be swift and violent.

In a chapter on Soviet–American rivalry, the question of arms sales cannot be entirely ignored, although it resides somewhat uneasily in a general discussion of who could do what to whom. Clearly the economic imperatives to sell arms are not unimportant, but more is implied by such sales (in most cases) than the simple recycling of petrodollars. Sales generally imply approval and *may* confer influence on the seller of arms. Although the latter proposition has been somewhat dented by recent events in Iran and by the Iran–Iraq war, there remains both in Washington and in Moscow at least some expectation that regional regimes will be dependent on them to a politically useful extent once they have become substantial purchasers of arms. This is a far cry from the Nixon Doctrine and there is no obvious candidate to replace the Shah's Iran as a regional military bulwark against the Soviet Union. Certainly Saudi Arabia cannot perform that role. Nevertheless an equation will continue to be made between arms and influence despite clear evidence to the contrary. Even if it were not made, it would be extremely difficult for either superpower to resist requests for weapons backed by petrodollars when the denial of those demands is likely to be interpreted as an important political signal, and when the prospective purchaser can go elsewhere – thus making a very important political gesture of his own.

However, while noting rivalry over arms sales (not just between the superpowers but also between them and other smaller producers), it is hard to see how this rivalry will affect the ability of one superpower to limit the military extension of the other. Both could, as a result of arms sold by either, be faced with somewhat greater regional resistance than would otherwise be the case, but this resistance is unlikely to be decisive even if it may raise the cost of intervention. There are other and more powerful constraints to be considered.

The military constraints

The USSR
Proximity is a geographical fact conferring undeniable advantage to the Soviet Union in most hypothetical confrontations between the superpowers in the Gulf region, but it is an advantage which diminishes quite rapidly with distance from the Soviet Union. This makes intervention in Azerbaijan look a very different proposition from intervention in Saudi Arabia or Oman. Nevertheless, the Soviet Union has the advantage of a number of clients prepared to

confer upon it some use of territory. Ethiopia and the People's Democratic Republic of Yemen (PDRY) provide some assistance in naval operations and in the use of land-based airpower, and, as noted earlier, Afghanistan allows airpower to be brought closer to the region. While still being reluctant to be tied to scenarios, there is nevertheless a clear possibility that the rapid movement of troops by air to the southern entrance to the Red Sea could greatly complicate any Western military initiative. Moreover, the regional states remain acutely conscious of the opportunities available to put pressure on Saudi Arabia and Oman through the PDRY.

Whereas in the past the Soviet Union was not particularly well placed to generate large forces quickly in its southern republics, having other and higher priorities to attend to, the demands on Afghanistan appear to have led to considerable improvement in infrastructure and in transport links generally to the area. Moreover, increasing emphasis on airborne forces and airlift capacity has quite dramatically improved rapid interventionary capability for *coup de main* when operating in conjunction with special forces designed for rapid insertion and deep raiding. Over-flying of adjacent territories now looks substantially less risky than before. None of this is intended to discount the costs to the Soviet Union of the *occupation* of a hostile state, but a move to deny oil to the West does not necessarily imply that they would, at least at the outset, have to cope with widespread civil disorder.

At sea, there is no need to dwell on the change in maritime capability. The ability of the Soviet navy to maintain strength in distant waters is sufficient, at the least, to raise substantially the threat to any Western naval presence and to raise also the costs of military intervention by the United States. This is probably why Soviet ships are in the Indian Ocean. Traditionally the Soviet Union has deployed anti-carrier task forces to match American carrier task forces, not least because the latter are seen as posing a nuclear threat to the Soviet homeland. It would probably be wrong to see Soviet naval power as dependent on anchorages and shore facilities in the north-west Indian Ocean for sustained operations, but some of the difficulties of maintaining a substantial naval presence in this particular area are eased by access to the PDRY's Aden and Socotra, and most recently to Ethiopian ports and anchorages. It was clear that the investment in the Somali port of Berbera was quite considerable, and it is reasonable to suppose that Aden now provides the same kind of fleet support. Moreover, even if Soviet units are drawn from other fleets, the Soviet navy is now sufficiently large and competent for that to be done without undue strain.

Yet in two respects, the Soviet maritime presence is deficient. The Soviet Union cannot in any sense match American amphibious capability; the Soviet naval infantry remains a small and not particularly impressive force, dedicated primarily to securing those choke-points considered vital to Soviet naval operations in war. Nor can the Soviet Union deploy significant carrier-based airpower, having to rely instead on land-based aircraft. Although the improvements in range and payload of Soviet Frontal Aviation are impressive, without airfields in the Gulf, air operations would present considerable problems for the USSR, especially against US carrier-based airpower.

Nevertheless, the military reality is that the Soviet Union could bring preponderant power to bear, especially on the countries of the Northern Tier, without great difficulty and without significant diversion of forces from other high-priority tasks. Moreover, it could generate that power in a relatively short time. Some warning of an impending move would certainly be obtained but, by almost any calculation of time and space, the Soviet Union could mobilize and move military forces across her borders more rapidly and in greater strength than the United States could reinforce the region. Subsequent development would be impossible to predict, depending crucially upon the local opposition encountered, but it is not hard to imagine Soviet forces moving overland to link up with airborne forces dropped into the critical area of the upper Gulf in a matter of ten days to two weeks. Extensive use would also be made of helicopters and heliborne forces to secure routes and airfields. Not much has changed in this respect since Sir Mortimer Durand wrote in 1886: 'Russia has much in her favour . . . She is coming overland with nothing to overcome but geographical difficulties – a big nation absorbing a number of small weak tribes.'[6]

The United States

It may be that the United States would, in the event, attract some military support from allies, but such support could only be marginal. This is not to deride what other Western powers are trying to do, which may have very great political significance. The genesis of the US Rapid Deployment Force (RDF) is well known and its deficiencies widely advertised. Attempts to remedy those deficiencies are being made, but in many respects the United States will continue to suffer major disabilities. These can be summarized as: distance from the theatre of war; lack of secure access and forward bases for shortening intervention times; shortage of long-range airlift and amphibious shipping; and acclimatization.

These points hardly need elaboration. Considerable attention has already been paid to short-term remedies such as the acquisition of roll-on/roll-off shipping to carry heavy equipment based on Diego Garcia, which at present is being developed. The current US air-transport fleet is being enhanced by in-flight refuelling, strengthening and stretching, but no new American transport aircraft can enter service until the late 1980s, assuming that procurement of a new transport aircraft (C–X) goes ahead. Negotiations have been completed to allow America conditional use of airfields and harbours in Oman, Somalia, Kenya and Egypt, but much work remains to be done to bring these facilities up to standard. Moreover, the conditions imposed are likely to be very restrictive. For instance, it appears that the Egyptian government would allow American use only if the US is involved in helping to resist aggression against another Arab state; if the state concerned has asked for American assistance; and if the use of the facility terminates when the aggression terminates.

Even such limited and contingent access may be hard to sustain in the face of declarations such as that contained in Saddam Hussain's proposed Pan-Arab Charter of February 1980 (Principle One): 'The presence in the Arab homeland of any foreign troops or military forces shall be rejected and no facilities for the use of Arab territory shall be extended to them in any form or under any pretext or cover.'

Turkey too has indicated very clearly to the United States that it cannot permit the use of American facilities in Turkey for a Middle Eastern contingency of which it did not approve. The Turkish leaders, having pressing energy needs and seeking financial support from oil-rich Arab states, are unlikely to do anything which might offend their Arab neighbours.

Of course such coyness and inhibitions could evaporate under threat, but the Arab states seem determined to avoid paying a political price in advance, thus making American preparations and planning for intervention very difficult and uncertain. Most certain and most difficult to obstruct is the US maritime presence, yet this is the one most difficult and expensive presence to sustain, given current US naval force levels, and the slowest to improve substantially. The US navy is finding it hard to maintain two carrier task forces on station in the Indian Ocean, and the marine contingent embarked is only some 1,800 men. The Americans could greatly increase their marine forces, but not quickly, given steaming times from Okinawa and the United States. Moreover, it is not easy to maintain marines on station for long periods, especially in the climatic conditions prevailing to the north-west Indian Ocean. However, the alternative, which is to fly the marines to marry up with heavy equipment held on the floating stockpiles, not only requires a place to do it, but also implicitly denies an assault capability. That requires specialized shipping. Few military operations are easy, but such an operation is extremely complex, requiring a combination of adequate warning time and good fortune that is unlikely to be present. If the shooting has already started by the time the operation is being mounted, the Soviet naval force will be in a position very seriously to interfere with the preparations. Moreover, all operations of this type can have the opposite effect to that intended. Rather than deter Soviet moves by pre-emption, they could indeed encourage the Soviet Union to pre-empt. Rather than alleviate regional tensions, such preparatory deployments could exacerbate those tensions.

To keep matters in perspective, the United States has always maintained a substantial strategic reserve of army formations and marines, and could draw on front-line and logistic units up to some 200,000 men. However, over time that force has tended to be earmarked for the reinforcement of the more traditional prospective theatres of conflict – Europe and the Far East. Very little thought has been given to contingency planning for other tasks, which could come to appear much more daunting in terms of climate, terrain and logistic support. It is reasonable to assume that such planning is now taking place, at least to the extent of facing up to the problems of providing logistic support, routing, training and appropriate command and control. The last is proving difficult to resolve, for the responsibilities for preparing the RDF are divided and it is far from clear under whose operational command the force would be deployed. To say the least, US interservice rivalry is not making it any easier to solve the problem. In April 1981 it was reported that the Secretary for Defense had approved plans to establish a new combat command for the Gulf, answering directly to the Joint Chiefs of Staff (JCOS).[7] Much remains to be worked out, and it is not easy to see how training and preparation of the force can be rationalized, in that the forces would only be assigned to the new command when need arises. Nevertheless, there is some logic to this redrawing of the boundaries of US overseas commands, given that currently SACEUR's responsibility extends to the eastern border of Iran while Commander-in-Chief Pacific's (CINCPAC) area runs westwards to the Straits of Hormuz and Bab al-Mandeb.

Capabilities compared

The objective conclusion to any comparisons of *rates* of build-up within the Gulf is that they must favour the Soviet Union, and that the aggregated difficulties facing the United States exceed by a considerable margin those facing the Soviet Union. If 'getting there fastest with the mostest' (General Nathan B. Forrest's ultimate reduction of the principles of war to one simple formulation) is likely to be decisive, it is quite hard to see the United States doing that in terms of conventional forces on land. Moreover, the political implications of such perceptions are likely to be profound in crisis. It makes little sense to start a race that you have little prospect of winning.

Yet the calculations made by both superpowers will be profoundly affected in a crisis by the knowledge that the other could not be pre-empted. From the Kremlin's perspective, this still would be true even if it were to look as if the Soviet Union might be strong enough to overcome such resistance as the United States could sustain. The implications of having to overcome American resistance, of forcing an American withdrawal and of killing Americans to secure objectives, feed back into the original political calculations. The United States must be able to convince the Soviet Union that it would be prepared to escalate rather than resign the field – with all that implies in terms of the risks of losing control of events. Clearly it is undesirable to have to defend an interest by the threat to escalate the violence (rather than by evincing a manifest capability of defending the interest itself), but there is no realistic alternative in prospect in this case. The determination to defend the interest against Soviet attack, and the positioning of American forces in the path of that attack, place the onus of escalation on the Soviet Union. If the Soviet Union has nothing to fear from the consequences of escalation (implied by killing Americans), it will presumably continue the aggression. Moreover, it is unlikely to embark on aggression in the first place unless it is prepared to raise the level of violence should that prove necessary.

Some in the West might now pessimistically conclude that the Soviet Union, possessing escalation dominance, would be prepared to kill Americans and challenge the United States to raise the level of violence, believing that the Americans would not respond effectively and would be forced to back down. Others, myself included, do not believe that the military balance between East and West is sufficiently adverse for the Soviet Union to have any confidence that it could dominate the United States in a crisis. What flows from this latter judgement (and it is only a judgement) is that American willingness to risk escalation would adequately define the interest as it does in the European theatre. Furthermore, the prior definition of that interest (the exclusion of Soviet military power from the Gulf) by announcement, and by the attention paid to the RDF, would appear to be credible. The rapid deployment of *some* American power into the region would make it certain that Soviet calculations of risk and benefit would be substantially affected.

However, it is not certain how the Soviet Union defines her interests in the Middle East. This question has been addressed by others in this book. If those interests are limited to the exclusion of American military power from regions close to the Soviet Union, that might seem to make superpower accommodation possible. If, on the other hand, the acquisition of territory or resources or influence through the deployment of military power becomes a first-order interest, accommodation is clearly impossible over the longer term. The signs are that the Soviet Union is prepared to admit Western interest in oil and is in no mood to assume additional burdens of occupation at the present time. This will not, presumably, mean that it will desist from low-level non-military probing, or cease to express support for leftist forces, or acquiesce in any expansion of Western influence in the region. However, there does not seem to be any obvious desire on the Soviet Union's part to run the risk of starting a world war over the Gulf. It seems, therefore, that, for all its weakness and difficulty, the RDF as an expression of US commitment is probably a sufficient deterrent at present to any Soviet military adventure.

More worrying perhaps is that the Middle East constitutes an enduring vulnerability for the West which cannot, for reasons already outlined, be adequately protected in war. In other words, should an unintended war occur through some catastrophic error of judgement, miscalculation or sheer accident, the West, as Abba Eban has put it, with 'one lung outside the body', could be forced to concede, if not capitulate, by a Soviet move against oil, whether at source or in transit. Whereas the United States might be able to ride out supply interruption, Europe and Japan could not do so for long. It would not be hard for the Soviet Union either to mount an operation against the oilfields with the aim solely of preventing pumping, or to attack tankers in transit (thus forcing the Western navies to stretch – even overstretch – their protection to the Gulf), or both. It is worth remarking at this point that the widening and deepening of the Suez Canal will cause a substantial part of European tanker traffic to be diverted up the Red Sea, and this will have the effect of creating yet another choke-point at the Straits of Bab al-Mandeb, which the Soviet Union is now well placed to block. As part of a concerted attack on the West, such tactics would not only produce positive results contributing to the defeat of the West but even the threat of such operations could cause the diversion of

Western (American) military power away from Europe (and the Far East). One distinct advantage possessed by a continental power is that it can rather easily shift weight on interior lines to press at different points on its periphery. When several of those points are likely to be defined as 'vital' to Western security, the rather loose maritime coalition which is 'the West' will not only find it difficult to shift its strategic weight as rapidly but may indeed collapse under the psychological pressure imposed by trying to resolve conflicting interests and priorities.

Conclusions

In a rather short analysis of the problem it is not possible (nor would it be wise) to enter a discussion of scenarios. They are easily imagined. Yet a restless search for scenarios, and the failure to find any which not only are unimpeachable but allow Western military power to prove decisive, has tended to obscure a number of important political points about perceptions of power and about Soviet calculations with respect to risk. It is indeed quite hard to see what the RDF can do beyond raising the stakes, but that in itself is not an insignificant contribution to stability. Although it is not at all easy for us to see how the RDF can contribute to the resolution of domestic or regional conflict, the belief that it *might* can give friendly regimes a ring of confidence that would otherwise be absent.

The RDF can certainly prevent easy pickings for the Soviet Union and almost certainly does so now. The faster that some American forces can be moved into the region in a crisis the better that will be, and it must be possible to sustain them in place as a continuing deterrent until the crisis is resolved. The kind of presence which is least intrusive, most flexible and most reassuring in the region is a maritime (including amphibious) one. The United States will therefore have little alternative to an expensive long-haul improvement in maritime capability, given that new tasks have now been added to the traditional (Atlantic, Pacific and Mediterranean) tasks of the US navy. The more persistent vulnerability is that of oil strangulation in a general war. In this case, the danger can be reduced through extensive stockpiling, conservation policies and diversification. That is something we must admit to and learn to live with. The alternative would be a massive (and politically unsustainable) military investment in the region, which would risk the diversion of attention from what most would regard as being of even higher priority – the territorial defence of Europe and Japan.

Notes

[1]   William Shakespeare, *King Lear,* II. iv. 282.
[2]   J. A. Norris, *The First Afghan War, 1838–1842* (Cambridge, Cambridge University Press, 1967), p. 24.
[3]   Arthur Swinton, *North-West Frontier: People and Events, 1939–47* (London, Hutchinson, 1970), p. 142.
[4]   G. D. Clayton, *Britain and the Eastern Question* (London, University of London Press, 1971), p.126.
[5]   See Shahram Chubin, *Soviet Policy Towards Iran and the Gulf,* Adelphi Paper No. 157, (London, International Institute for Strategic Studies, 1980), p.11.
[6]   Quoted by Robert Fisk in *The Times,* 24 January 1980.
[7]   *International Herald Tribune,* 27 April 1981.

10 The Correlation of Forces and Soviet Policy in the Middle East
Karen Dawisha*

For a country whose foreign policy is proclaimed by its leaders to be based on the scientific principles of Marxism-Leninism, the Soviet Union has had its fair share of setbacks in the Near and Middle East. Kicked out of Egypt in 1972, largely excluded from the Arab-Israeli peace process after 1973, astride the wrong horse in the Horn of Africa until 1977, and bewitched and bewildered by the Iranian revolution, the Kremlin cornucopia is hardly overflowing with the fruits of victory. Of all the glittering prizes the area offers any greedy power, prizes of oil, power, wealth and prime-site real estate for the erection of a strategic colossus, the Soviet Union, at the beginning of the fourth decade of post-war interest and involvement in the area, has only Ethiopia and South Yemen (the PDRY) to show as firm and voluntary adherents to an avowedly Marxist-Leninist course. Afghanistan is being shepherded in the same direction by Soviet troops, but their presence, while marking the victory of Soviet power, also surely demonstrates the frailty, if not the failure, of Soviet influence. Even in Iraq and Syria, both signatories of friendship treaties with the Soviet Union, a quarter-century of dealing with Moscow has enhanced neither the pull of communist ideas nor the position of local communist parties in the two countries. Nor has the Soviet Union found the navigational tools supposedly provided by its ideology sufficient to prevent its goal of building an impregnable phalanx of progressive states from floundering in a sea of regional disputes, conflicts and coups.

None of these caveats is meant to deny that had the USSR not been prepared to 'reap the whirlwind' of Western decline, the West

*A shorter version of this chapter was delivered at a conference held jointly by Chatham House and the Istituto Affari Internazionali in Rome on 10–12 July 1981. For their many helpful comments, I am indebted to the members of the two delegations.

might have been able to contain, if not prevent, the damage wreaked by the post-colonial storm. Equally, cognizance must be taken of the almost inexorable rise of Soviet military power and the global and regional manifestations and repercussions of that power. Yet it is remarkable that a state such as the Soviet Union, contiguous to the Middle East, with long-standing interests there even in pre-revolutionary days, should be described by so many analysts, including contributors to this volume, as a state without a clear policy, reacting to situations, taking advantage of opportunities, veiling accident as strategy.

While to Western analysts Soviet policy may appear to be inconsistent or even haphazard, this is not how it is portrayed in the Soviet Union. Similar inconsistencies in Western policy are accounted for, or at least disguised by, the disruptive effects of elections and inter-alliance differences. The Soviet leadership has no similar excuses to hide behind, and its policy must be presented to the public as a cogent and coherent application and development of Marxist principles.

This chapter will examine, therefore, Soviet policy as it is seen in Moscow. In particular it will look at the concept of correlation of forces and the various components of that concept as applied to the Middle East. Any great power wishing to exercise influence in an area such as the Middle East will have to overcome diverse and conflicting religious, tribal, national and ideological crosscurrents. But is Moscow any better equipped than the West to understand these problems? With the constant growth of Soviet power, particularly in the military field, Moscow need no longer be constrained by incapability. Are there any other constraints built into Soviet policy, therefore, and if so how can the West exploit them to its advantage? In particular, at a time when the Middle East has been elevated to an area of vital strategic importance to the West, what risks is Moscow likely to take in order to expand its own presence in that area?

Correlation of forces
In the USSR, the application of Marxian ideology to current operative policy issues is determined through the calculus of the correlation of forces (*sootnoshenie sil*). Lenin once called it 'the main point in Marxism and Marxian tactics', further stating that 'we, Marxists, have always been proud of the fact that by a strict calculation of the mass forces and mutual class relations we have determined the expediency of this or that form of struggle'.[1] In the West, while the systematic comparison of one's own capabilities relative to those of one's enemies is usual in military affairs, it is only the Soviets and

other socialist countries who carry this concept over into policy-making in the sphere of international relations. The calculation includes both actual and potential shifts in the alignment of forces, thus allowing incredible flexibility of interpretation. The Soviet leaders are accorded, and they claim for themselves, the right to be the ultimate, if not the sole, diviners of policy at any given time, on the basis that it is they who are the most steeped in historical insight and Marxist teachings.

At the centre of the concept, distinguishing it from Western notions of balance of power, is its dynamic and manipulative character. It is as much a definition of power as it is a calculus for the application of power. It is, above all, a concept based on the notion not of maintaining the *status quo* but of transforming it, and the leadership is under the compulsion not only to consider the correlation of forces but also to act upon it as the basis both of grand stategy and of day-to-day policy.

In the Middle East, it is possible to observe four major elements of the Soviet view of the correlation of forces at work:

1. Soviet policy must take into account, and seek to manipulate, the total correlation between class forces, and not just the balance of power between states.
2. Short-term policy must serve long-term goals.
3. Regional policy should be determined with reference to global strategy.
4. The interests of Soviet socialism must take precedence over the interests of national liberation movements, and similarly the maintenance of the security of the borders of socialism must take precedence over national liberation movements, and in itself forms a basic principle of Soviet strategy.

Correlation of class forces

The first aspect in the 'classical' Soviet conception of the correlation of forces is that international relations is concerned with the interaction not primarily between states and governments, as in the Western conception, but between class forces – socialism, capitalism, feudalism, etc. It goes without saying that interaction between these forces is often expressed in the form of state-to-state relations. But the important point here is that because the focus of the Soviet perspective is on the dialectical relationship between class forces, the USSR has absolutely no qualms about openly supporting any communist party, national liberation movement or separatist group which helps to 'tilt the balance in favour of socialism'. Looking at the Middle East, one has the example of Soviet support at different times for the Kurds, the Palestinians, the Dhofari rebels in the Sultanate of Muscat and Oman, the Eritreans (while

Haile Selassie was in power) and of course all the various communist parties and progressive groupings which fought against British and French rule in Aden, Algeria and other countries during colonial wars. The point that needs to be made is not that the USSR has always been a selfless and tireless supporter of these groups, because it has not, or that it conducts all its relations 'in the open' without needing to resort to clandestine methods, since this also is clearly not the case. Rather, the fact of the matter seems to be that its view of international relations allows it to lend support freely and openly if the cause is deemed deserving.

The West, with a different view of international relations, is considerably more constrained, since support for 'non-state actors', however just the cause, goes against the dominant conception that state-to-state relations reflect and support the *status quo* and are thus the only truly legitimate form of international politics. The West has not lent open, direct and non-clandestine military support to a single non-state actor in the Middle East, which is presumably why the picture of former National Security Advisor Zbigniew Brzezinski holding a gun in an Afghan refugee camp in Pakistan in 1980 created such a furore at the time. The West's support tends to be clandestine or through third parties, such as in the case of arms to the Kurds via Iran in the early 1970s (after they no longer received Soviet support) and to the Afghan rebels via Pakistan. Even in the case of aid to a state, the West has often felt constrained to go through third parties or find a means by which its aid can be disguised, as when British aid to the Sultanate of Muscat and Oman to put down the Dhofari rebellion, again in the early 1970s, was either channelled through Iran or took the form of sending contract or loan service personnel from British forces to fight there. The low level of publicity given in the West to the large number of its own personnel stationed throughout the Middle East is in marked contrast to the Eastern bloc, including Cuba, where the press hails the stationing of military personnel and advisers overseas as proof that these countries are fulfilling their international duties.

Short-term policy serves long-term goals

Examining the second maxim, that short-term policy must always be made within the framework of long-term goals, application of this principle, if successful, would give Soviet policy an overall coherence often lacking in Western strategy. The provision of massive quantities of economic and military assistance, either gratis or at favourable rates, also could be justified in terms of long-term benefits. Equally, setbacks could be accepted as temporary or tactical retreats on the way to the achievement of more fundamental goals.

In the Middle East, as elsewhere, Moscow's long-term goal is the establishment of Marxist-Leninist regimes integrated into the Soviet-led world communist system; and it has been a feature of Soviet policy since the mid-1970s, perhaps as a result of the reverses suffered in Egypt, that Moscow has devoted much more time to the elaboration of the means by which this long-term goal is to be achieved. There are first of all, certain obligatory steps which a regime must follow before it can embark on 'the road of socialist orientation'. Articles published in the Soviet press to mark the 26th CPSU Congress have outlined the steps as follows:[2] left-wing elements (by no means necessarily communist) within the leadership must seek to eliminate their opponents from control over 'the levers of political power' (the police, army, bureaucracy) and put into effect economic measures (confiscation, nationalization and regulation) designed to eliminate the influence of the bourgeoisie and Western capital. These are measures which have become almost commonplace in the Middle East, but the Soviet Union no longer recognizes them as sufficient guarantees of the continued left-wing orientation of a regime. To this end, the leadership must embark upon a second stage of reforms in which it enacts a wide range of progressive socio-economic measures, dissociates itself from Maoist-style leftism, and sets about forming a vanguard party in collaboration with local communists using a Soviet-type organizational structure. The establishment of a vanguard party has become a *sine qua non* of Soviet policy, with it now openly being stated that 'no group of revolutionaries . . . can ensure the socialist orientation of the bulk of the population and the work of the entire state apparatus without the existence of a vanguard revolutionary party of fellow-thinkers'.[3]

Yet Moscow has long realized that it is faced with many problems in trying to achieve its long-term goals in areas such as the Middle East. One Soviet analyst noted some time ago that 'here nothing is automatically certain in advance, every step forward has to be won in battle and progress is often attained at the price of bitter disappointments, mistakes and searches'.[4]

One of Moscow's most intractable problems is that while many Middle Eastern leaders might agree that there is a basis for short-term cooperation, they would totally reject any correlation between short-term and long-term objectives. Thus, Soviet willingness to invest large sums of money in the Middle East was based on the assumption that short-term investment would reap long-term benefits. Yet when Egypt's President Sadat abrogated the

Soviet–Egyptian Treaty of Friendship, leaving an unpaid debt of $11 billion, this was shown to be a fallacious assumption. The result has been that Moscow has reappraised the notion of the 'irreversibility' of socialist gains. In the economic field this shift has manifested itself in a greater emphasis on the principle of 'mutual economic advantage' and, as a result, the Soviet Union has become less and less willing to sink large sums of money into states where it enjoys little political control.

Moscow's difficulties become most apparent at the moment when it tries to encourage a regime to make the transition from the first 'progressive' and 'anti-imperialist' stage of development to the second 'socialist' and 'pro-Soviet' stage, involving, as mentioned earlier, dissociation from both 'rightist' and 'leftist' excesses, cooperation with local communists and the establishment of a vanguard party. The vast majority of the countries of the Middle East have passed through the first stage of development at some time or other since the Second World War, but very few have made the crucial transition to socialism.

Moscow has suggested that there are four main reasons why states of the Middle East have failed to make this crucial transition. The first, but not necessarily the chief, problem is that elements within the leadership are influenced by 'adventurist' and pro-Chinese notions of going 'too far, too fast'. A basic Soviet work on the Third World, thus explicitly stated that 'the concept of violent revolution, which the ultra-left opportunists seek to impose upon the national-liberation movement, has nothing in common with Marxism-Leninism . . . Such "revolutionary" postures can merely produce a schism in the united anti-imperialist front . . . and hold up its further development'.[5] In the Middle East, during the 1970 civil war between the Jordanians and the Palestinians, *Pravda* explicitly condemned 'crazy extremists amongst the fedayeen, governed by the slogan "the worse it is, the better it is" '.[6] Soviet accounts of the situation in Afghanistan prior to the Soviet intervention similarly make it clear that Amin's major failing had been in pursuing a leftist policy. The following analysis deserves to be quoted in some length:

The damage that can be inflicted on society if such elements grasp the political initiative is illustrated best by the example of the 'great leaps' and 'cultural revolution' in China. Still manifestations of leftism and adventurism did take place in some countries of socialist orientation even in the recent past. In Afghanistan, for example, a part of the former leadership tried without justification to accelerate social transformations and to raise them immediately to the level of the people's democratic revolution. This brought about a serious aggravation of the situation which not only internal but also external counter-revolutionary forces were quick to use to their advantage. The country's present leadership made vigorous efforts to rectify the situation, to form a broad front of national-patriotic forces for a consistent solution of the tasks of the national-democratic revolution.[7]

A second problem in achieving the correlation between short-term and long-term policy lies in the attitude towards a regime's collaboration with local communists. In order to maintain its influence in the short term, Moscow has shown itself more than willing to gloss over the regime's suppression of its communists. The most graphic example, as discussed in Robert Patman's contribution, occurred in Ethiopia in May 1977, when 500 communists were slaughtered on the very weekend that then-President Podgorny arrived in Addis Ababa to consolidate Moscow's shift from Somalia to Ethiopia. In Iraq, the Soviets also initially remained mute to the suppression of local communists by the ruling Baath regime after 1978, although evidence of a shift in Moscow's attitude was evoked by the decision to allow Aziz Muhammad, exiled leader of the Iraqi Communist Party, to use the platform of the 26th CPSU Congress to condemn the 'cruel repression and persecution' unleashed on the ICP by Saddam Hussein's 'reactionary and dictatorial' regime.[8]

A third and major problem arises out of differences over regional rivalries and conflicts which Moscow feels unable to support because they are not directed against Western interests. Thus, for example, having established some considerable influence in both Iraq and Somalia largely through the supply of weaponry, when those weapons were used not against Western interests but against regimes which the USSR sought to nurture (Iran and Ethiopia respectively), the Soviet Union made its objections clear. But, in doing so, its chances of achieving its long-term goals were considerably reduced. In the case of the Somali–Ethiopian conflict, Soviet losses were minimized by the fact that the shift to Ethiopia represented a net gain in Moscow's eyes. In the case of the Iran–Iraq war, however, failure to support Iraq did not eliminate Iran's suspicions of Soviet motives, and, as I have argued elsewhere, Moscow felt itself to be in a 'no-win' situation.[9] Despite the Soviet leaders' determination to prevent any further deterioriation which might lead to the abrogation of the Iraqi–Soviet Friendship Treaty, and their claims that it should be preserved because it served 'the fundamental *long-term* interests' of the two countries,[10] the Iraqis made it clear that Soviet refusal to supply arms during the war with Iran would not quickly or easily be forgotten.[11]

Regional conflicts also impede the achievement of another of the

Soviet Union's aims, namely the establishment of a united front amongst all of its allies in the region. Article 10 of its 1979 treaty with the USSR specifically commits the PDRY to the formation of a bloc of progressive states in the region, and to this end a friendship treaty between Ethiopia and the PDRY was indeed signed on 3 December 1979. All of Moscow's other efforts in this direction have ended in failure, however. Attempts before 1977 to encourage the formation of a Marxist-Leninist confederation taking in the PDRY, Ethiopia, Somalia and Djibouti were doomed from the outset, and only displayed the Soviet leadership's own ignorance of national and ethnic rivalries in the Horn. Elsewhere, as of the autumn 1981, Syria and Iraq are arch-rivals; Iraq is publicly committed to the overthrow of the PDRY on account of the latter's support of communist subversion in Iraq; Syria is unlikely to sign a treaty with the PDRY for fear of alienating her Saudi backers; and all of these regimes, anxious to protect their Islamic credentials, will provide the minimum support possible to the Soviet Union's other treaty ally in the area – Afghanistan.

As for Libya's President Gaddafi, even Moscow has kept some distance between itself and this quixotic leader, as manifested by the absence of a friendship treaty between the two states. Indeed, on the occasion of Colonel Gaddafi's visit to Moscow in April 1981 (his first since 1976), President Brezhnev took the opportunity to stress not growing friendship but continuing, if accepted, differences: 'Between us there is a defined difference and ideological order. But that does not interfere with our being good comrades . . .'[12] Equally, Moscow has not been an outspoken supporter of Libya's intervention in Chad, and interestingly, on the occasion of the shooting-down of two Libyan-piloted SU-22s by US F-14s in August 1981, Tass presented both the Libyan and the Pentagon version of the events.[13] While it appeared for some time that a radical coalition of Iran, Syria, Libya, Algeria and the PLO might be emerging, particularly in opposition to the nascent Baghdad–Riyadh axis, Israel's actions in bombing the Iraqi nuclear reactor in summer 1981 and supplying arms to Iran diminished the support which radical Arab states could openly show for Iran's war effort against Iraq. However, the announcement of a unified defence pact between Libya, the PDRY and Ethiopia in August 1981, clearly designed to isolate and encircle Egypt, did represent a step forward for Moscow; and it was hailed by *Pravda* as ushering in a 'relatively new stage' in relations between the three signatories.[14]

It is clearly in the Soviet Union's financial interests to promote closer relations with any country, such as Libya, which can pay in hard currency both for its own weaponry and for the Soviet equipment supplied to other Arab states (for example, with $1 billion reportedly transferred by Gaddafi to Moscow in September 1980 to pay for Syrian arms). It is rather surprising, therefore, that Moscow continued to distance itself from some of Gaddafi's more excessive policies. Ethiopia too has been rather sceptical of Libya's regional intentions, and has been keen both to guard its own pre-eminent position in the OAU hierarchy against Libyan challenge and to thwart Gaddafi's hegemonistic regional plans by maintaining its own links with both Egypt and the Sudan.[15] Libya's support for Islamic radicals in Eritrea, as elsewhere, also naturally has impaired the friendship between Ethiopia and Libya. These latent conflicts of interest between Moscow's regional allies continue to represent formidable obstacles to the achievement of Moscow's long-term goals. In the case of Libya at least, it seemed that excessive Western pressure on that regime might actually serve Moscow's interests by limiting Gaddafi's options and making him more amenable to Soviet control. Thus, in the wake of the downing of the two Libyan SU-22s, Libyan officials stated that while the USSR had no bases in Libya at the moment and while 'Libya will try everything to keep from accepting foreign bases, . . . they could be accepted to defend our freedom'.[16]

The fourth and final problem seen in Moscow as jeopardizing the chances of a revolutionary regime fully establishing itself is Western interference. The current Soviet formulation would appear to allow for all forms of Soviet assistance, including direct military intervention, if a regime which is already 'oriented' towards socialism is threatened by 'external or internal reaction'. In his 26th Congress speech, Brezhnev made it clear that the USSR reserved the option to lend direct military aid if the situation required it. At the same time, however, he did not give an unequivocal guarantee that the Soviet Union would intervene if socialism were in fact threatened in a client state. He gave only the following assurance:

We are also helping . . . in strengthening the defence capability of the liberated states . . . for example, in Angola and Ethiopia. Attempts were being made to deal with the popular revolutions in these countries by encouraging internal counter-revolution or aggression from outside. We are against the export of revolution but we cannot agree either with the export of counter-revolution. Imperialism unleashed a real undeclared war against the Afghan revolution. This also created a direct threat to the security of our southern border. This situation forced us to render the military assistance asked for by that friendly country.[17]

By drawing a distinction between Ethiopia and Angola on the one hand and Afghanistan on the other, Brezhnev failed to make an unequivocal statement that established Marxist-Leninist regimes in the Middle East and the Horn of Africa would be protected with the force of Soviet arms and soldiers if necessary. Thus Moscow showed itself unwilling firmly to commit its resources to the forcible achievement of the transition between short-term and long-term objectives. Clearly other factors in the correlation of forces would have to be taken into account.

Regional ambitions and global strategy

Two extremely important factors in determining Soviet policy in the Middle East at any given time are Soviet strategy and Soviet priorities at the global level. It is interesting that while Moscow resolutely denounces US efforts to establish any linkage between East–West relations and Soviet conduct in the Third World, nevertheless Moscow carefully assesses the relationship between these two policy sets and considers them in their entirety. As outlined at the beginning of the chapter, there are three basic principles that follow on from the Soviet view of the correlation of forces: regional policy should serve global strategy; the interests of Soviet socialism should take precedence over the interests of national liberation movements; and similarly the security of the borders of socialism takes precedence over national liberation movements and itself forms a basic principle of Soviet global strategy. These three principles are seen in Moscow as forming a single unit, and while open to wide and various interpretation are central to the determination of Soviet policy in the Middle East.

If we look first at the correlation between the USSR's regional and global policy, many commentators have concluded that with the clear establishment of détente in the early 1970s, the Soviet Union would not take any action at the regional level in the Middle East which would jeopardize the steady improvement of relations with the United States. This was the firm policy adopted at both the 24th and the 25th Party Congresses, and despite anticipation that détente would be scrapped in favour of proletarian international-ism as the basis of Soviet global strategy, Brezhnev announced at the 26th Congress that the USSR remains firmly committed to détente as the overarching principle governing East–West rela-tions, despite recent setbacks.

At the same time, however, Brezhnev emphasized that while the USSR was not in favour of the export of revolution, neither could Moscow any longer 'agree' with the export of counter-revolution. In clear terms, the Soviet Union would not invade a country in order to put a socialist government in power, but it reserved the right to provide 'fraternal assistance' if an established socialist regime were threatened by counter-revolution. With the extension and devlopment of Soviet military power, the USSR clearly does have the capability to defend the 'gains of socialism' in Afghanistan, Ethiopia, the PDRY and elsewhere in the Middle East if it chooses to do so. Thus it can be seen that both détente and proletarian internationalism are juxtaposed uncomfortably in current Soviet global strategy.

There are two further aspects of that strategy which influence Soviet policy in the Middle East. One is the protection of Soviet borders and the other is the strengthening of Soviet military capability. The enhancement of Soviet military power not only provides the means to pursue a more active policy of proletarian internationalism, but also becomes an end in itself, generating its own dynamics and requirements independent of, or even in contradiction to, other aspects of Soviet global strategy, including both détente and proletarian internationalism. Thus, for example, the continued interest of the Soviet navy in obtaining deep-sea ports has to be seen as a prime motivator of Soviet policy in the Middle East, as shown in the case of Soviet offshore bombardments of positions held by the Marxist-oriented Eritrean liberation movements. This Soviet action illustrated more clearly than most the Soviet adherence to the view that the interests of socialism, defined in this case in terms of military interests, must take precedence over the interests of national liberation movements.

Up to the mid-1970s, Soviet adherence to détente dominated other aspects of Soviet global strategy, and produced a policy in the Middle East that was roundly criticized by progressive leaders in the area for being over-cautious. Thus, in the case of the Arab–Israeli conflict, many Arab leaders complained that the Soviet interest in détente took precedence over Soviet support for the Arab cause against Israel. In particular, Soviet reluctance to supply the Arab states with sufficient quantities of the most sophisticated offensive weapons so as to ensure victory against Israel, either prior to the outbreak of hostilities or during a war, was a major cause of disputes between the Arab states and the USSR, and was the chief factor in the expulsion of Soviet advisers from Egypt in 1972 and the gradual exclusion of all other forms of Soviet influence from that country after 1973. Despite continued and long-standing criticisms both from Middle Eastern leaders and from radical elements within the world communist movement itself, notably the Chinese, that the Soviet leaders 'are sorely afraid of the revolutionary storm',[18] Moscow continued to insist that détente, by decreasing imperialist aggression, actually increased the chances of success for national liberation movements.

What creates particular difficulties for Moscow is the Soviet precept that in the event of a clash between what is good for a national liberation movement and what benefits the USSR, the latter must always take precedence. Soviet adherence to this view was most forcefully stated in response to the Maoist doctrine, developed in the mid-1960s, that the revolutionary forces had shifted to the Third World (of which China then considered itself a member). The Soviet response was unequivocal:

> The contentions are designed to refute the Marxist characterization of the current epoch and to substitute for the basic contradiction of our day, which is that between socialism and capitalism, the contradiction between . . . 'rich' and 'poor' nations . . . These conceptions in reality seek to push into the background and play down the significance of the revolutionary struggle waged by the peoples of the socialist community of nations . . . They are completely alien to a class interpretation of the nature of the present epoch.[19]

Yet it is not only the Chinese who have objected to the USSR putting the 'interests of socialism' above that of the national liberation movement. Moscow itself concedes that criticism has also come from the Third World, where 'leaders of nationalist leanings . . . are fanning a useless argument over which of the two trends are of greater importance'.[20] It is a useless argument only in the sense that there is no chance of Moscow changing its view, although it is willing to concede that 'the objective fact that the socialist system is a leading factor in the world revolutionary process must in no way be taken to belittle the importance of the . . . fight the oppressed people are waging'.[21]

Clearly, until the mid-1970s, Moscow considered the 'interests of socialism' to be served by the policy of détente. The strategic and cooperative relationship between Washington and Moscow brought the Soviet Union numerous benefits in terms of technology, trade, disarmament negotiations, and the containment of Chinese efforts to transform the international system from bipolarity to tripolarity.

By the beginning of the 1980s, it certainly was no longer apparent that the 'interests of socialism' could be furthered by such a single-minded adherence to détente. In particular, the collapse of the SALT negotiations, the intensification of the arms race, and the diminution of East–West trade and technology transfer, all led Moscow to believe that the benefits on the global level of restraint at the regional level had been minimized. Further, Moscow viewed with great alarm the enthusiasm with which Washington set about constructing a special relationship with the Chinese designed, in the Soviet view, to resurrect the policy of containment and to challenge the Soviet Union not just at the global and strategic level but also at the regional and conventional level.

The enunciation by Zbigniew Brzezinski of the 'arc of crisis' theory was considered by Soviet analysts to be a turning-point in US policy. This theory, according to Moscow, became a 'factor in the intensification of the military element in US policy toward the region *adjacent to the Soviet Union's frontiers*'. It also 'formed the pretext for stepping up US military activity, primarily in the region of the Red Sea, the Persian Gulf and the entire Middle East'.[22] As a result of the growing military involvement of the USA (along with that of the Chinese) in the 'arc of crisis' and the US policy of linkage, Moscow was no longer able to pursue a policy of cooperation at the global level and activism at the regional level. Not only had the two levels become linked but, contrary to Soviet interests, the regional level had itself become 'globalized'. The Middle East had once again become a central arena for East–West rivalry and confrontation in a way which had never seemed possible during the days of détente.

The globalization of the area became most apparent following the Soviet invasion of Afghanistan. Of course, détente already had been seriously damaged before December 1979, and Moscow had already become sensitive to the implications for its posture in the Middle East and South and South–East Asia of the normalization of relations between Peking and Washington. Whereas in the previous twenty years the principle that the security of the borders of socialism was an inalienable part of overall Soviet global strategy had been tested only in Czechoslovakia in 1968, the Soviet Union found that first with the Iranian revolution, and then with the growing turmoil in Afghanistan, the security of its own southern borders was being jeopardized.

Anyone familiar with the Soviet attitude towards conflict on or near its southern borders knows that, in the event of conflict breaking out, almost inevitably Moscow is sooner or later going to issue its time-honoured statement about the USSR being 'unable to remain indifferent to acts of unprovoked aggression in an area adjacent to its borders, and it reserves the right to take the necessary measures dictated by the security interests of the Soviet Union'. The Soviet interest in maintaining border security arguably has played a part in the formulation of two rather contradictory policies, including on the one hand the Soviet intervention in Afghanistan, of which more will be said below, and on the other hand the long (if not entirely unbroken) tradition of 'good neighbourly relations' with Turkey and Iran, both discussed by Malcolm Yapp in Chapter 3. In the case of Iran, relations date back to the early 1920s, when Moscow unceremoniously allowed the collapse of the newly founded independent Soviet Republic of Gilan in northern Iran in return for the 1921 Treaty of Friendship between Moscow and Iran's Reza Shah, the founder of the Pahlevi Dynasty. In the late 1970s, even as opposition to the Shah was growing, the USSR initially refrained from openly supporting his overthrow. Indeed, when on 19 November 1978, Brezhnev delivered the first major statement of Soviet concern over Iran, he made no mention, as one might have expected, of supporting the 'democratic aspirations of the peoples struggling to free themselves from imperialist oppression'. Rather, his sole concern was that any US attempt to interfere militarily in Iran would constitute a threat to Soviet security interests.[23]

Of course the Soviets were impeded in developing a clear view of the Iranian revolution by virtue of its Islamic character. Prior to the overthrow of the Shah, Moscow considered that Islam had almost always been used in the service of reactionary movements and leaders. The emergence of virulent anti-Western Islamic radicalism made it apparent that this view would have to be altered. The end-process of that review was signalled by Brezhnev at the 26th Party Congress when he described the Iranian revolution as 'a major international event' and stated that 'for all its complications and contradictions, it is fundamentally an anti-imperialist revolution'. The broader lessons to be learned from Iran were that 'the liberation struggle can develop under the banner of Islam'[24] and that therefore it should no longer be condemned. Indeed, one of the crimes committed by Afghanistan's Hafizullah Amin was that he put into effect reforms which 'impinged upon the interests of . . . patriotic elements of the clergy'.[25] On the other hand, Brezhnev cautioned that 'history shows that reaction also operates with Islamic slogans . . . Consequently, what really matters is the actual content of a particular movement'.[26] As long as the Islamic content of the Iranian revolution works against American interests and does not produce a threat to the security of Soviet borders, Moscow can be expected to support Khomeini, even though the Soviet Union has little opportunity of transforming that revolution along Marxist-Leninist lines. Soviet policy towards Iran is therefore also an illustration of the difficulty faced by the Soviet Union in directing its short-term policy to accord with its long-term goals.

To turn to the case of Afghanistan, the Soviet intervention there certainly was prompted by several of the principles underlying Soviet global strategy, including both proletarian internationalism and Soviet concern for border security. It certainly was not constrained by what remained of détente, although almost all Soviet accounts of that period emphasize that 'US attacks on the policy of détente began long before the events in Afghanistan'.[27] Nevertheless, the Soviet leaders are willing to concede both that their actions in Afghanistan certainly had a whole series of negative repercussions and that they were 'surprised' by the vehemence of Western reaction. The previous constraints on Soviet activism in the Middle East presented by Moscow's adherence to détente were considered to have been removed before the invasion. But what Soviet leaders did not expect, and what they had to deal with after December 1979, was the globalization of Soviet policy towards not only Afghanistan but the whole of the Middle East. The area had become a front line of East–West competition, with Soviet behaviour affecting, if not entirely determining, American attitudes to the Soviet Union in other spheres. Thus Soviet efforts to compartmentalize their regional policy and use it in the service of their global strategy had all but failed.

While the globalization of Soviet behaviour in the Middle East has been resisted by Moscow, the Soviet Union has itself been responsible for the occurrence of this phenomenon in three ways. First, the increased emphasis on conventional military competition between the superpowers has led to the elevation in importance of areas such as the Middle East and Indian Ocean. Second, the increased emphasis in Soviet policy on military involvement in countries of the Middle East has further alarmed the United States at a time when Middle East oil has become a major strategic commodity. And, finally, Soviet actions in Afghanistan demonstrated to the West the risks Moscow was willing to take in the pursuit and protection of its interests. Thus while Brezhnev may have been genuine in his attempts to reassure the West, in his 26th Congress speech, that the Soviet Union has 'no intention' of encroaching on 'the oil riches of the Near and Middle East or on the oil transport routes', yet the increased emphasis on both the military instrument and military aspect of Soviet policy hardly provides visible proof of pacific intentions.

Military aims and instruments

The preceding discussion has suggested that in several respects the correlation of forces calculus has fallen far short of providing Moscow with a foolproof, scientific framework for the formulation of policy. In particular, Soviet leaders continue to find it extremely difficult to translate short-term policy into long-term gains, often as a direct result of pursuing policies which meet immediate requirements but which, as is shown for example in Chapter 2, at the same time are deleterious to long-term interests. Equally, the USSR has failed to use its regional policy in the service of its global strategy, with its behaviour in the region being used by the West as a litmus test of its intentions at the global level. And given the direction of Soviet policy, with its emphasis on the use of the military instrument and the salience of military and security considerations in its strategy, this situation is unlikely to improve.

If one looks first at the use of the military instrument, this can be divided into arms supplies and direct Soviet involvement. The USSR uses arms supplies both to establish and maintain influence and, increasingly, as Alan Smith points out in Chapter 8, to earn either petrol or petrodollars. Yet the economic imperatives to supply arms may confer on the recipient some considerable reverse influence on the supplier, in addition to the fact that the Soviet Union has found it extremely difficult to turn arms supplies into political influence. Thus, a massive influx of Soviet arms into one client state will almost inevitably generate similar demands amongst Moscow's other client states in the region, with failure to meet these demands becoming a major issue in bilateral relations and leading to a diminution of Soviet influence. Secondly, having supplied the weapons, Moscow has often had no control over the end-use of the weapons. As with the cases of the Somali offensive in the Ogaden and Iraq's war with Iran, Moscow was faced with the stark choice of either supporting actions which it did not condone, and which ironically would not have been possible without initial Soviet supplies, or losing influence altogether. And as both of these examples illustrate, although Soviet refusal to continue supplying weapons did prevent the crises from escalating, it did not lead either to the cessation of hostilities or to the reaffirmation of Soviet control. Rather, influence disappeared almost immediately once supplies ceased. A similar problem relating to the lack of control over end-use is that arms are also often supplied to bolster the internal security of a regime against rightist, separatist or Islamic fundamentalist groups. Yet Moscow on numerous occasions in the past appeared powerless if the regime turned the army or the security apparatus against the communists and other pro-Soviet groups.

Moscow has attempted to resolve some of these problems by increasing its direct military presence in countries of the Middle East, both in pursuit of greater political control and in the protection of its own distinct military interests in the area. As Edwina Moreton suggests in Chapter 6, East German and Cuban assistance in the organization and running of the military and the internal security services in countries such as the PDRY, Ethiopia and Afghanistan has done much to bolster Moscow's political control in countries of the so-called 'Communist Third World'.

The growth of the Soviet Union's military capabilities undoubtedly has produced a greater confidence amongst its allies in the Middle East that it will come to their assistance in the case of need. Thus, for example, while previous treaties between the USSR and states of the Middle East make only general reference to mutual consultation in situations which threaten peace, Article 6 of the October 1980 treaty with Syria does take the formulation one important step further by declaring that in the event of a crisis the two parties 'shall immediately enter into contact with each other with a view to coordinating their positions *and cooperating in order to remove the threat which has arisen* and to restore peace'.[28] And the Syrian Minister of Information has made it clear that Damascus welcomes the treaty as a guarantee of Syrian security providing for the dispatch of Soviet troops to Syria in case of need.[29]

While increased Soviet military capability multiplies Moscow's options for the support of local clients and the promotion of its interests, in any sense, the very growth of that influence presents almost equally severe problems for the future of Soviet policy in the area. First, the enhancement of Soviet capabilities means that Moscow will no longer be able to beg lack of capability as the reason for its non-support of local clients if they get involved 'above their heads' in regional conflicts which Moscow really does not want to support. As a result, tension between Moscow and its clients certainly need not disappear with the growth of Soviet military power and may indeed even increase. Second, the physical presence of Soviet troops in the various states of the Middle East almost without exception has produced not only widespread anti-Soviet (specifically anti-Russian) sentiments, but also the feeling that local independence is being infringed. These feelings manifest themselves both at the popular level and, more important, in the army, thus often producing a subsequent anti-Soviet backlash, the most notable example being the transition from Nasser to Sadat. Third, the growth of Soviet naval power, while used successfully in the support of local clients in Ethiopia and Syria (when joint manoeuvres in the summer of 1981 were part of the minatory diplomacy employed by Moscow to remind the Israelis of the dangers of escalating the Lebanese crisis), also increasingly creates its own demands in terms of requirements for ports and onshore facilities, a subject of considerable tension in negotiations between Moscow and its Middle Eastern clients, whose determination to protect their hard-won sovereignty persists. And, of course, sensitivities of this type were not allayed by the Soviet invasion of Afghanistan, which did more than anything to signal to the Middle Eastern states the length to which Moscow was willing to go to protect its own interests.

Military aims and instruments have thus come to the forefront of Soviet policy in the Middle East. While undeniably establishing the USSR as a superpower in the area, the promotion of Soviet military power has emphasized the failings of Moscow's political and ideological offensive, and itself has brought with it problems which the Soviet leaders have yet to resolve. Unless they are resolved, Moscow's optimism that the correlation of forces is shifting in its favour may be misplaced.

Notes

[1]   V.I. Lenin, *Sochineniya*, vol. 22 (2nd edn, Moscow, 1929), p. 265.

[2]   See in particular E. Primakov, 'Zakon neravnomernosti razvitiya i istoricheskiye sud'by osvobodivshikhsya stran'm *Mirovaya ekonomika i mezhdunarodnyye otnosheniya*, vol. 12 (1980), pp. 28–48; Yu. N. Gavrilov, 'Problemy formirovaniya avangardnoy partii v stranakh sotsialisticheskoy orientatsii', *Narody Azii i Afriki*, vol. 6 (1980), pp. 10–24; and the articles by N. Simonya, A. Iskenderov and Anatoly Gromyko on the 26th CPSU Congress and the International Liberation Movement in *Asia and Africa Today*, vol. 3 (1981), pp. 2–11.

[3]   N. Simoniya, 'The Present Stage of the Liberation Struggle', *Asia and Africa Today*, vol. 3 (1981), p. 4.

[4]   K. Ivanov, 'The National-Liberation Movement and the Non-Capitalist Path of Development', *International Affairs* (Moscow), vol. 2 (1966), p. 12.

[5]   Yu. Zhukov, L. Delynsin, A. Iskenderov and L. Stepanoy, *The Third World* (Moscow, Progress Publishers, 1970), pp. 23–4.

[6]   *Pravda*, 17 October 1970.

[7]   Simoniya, 'The Present Stage', p. 4. This view was also expressed by Evgeni M. Primakov, 'The USSR and the Developing Countries', *Journal of International Affairs*, vol. 34 (1980/81), p. 276.

[8]   *Pravda*, 2 March 1981.

[9]   Karen Dawisha, 'Moscow's Moves in the Direction of the Gulf – So Near and Yet So Far', *Journal of International Affairs*, vol. 34 (1980/81), pp. 219–35; Karen Dawisha, 'Moscow and the Gulf War', *The World Today*, January 1981, pp. 8–15.

[10]   Message of congratulations to Saddam Hussain from Brezhnev and Tikhonov on the ninth anniversary of the signature of the Soviet–Iraqi Friendship Treaty, *Pravda*, 11 April 1981 (italics mine).

[11]   Press conference of Saadoon Hammadi, Iraqi Foreign Minister, in London, 11 March 1981, Arabic transcript issued by the Iraqi embassy, pp. 7–8.

[12]   *Pravda*, 27 April 1981.

[13] *The Times*, 20 August 1981.

[14] *Pravda*, 24 August 1981.

[15] The links between Ethiopia and Sudan were recently cited by Moscow as an example of how 'the coming to power of progressive regimes contributes to lower tension on a regional level and has a stabilizing effect on international relations as a whole'. Evgeni M. Primakov, 'The USSR and the Developing Countries', p. 272.

[16] *The Guardian*, 26 August 1981.

[17] Brezhnev's 26th Congress speech, 23 February 1981, BBC, *Summary of World Broadcasts (SWB)*, part 1, SU/6657/C/8.

[18] *Jen-min Jih-pao*, 22 October 1963, quoted in Raymond Garthoff, *Soviet Military Policy* (London, Faber, 1966), p. 212.

[19] A. Iskenderov, 'The National Liberation Movement in Our Time', *The Third World* (Moscow, Progress Publishers, 1970), p. 30.

[20] L. Delynsin, 'Socialism and the National-Liberation Struggle', ibid., p. 247.

[21] A. Iskenderov, 'The National Liberation Movement', p. 31.

[22] Primakov, 'The USSR and the Developing Countries', p. 274 (italics in original).

[23] *Pravda*, 19 November 1978.

[24] Brezhnev's 26th Congress speech, 23 February 1981, *SWB*, SU/6657/C/8.

[25] Primakov, 'The USSR and the Developing Countries', p. 276.

[26] Brezhnev's 26th Congress speech, 23 February 1981, *SWB*, SU/6657/C/8.

[27] Primakov, 'The USSR and the Developing Countries', p. 275.

[28] *Pravda*, 9 October 1980 (italics mine).

[29] Interview with Syrian Minister of Information, Ahmed Iskandar, in *al-Moustaqbal* (Paris), 26 September 1980.

Index

Abu Dhabi, 48, 52
Aden, 150
Afghanistan
  arms supplies, 62
  border with USSR, 3, 32–3, 159,
    160–1
  CMEA
    observer status, 27, 103, 108, 109
    possible membership, 114, 120–1
  economic aid from
    CMEA, 114
    USSR, 109, 113–14
  military assistance from
    GDR, 75, 162–3
    USSR, 26, 62, 64
  military facilities for USSR, 5, 133
  revolution, 25, 27, 40
  Soviet attitude towards, 24–42, 147,
    152–5
  Soviet invasion, 1, 14, 17, 24, 33, 63,
    164; attitude of
    Angola, 74
    East European countries, 81
    India, 29
    Iraq, 17
    Saudi Arabia: aid to rebels, 21
    US, 130
    Western countries; aid to rebels,
      150
  trade with USSR, 27, 92, 108, 109,
    113–14, 121; (table), 112
Algeria
  military assistance from East
    European countries
    and Cuba, 64, 68–70, 75
  military facilities for USSR, 14
  Soviet attitude towards, 12, 13, 150
Amin, Hafizullah, 152, 160
Angola
  arms supplies, 70–1

attitude towards Soviet invasion of
    Afghanistan, 74
  military assistance from
    Cuba, 64, 68–74
    GDR, 75
    Romania, 63, 65
    USSR, 155–6
Arab-Israeli conflict, 13, 15, 130, 157;
  see also Israel, Palestine issue
Arab League, 48
Arafat, Yasser, 18, 76
Arms supplies to Middle East, 5, 135,
  138; from USSR and East European
  countries, 2, 8–9, 11, 15–18, 62–3,
  65, 69–71, 120–1, 153–5
Asad, Hafiz al-, 17, 18, 21
Aswan Dam, 10

Baghdad Pact, 8–9
Bani Sadr, A.H., 41
Barre, Siad, 21, 45–50, 52–9, 73
Black Sea, 29, 31–2
Border security of USSR, 3, 24–42,
  157, 159–61
Bosphorus, 31–2
Boumédienne, Houari, 21
Brezhnev, L.I., 12, 18, 29, 95, 114, 154,
  155, 156, 160, 161
Brzezinski, Z., 150, 159
Bulgaria
  attitude towards Soviet invasion of
    Afghanistan, 81
  military assistance to Middle East
    countries, 51, 65

Camp David agreement, 78
Carter, President J.E., 51
Carter Doctrine, 125
Castro, F., 49–50, 58, 68–74

Central Intelligence Agency, 18, 104, 105
Central Treaty Organization (CENTO), 26
Chad, 154
China, 158–9
  economic aid to Somalia, 48, 49, 56
  military assistance to Middle East countries, 159
Coal in USSR
  consumption, 93
  production, 87–8
  trade, 92–3
  see also Energy
Communism in Middle East, 10–12, 14–15, 147, 153
Communist International, 8
Congo-Brazzaville, 68, 74–5
Council for Mutual Economic Assistance (CMEA)
  cooperative agreement with Iraq, 109
  economic aid, 113–14
  energy imports by Eastern Europe from USSR, 91, 93, 97
  members and observers, 27, 103, 108, 109, 113–14, 120–1
  see also East European countries
Cuba
  economic aid from CMEA, 113
  Ghana: guerrilla training base, 68
  military assistance to Third World, 4, 62–82, 133, 163
    Algeria, 64, 68–70
    Angola, 64, 68–74
    Congro-Brazzaville, 68
    Eritrean guerrillas, 51, 70, 74
    Ethiopia, 45, 52, 64, 68–70
    Jordan, 68
    Somalia, 69
    Syria, 68, 70
    Zaire, 68
Czechoslovakia
  arms supplies to
    Egypt, 8–9, 62–3
    Israel, 63
  attitude towards Soviet invasion of Afghanistan, 81
  military assistance to Middle East countries, 65, 66
  trade with USSR, 93

Dardanelles, 31–2
Da'ud, Muhammad, 27
Détente, 156–61
Dulles, J.F., 9

East European countries
  involvement in Middle East, 62–68, 74–82
  trade with Middle East, 67–8, 115
  see also Council for Mutual Economic Assistance
Egypt
  arms supplies from
    Czechoslovakia, 8–9, 62–3
    USSR, 15
  communism, 11–12
  expulsion of Soviet advisers, 15, 65, 157
  Israel: disengagement agreement, 15
  military and naval facilities for USSR, 14, 15, 141
  military assistance from USSR, 64
  relations with Ethiopia, 155
  relations with US, 15
  repudiation of Soviet debt, 11, 16, 152
  Soviet attitude towards, 11, 13–16, 18, 20
  trade with USSR, 108, 118
  Treaty of Friendship with USSR, 14; abrogated, 15, 151–2
Eisenhower Doctrine, 9
Electricity: Soviet production, 87–8; see also Energy; Hydroelectric power
Energy, Soviet
  conservation prospects, 95
  consumption (table), 94
  energy balance, 85–101
  production (table), 86
  trade, 89–93; (table), 90
Eritrea
  assistance to guerrillas from
    Bulgaria, 51
    Cuba, 51, 70, 74
    Libya, 155
    Saudi Arabia, 21
  Soviet attitude towards, 49–51, 53–4, 60
Ethiopia
  arms supplies, 69
  communism, 147, 153
  CMEA: observer status, 103, 109, 120
  coup in 1974, 49
  coup in 1977, 19, 49
  economic aid from
    CMEA, 114
    US, 47–9
  military and naval facilities for

USSR, 5, 60, 132–3, 139
military assistance from
  Cuba, 45, 52, 64, 69–70, 162–3
  East European countries, 64, 163
  GDR, 52, 75, 163
  USSR, 3, 45, 49–60, 155–6
relations with Egypt and Sudan, 155
Soviet attitude towards, 19, 30,
  45–60, 132, 153
trade with USSR, 109
Treaty of Friendship with
  GDR, 76
  USSR, 1, 59
  see also Ogaden
European Economic Community, 41

Fahd, Crown Prince, 21
Faisal, King, 21
Federal Republic of Germany (FRG)
  Saudi Arabia: security links, 136
  Turkey: economic aid, 131
France
  Saudi Arabia: military assistance,
    135
  Somalia: military assistance, 51
  Turkey: economic aid, 131

Gaddafi, Mu'ammer, 18, 79, 154–5
Gas, Soviet
  consumption, 93
  production, 4, 87–8
  trade, 91–2, 115; imports from
    Afghanistan, 27, 92, 108–9,
    113–4, 121
    Iran, 27, 92, 98–9, 108, 117, 121
  see also Energy
German Democratic Republic (GDR)
  arms exports, 75
  attitude to Soviet invasion of
    Afghanistan, 78–9, 81
  military and technical assistance to
    Middle East countries, 74–5, 133;
    to
    Afghanistan, 75, 162–3
    Algeria, 64, 75
    Ethiopia, 52, 75, 163
    PDRY, 162–3
  relations with PLO, 77
Ghana: Cuban guerrilla training base,
  68
Gromyko, A.A., 56
Guevara, Che, 68
Guinea, 68

Hanson, Philip, 104, 105
Heikal, Mohamed, 56

Honecker, Erich, 76, 77
Hungary: attitude to Soviet invasion of
  Afghanistan, 81
Hussein, Saddam, 17, 21, 153
Hydroelectric power: Soviet
  production, 4, 87, 89;
  see also Electricity; Energy

India, 29
Indian Ocean
  Soviet naval presence, 2, 5, 27–9, 54,
    131, 133, 139–40, 163
  Western naval presence, 131,
    139–42, 145
  zone of peace, 28–9, 131
Iran
  border with USSR, 32–3, 159
  economic aid from USSR, 67
  revolution, 14, 25, 27, 40–1, 159;
    Islamic
    character, 160
  Soviet attitude towards, 24–42, 132,
    137–8
  trade with USSR, 27, 92, 99, 108,
    117, 121; (*table*), 112
  Treaty of Friendship with USSR, 25,
    160
Iran-Iraq war, 41, 109, 153, 162
Iraq
  arms supplies, 16, 153
  attitude towards Soviet invasion of
    Afghanistan, 17
  communism, 6, 12, 16–17, 153
  CMEA: cooperation agreement, 109
  economic aid from USSR, 67
  military and naval facilities for
    USSR, 14
  military assistance from East
    European countries, 64, 75
  relations with Syria, 154
  revolution, 10
  Soviet attitude towards, 10, 13, 14,
    16–18, 132
  trade with USSR, 91, 99–100, 108–9,
    118; (*table*), 112
  Treaty of Friendship with GDR, 76
  Treaty of Friendship with USSR, 1,
    14, 16–17, 153
Islamic Conference at Islamabad, 21
Israel
  arms supplies, 63
  disengagement agreement with
    Egypt, 15
  recognition by USSR, 8, 11
  US support, 130, 135
  see also Arab-Israeli conflict

Jadid, Salah, 21
Jordan
  Cuban military advisers, 68
  trade with USSR, 108

Khomeini, Ayatollah, 40, 160
Khrushchev, N.S., 8, 10–11, 46
Korea, South, 21–2
Kurds, 149–50
Kuwait
  aid to Somalia, 48
  British military advisory missions,
    131
  Soviet attitude towards, 128, 132
  trade with USSR, 108

Lamberz, Werner, 79
Lebanon
  Syrian invasion, 17–18
  trade with USSR, 108
Libya
  arms supplies, 154–5
  Eritrea: support for guerrillas, 155
  intervention in Chad, 154
  military assistance from Cuba and
    East European countries, 64, 75
  Soviet attitude towards, 14, 18, 21,
    154–5
  technicians from East European
    countries, 67
  trade with USSR, 108, 118

Machel, Samora, 114
Mediterranean: Soviet naval presence,
  2, 14, 31–2
Mengistu (Haile Mariam), 49–52,
  59–60, 73
Military and naval facilities in Middle
  East for USSR, 5, 14–15, 47, 60,
  132–3, 141, 157, 163
Military assistance to Middle East from
  China, 159
  East European countries and Cuba,
    4, 62–82, 133, 163
  USSR, 3, 26, 45–60, 64, 149, 155–6
  Western countries, 47, 49, 51, 131,
    135–6, 150
Military balance in Middle East, 124–7,
  131–2, 134, 138–45, 148–50
Military technicians in Middle East
  from East European countries and
  Cuba (*table*), 64
Military training of Middle East
  personnel in USSR and Eastern
  Europe (*table*), 66
Mirsky, G., 59

Mongolia, 113
Montreux Convention, 31–2, 33
Mozambique
  CMEA: observer, 113–14
  military aid from GDR, 75
Muhammad, Aziz, 153
Muscat and Oman, 149, 150
Muslims in USSR, 33–8, 40, 104

Nasser, Gamal Abd al-, 8–9, 10,
  13, 20–1, 62
Neto, Agostinho, 73
North Atlantic Treaty Organization
  (NATO), 32
nuclear power: Soviet production, 4,
  87–9; *see also* Energy
Numeiry, Jaafar, 14–15, 21, 50, 56

Ogaden: Ethiopia-Somalia conflict, 3,
  19, 45–7, 49, 52–3, 58, 69–70, 73–4,
  162
Oil, Soviet
  consumption, 93
  production, 4, 87
  trade, 90–2, 97–8, 115, 121
  see also Energy
Oman
  British military assistance, 131, 135
  naval and air facilities for US, 132,
    141
  Saudi economic aid, 21
  US advisory missions, 131
Organization of African Unity (OAU):
  immutability of states' boundaries, 3,
  46, 51

Pakistan, 29, 150
Palestine issue, 11, 126–8, 130, 149; *see
  also* Arab-Israeli conflict
Palestine Liberation Organization
  (PLO), 18, 77
People's Democratic Republic of
  Yemen (PDRY)
  communism, 147
  CMEA: observer status, 103, 109,
    120
  economic aid from CMEA, 114
  military and naval facilities for
    USSR, 5, 14, 132–3, 139
  military assistance from
    Cuba, 69, 162–3
    East European countries, 64
    GDR, 75, 162–3
  Soviet attitude towards, 13–14,
    18–19, 21–2, 30, 39, 132
  trade with USSR, 109

treaty with GDR, 76
treaty with USSR, 1
Persian Gulf security, 125–33
Petrov, V.I., 53
Podgorny, N., 50, 57, 153
Poland
  attitude towards Soviet invasion of
    Afghanistan, 81
  military assistance to Middle East
    countries, 66

Rapid Deployment Force, 6, 125,
  140–2, 144–5
Ratanov, A., 52
Red Sea, 50
Rodriguez, C., 70
Romania
  Angola: assistance to guerrillas, 63,
    65
  attitude towards Soviet invasion of
    Afghanistan, 81

Sabri, Ali, 20
Sadat, Anwar, 11, 15, 20–1, 151
Samsonov, G., 45
Saudi Arabia
  economic aid to anti-communist
    governments and groups, 21–2
  economic aid to Somalia, 48, 50
  FRG: security links, 136
  military assistance from France, 135
  trade with USSR, 108
Selassie (Haile), 47–9, 150
Somalia
  arms supplies, 153
  economic aid from
    Arab League countries, 48
    China, 48–9, 56
    USSR, 3, 56
  expulsion of Soviet military advisers,
    45
  military assistance from
    Cuba, 69
    East European countries, 64, 75
    USSR, 45–8, 50
    Western countries, 45, 51
  naval and air facilities for US, 47,
    141
  naval facilities for USSR, 14, 139
  Soviet attitude towards, 14, 18, 19,
    45–60, 132, 153
  trade with USSR, 108
  Treaty of Friendship with USSR, 48;
    abrogated, 53, 73
  see also Ogaden

Sudan
  communism, 14–15
  explusion of Soviet military advisers,
    50
  relations with Ethiopia, 155
Syria
  arms supplies, 2, 17–18, 62, 155
  communism, 12
  economic aid from USSR, 67
  invasion of Lebanon, 17–18
  military assistance from East
    European countries
    and Cuba, 64, 68, 70, 75
  military facilities for USSR, 14
  relations with Iraq, 154
  Soviet attitude towards, 13, 17–18
  trade with USSR, 108
  Treaty of Friendship with USSR, 1,
    11, 17, 163

Taiwan, 21–2
Tikhonov, N.A., 95
Trade
  East European countries with
    Middle East, 67–8, 115
  USSR with Middle East, 4–5,
    103–122; (*tables*), 110, 111, 112,
    116, 118, 119
  political factors, 105, 108, 109
  unspecified components, 106–8,
    115, 117; (*tables*), 107, 116

USSR with
  Afghanistan, 27, 92, 109, 113–4,
    121; (*table*), 112
  Iran, 27, 92, 99, 108, 117, 121;
    (*table*), 112
  Iraq, 17, 91, 99–100, 108–9, 118;
    (*table*), 112
  Turkey, 100–101
  see also Arms supplies
Turkey
  border with USSR, 32–3, 160
  economic aid from
    USSR, 67
    Western countries, 41, 131
  naval and air facilities for US, 141
  sovereignty over Bosphorus and
    Dardanelles, 31–2
  Soviet attitude towards, 24–42
  trade with USSR, 100–101

United Kingdom
  military assistance to
    Kuwait, 131
    Oman, 131, 135

Somalia, 51
United Arab Emirates, 135
United States
  attitude towards Soviet invasion of
    Afghanistan, 130
  economic aid to Ethiopia, 47–9
  naval and air facilities in Middle
    East, 132, 141
  naval presence in Indian Ocean,
    131, 139–41
  Rapid Deployment Force, 6, 125,
    140–2, 144–5
  relations with Egypt, 15
  relations with Israel, 130, 135
United Arab Emirates
  British military assistance, 135
  trade with USSR, 108

Venice Declaration, 130
Vietnam, 113

Warsaw Pact, 62, 65

Yemen
  arms supplies, 62
  Soviet attitude towards, 13, 16, 18
Yemen, North
  economic aid from Saudi Arabia, 21
  Soviet attitude towards, 14, 19, 132
Yemen, South: *see* People's Democratic
  Republic of Yemen

Zaire
  Cuban military assistance, 68
  economic aid from Saudi Arabia,
    21–2

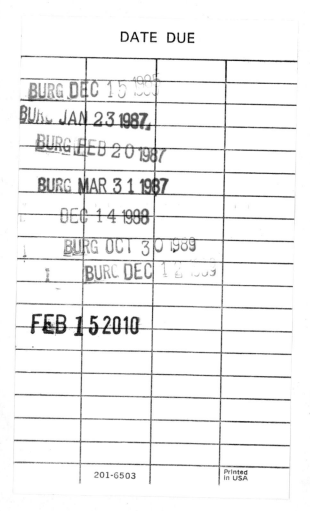

DATE DUE